Welcome to the EVERYTHING® series!

These handy, accessible books give you all you need to tackle a difficult project, gain a new hobby, comprehend a fascinating topic, prepare for an exam, or even brush up on something you learned back in school but have since forgotten.

You can read an *EVERYTHING*® book from cover to cover or just pick out the information you want from our user-friendly format. We literally give you everything you need to know on the subject, but we throw in a lot of fun stuff along the way, too.

We now have well over 100 *EVERYTHING*® books in print, spanning such wide-ranging topics as weddings, pregnancy, wine, learning guitar, one-pot cooking, managing people, and so much more. When you're done reading them all, you can finally say you know *EVERYTHING*®!

THE
EVERYTHING®
Series

Dear Reader,

You can find romance just about anywhere, any time of year, or any time of day. There are an amazing number of ways to spice up a romantic life with that special person. We turned the writing of this book into our own enjoyable, romantic adventure. Now we're ready to share the results with you!

The Everything® Romance Book is filled with creative ways to include romance in your life. Single teens to Grandma and Grandpa all have great romantic potential. We're here to help you unleash yours! From fabulous foods to adventuresome outings, you can use your senses of hearing, taste, touch, smell, and sight to enhance your love life. Music, food, nature, and poetry are just some of the romance-building items that should be on your agenda.

We are excited to share not only some personal insights but also ideas and information we discovered while doing our "research" and talking to friends about their romantic lives. These tips range from small, kind, inexpensive expressions of love to grandiose gestures for major occasions.

We hope you have as much romantic fun reading our book as we had writing it!

Sincerely,

Donald Baack

Pam Baack

THE EVERYTHING ROMANCE BOOK

From drive-in movies and long walks to
candlelit dinners and getaway weekends–
create passion, intimacy, and
excitement in your relationship

Donald and Pamela Baack

Adams Media Corporation
Avon, Massachusetts

EDITORIAL
Publishing Director: Gary M. Krebs
Managing Editor: Kate McBride
Copy Chief: Laura MacLaughlin
Acquisitions Editor: Bethany Brown
Development Editor: Lesley Bolton

PRODUCTION
Production Director: Susan Beale
Production Manager: Michelle Roy Kelly
Series Designer: Daria Perreault
Layout and Graphics: Arlene Apone,
Paul Beatrice, Brooke Camfield,
Colleen Cunningham, Daria Perreault,
Frank Rivera

An Everything® Series Book.
Everything® is a registered trademark of Adams Media Corporation.

Published by Adams Media Corporation.
57 Littlefield Street, Avon, MA 02322, U.S.A.
www.adamsmedia.com

ISBN: 1-58062-566-5
Printed in the United States of America.

J I H G F E D C B

Library of Congress Cataloging-in-Publication Data
Baack, Donald.
    The everything romance book / by Donald and Pamela Baack.
        p. cm.
    Includes bibliographical references and index.
    ISBN 1-58062-566-5
        1. Courtship. 2. Dating (Social customs) I. Baack, Pamela. II. Title.
HQ801 .B1135 2001
646.7'7—dc21   2001046305

This publication is designed to provide accurate and authoritative information with regard to the subject
matter covered. It is sold with the understanding that the publisher is not engaged in rendering legal,
accounting, or other professional advice. If legal advice or other expert assistance is required, the services of a competent professional person should be sought.
                    —From a *Declaration of Principles* jointly adopted by a Committee of the
                    American Bar Association and a Committee of Publishers and Associations

Illustrations by Barry Littmann.

This book is available at quantity discounts for bulk purchases.
For information, call 1-800-872-5627.

Visit the entire Everything® series at everything.com

Contents

Introduction

Welcome to the wonderful world of romance! What you're about to read is a culmination of what we came to call our "book dates." We'd find a library or bookstore and go about our research together. We worked back and forth on individual chapters, teased each other, and generally had a grand old time. And yes, it was very romantic. It reminded us of past times. It also caused us to think up fun new things to try out.

The Difference Between Romance and Being Romantic

Before we get into the nature of romance, we'd like to spell out the difference between the terms *romance* and *romantic*. A romance is when some form of courtship or dating takes place. The bonding process may or may not end in a marriage. A romance can be two widowed senior citizens becoming romantic companions, even if they never officially tie the knot. A romance can be a passionate encounter with someone in college, even if the relationship does not last. A romance is more than a friendship, but it can also be something less than a lifelong relationship.

An evolving romantic life, or staying romantic, can be one of the most significant joys you'll ever experience.

On the other hand, anyone can be romantic. Young, single people do it, married people enjoy it, and older people can immerse themselves in romantic moments. Feeling romantic can even happen when you're alone, when you think fondly about that special person in your life. To summarize the differences, let's put it this way: Being romantic is something you can do while in a romantic involvement to heighten the emotions that are present, but romance can also be part of other life stages. In spite of these differences, however, we'll pretty much use the terms interchangeably in the upcoming pages.

Romance Is a Journey

Romance is a kind of journey, one that cannot be set in a single point in time. It grows, it changes, and it deepens and widens over time. Each step in your love together frames another episode in the journey—from dating, to more serious courtship, to marriage, to growing old together. Your trip will be different from the ones taken by every other couple you know. Throughout the course of your lifetime you will probably take several romantic "voyages" with different partners. As you travel together, remember that it's easy to get distracted and drift apart. As with anything that's good in life, real romance requires some effort to keep the flames of passion burning. And that's where this book can help. We'll give you lots of tips and ideas for keeping that spark of romance burning bright in your relationship.

Romance Is Sensuous and Seductive

Even though there is a significant sensual component to romance, this book is not a sex manual. If you need help in that area, many other titles are available that will better suit you and your partner. Our goal is to identify those tactics and techniques that you can use to get you into the bedroom in the first place, feeling not just randy, but also enamored with the romantic power of the moment. Most of you may feel you know the Xs and Os of intimacy, and now you are looking for ways to enhance your love environment. This book is directed toward you.

Romance Is Passionate

A passionate romance is much more than fervent lovemaking. It's caring and sharing an emotional bond that connects you no matter what you're doing. Everyone has the potential to build a partnership based, in part, on feeling things strongly, both separately and together. You can take that energy and use it to create a stronger bond with your partner.

Romance Is Fun

Part of the joy of living and loving comes from not taking things too seriously. It's always good advice to suggest that you should work hard, play hard, and love a great deal. Many of the romantic activities we mention in this book are as much fun as they are anything else. What makes them romantic is sharing the moment. Just think, for example, about the last time you attended a wedding by yourself. It was nice, but you probably didn't feel much more than that. On the other hand, when you go to a wedding as a couple, the same ceremony can easily take on a totally new and more profound meaning. You may recall your own wedding or you may be looking forward to the day when you get married. Dancing together at the reception is both fun and romantic. So it is with many events—from a day at the beach to a night under the stars.

The tools of romance described in this book include what may seem like some fairly mundane stuff: meals, music, and words— things that are part of everyday life. When you spice them up, however, they become new adventures. The secret to making them work is an open mind and a willing spirit.

Romance Is an Adventure

What separates a romantic journey from lots of other voyages is the adventure contained in the trip. You just never know how things are going to turn out, especially when you first start dating the person. That adds a great deal to the excitement of the process. There's also the thrill of learning about someone, discovering likes, dislikes, hobbies, and common interests. Once you're together and settled in, you never know where the next terrific romantic "zinger" will come from. Many memorable romantic moments come from spontaneous decisions, accidents, or just dumb luck.

Romance Is Both Big and Small Stuff

If you spend any time in bookstores, you've probably come across the popular *Don't Sweat the Small Stuff* books. That kind of thinking doesn't seem to apply when it comes to romance, because small stuff can make a big difference in how a relationship plays out. Throughout this book, we're going to suggest that doing the little things can make a major impression on your lover. Picking up dirty clothes just to be nice is a romantic gesture. Bringing a cup of coffee, fixed just right, to your lover in the morning when he or she is running late is small stuff, but it's a major step in the right romantic direction. Small stuff matters big-time.

The flip side is also true. Many seemingly small things can cause major damage to a relationship, particularly when they become chronic problems. A man who constantly looks at other women when he is with his romantic partner will argue it's just a small thing. Being critical can boil down to a single, small, hurtful statement. Inconsiderate acts may seem inconsequential, but they have great power, especially when they accumulate over time.

So, one of the first lessons we'll suggest about improving your romantic skills is to sweat the small stuff. Do as many nice little deeds as you can for your partner. They don't have to cost a thing or take a lot of time, but they'll make a big impression. It's a better way of living and dramatically improves the odds of a lifelong, loving relationship.

We'll also spend some time describing big events and activities that are part of romance: major anniversaries, birthdays, travels, holidays, and special gifts. We try to put our own little spin on each one. Big events build long-term memories. You enjoy them as they are happening and then again when you remember them. Both are great for accenting a romantic partnership.

Romance Is for Everyone!

It's not much of a stretch to say that romance can affect you as a small child, as a middle-aged adult, and in your golden years. How? As a child, your parents either were actively and emotionally involved with each other, providing role models for the future; or they sniped and griped and sent a totally different kind of message. The presence or absence of romance in your parents' marriage affects you. Children with parents who have divorced are forced (often painfully) to watch as Mom or Dad tries to construct a new romantic relationship, or, worse, tries to avoid forming emotional attachments with someone new.

Far too many people see romantic involvement as reserved for a fortunate few, usually young people and those celebrating Valentine's Day or anniversaries. It's really a shame when you put romance in a little box called "youth" or "special events" and leave it there the rest of the time. For those of you who do, or who live with someone who limits romantic contact to just a few key days per year, we hope some of the ideas presented in this book can help you climb out of that box and back into the game.

There's a fine line between suggesting some things are only for men (or women) and saying that everything matches everybody. So, some ideas apply *mostly* to one gender or another. But it's also fun to see if you can somehow make them work for both sexes.

You'll also probably notice that we'll talk in general terms about a relationship between things spiritual and things romantic. We believe one of the most profound connections you can make is with a spouse or partner. We also believe that this loving involvement can have a divine blessing attached to it that simply should not be ignored.

In addition to sharing our own experiences and insights with you, we'll tell you about couples we know who have done these wonderful romantic things that we were able to observe. When you combine their experiences, our ideas, and your intelligence, creativity, imagination, and passion, the net result is probably going to be some hot and heavy nights with your lover, both in the near future, and in the years to come. Enjoy!

CHAPTER 1

Are You Ready for Romance?

Our world is out of whack. That's because far too many people tend to value *immediate gratification* over *long-term gratification*. Seeking immediate gratification, many couples buy cell phones, CD players, big-screen televisions, designer clothes, and gourmet meals. They work two jobs and put in lots of overtime just to have these "lifestyle" goodies for themselves and their kids. Even worse, our culture seems focused on the immediate gratification of great sex. With all this immediate gratification going on, we are losing sight of the big picture. We are losing the glorious bonding that could have taken place along the way. This chapter is a short course in developing or rekindling an ability that exists in everyone—being romantic.

How Romantic Are You?

Before we get started on our romantic journey, take the following quiz to see how well you fare on our Love-O-Meter scale.

The Love-O-Meter Quiz

Answer the following questions honestly.

1. In the past year, how often have you given your romantic partner flowers?
   a. Never
   b. One to three times (birthday, Valentine's Day, and anniversary)
   c. More than three times

2. How often do you compliment your romantic partner? (It can be about anything from cooking skills to appearance to a special talent.)
   a. Once a day or more
   b. A few times per week
   c. Rarely

3. In a typical month, how often do you brag about your romantic partner in front of him or her?
   a. More often than not
   b. Rarely
   c. Every time we're out socially

4. How often do you try to cook one of your romantic partner's favorite meals?
   a. Once a month
   b. Once a week
   c. Whenever the ingredients are on sale

5. How many times each week do you do something nice for your romantic partner without expecting something in return?
   a. Once or twice
   b. Three or four times
   c. Practically every day

6. How often do you and your favorite special person plan a "date" alone?
   a. Once a month
   b. Once a week or more
   c. Not very often, we're too busy

7. How would you finish this statement? "A romantic evening should . . ."
   a. Always lead to sex
   b. Never lead to sex
   c. Lead to sex when the feeling is right

8. How many times a day do you kiss, hug, or touch your significant other for no apparent reason?
   a. Not very often
   b. Once or twice
   c. Too often to keep track, so I don't

9. How often per week do you and your romantic partner just sit and talk for twenty minutes or longer?
   a. Once or twice
   b. Three times or more
   c. There's never time, we always get interrupted

10. How often do you notice something (music, art, nature, television advertisement) that makes you feel romantic or makes you think about your special person?
    a. Not very often
    b. At least once a day
    c. A few times per week

Write your score here:

Question #1: a = 1 _____ b = 2 c = 3	Question #6: a = 2 _____ b = 3 c = 1
Question #2: a = 3 _____ b = 2 c = 1	Question #7: a = 1 _____ b = 1 c = 3
Question #3: a = 2 _____ b = 1 c = 3	Question #8: a = 1 _____ b = 2 c = 3
Question #4: a = 1 _____ b = 3 c = 2	Question #9: a = 2 _____ b = 3 c = 1
Question #5: a = 1 _____ b = 2 c = 3	Question #10: a = 1 _____ b = 3 c = 2

Add your scores together here: _____

If your total score is 25 to 30, you're practically a romantic genius (but you can still improve)!

If your total score is 15 to 24, you have romantic tendencies, but probably run into lots of distractions that keep you from fulfilling your love potential.

If your total score is 14 or less, it's time to change your ways and learn the language of love!

The Love-O-Meter quiz is designed to show you the many different aspects of a romantic life. You need to do much more than occasionally show up at your partner's door with a box of chocolates, a dozen roses, or a bottle of champagne. As you will soon see, it goes a lot deeper than that.

Being romantic also means being considerate, communicating, bragging about the special person in your life, taking time, and making time, as well as remembering those random acts of caring that make someone else's day just a little brighter.

Where Does Romance Fit into Your Life?

Music lovers regularly find ways to enjoy their passion throughout the day. They listen to the car radio or CD player on the drive to work or around town, at home on the stereo system, and on a portable player while they jog or walk. These deliberate efforts are designed to incorporate the music they love into their daily routine. Being romantic can work the same way. Take a look at this list, and consider the connection each entry has with romance:

- Being with friends
- Celebrating anniversaries
- Celebrating birthdays
- Dating
- Eating
- Falling in love
- Flirting
- Going on a honeymoon
- Marrying early
- Midlife
- Old age
- Practicing the art of seduction

For those who commit their minds and hearts to the goal of keeping the love light burning, a voyage through a romantic life begins early on and should never end. The journey might start as you watch your Mom and Dad smooch unabashedly or when you see love still shining in the eyes of your grandparents. Soon you're probably thinking, "Gee, I wish something like that would happen to me!"

Romance can be part of your entire life!

Before kids reach their teenage years, they've begun honing their romantic skills. Many girls experience their first romantic cravings as they read teen magazines and fantasize about a delicious kiss with the latest heartthrob. Boys usually start out with clumsy attempts at flirting and teasing, which soon evolve into something a little more sophisticated, such as note passing. Sure, early romance is often awkward and immature, but it is also exhilarating and a great training ground for what is to come.

Don't you wish you could recapture the fun and excitement that went along with those early crushes? The biggest bummer about innocence is that once you lose it, you can't get it back. Fortunately, what happens next is often grander. The dating years can be painful and filled with rejection, but they can also create some of our most powerful memories. Each new dating partner brings a unique kind of expectation, which is simultaneously tense, intriguing, and exciting. Think back to those days. Remember how you hoped to find your perfect match someday? Along the way, there were proms, movies, long walks and talks, and many other adventures. Teenage romance and the dating years usually add new depth to romantic feelings.

We're going to talk about youthful romance in some parts of this book, not only because some of our readers may be young, but also because it's part of the larger picture. We want those of you who are older to remember those times when romance was lighthearted and fun. Those feelings and activities can enrich your romantic life at all ages.

So, where does romance fit into your life? *Everywhere*, if you want it to!

Many people agree that the most romantic times in their lives took place (or will take place) during courtship and the early stages of marriage. Candlelit dinners, flowers, cards, notes, love letters, and lots of other romantic goodies seem to take place all the time when you're falling in love. You can't take your eyes off each other, and you ache when you're apart. For many people, it's one of the happiest times in their lives. Unfortunately, it is far too easy to fall into a rut in which passion cools and tender romantic moments occur less frequently. Life doesn't have to work that way!

If you are willing to try, and if you have the kind of partner who responds when you make a special gesture, you can use the upcoming pages to build or rekindle many tender, warm, romantic feelings. Of course, romance can never stay at the fever pitch it reaches during those early days. But good relationships deepen into something even better.

A Life of Love

Various studies done over the years comparing people in committed relationships with single people have yielded some interesting results:

- Married people tend to live longer.
- Married people tend to enjoy better health.
- Married people are more likely to report that they have consistent, satisfying sex with the same partner.
- Married people normally report that they are happier than single people.
- More than half of the people involved in some kind of long-term romantic relationship say that their "best friend" is their partner.
- Most divorced people remarry, which suggests that they are still looking for something associated with love and romance.
- The majority of people who are involved in a long-term romance say that if they were stranded on a desert island with just one person, they would choose their spouse or lover as that person.

Hungry for Romance

Take a look at these terms and ask yourself, "Which one is most like romance?"

- Spice
- Appetizers
- The main course
- Toppings
- Dessert
- Icing on the cake

The answer, not surprisingly, is "all of them." (Are you getting hungry yet?)

Romantic Love Is the Spice of Life

Why do we add pepper, salt, and other spices to our food? Because spices make food taste better. Romance is a spice. This is not to say there aren't other spices in life, like a meaningful job, a rich spiritual life, exciting hobbies, travel, adventure, and entertainment. But romance can (and should) be one of the tastiest, most potent spices in life. It can take a ho-hum relationship and make it magical. Being romantic can help you build a partnership and move it from one level (dating) to the next (an engagement). Romantic feelings add zest to everyday existence and deeper meaning to the longer-term memories that we store.

Romance Is an Appetizer

Along with regular meals, many restaurants offer a "sampler platter" as an appetizer. They do this to tease you into wanting more. They give you a chance to try out a few menu items on a smaller scale, hoping that next time you'll want a larger portion. Other appetizers set the stage for a more complete dining experience. Romantic involvements are the appetizers for courting, dating, and more involved relationships.

You can experience romantic feelings even when you're alone. Treat yourself to a special dinner or a soothing bubble bath at the end of a trying day!

Some restaurants are gaining popularity by offering "tapas." These little gems are appetizer-sized portions of main dishes. The point of the meal is to taste as many different tapas as you like. This eclectic eating experience is a great change of pace from the standard, appetizer– soup–main course–dessert approach to dining. Romantic adventures should be the tapas of the new millennium. A bite here, a taste there, and soon your entire adult life is filled with the riches of a variety of romantic (and culinary) encounters. Our tapas include musical experiences, movies, dinners, flowers, and dozens of ways to say, "I love you" or, "You are very special to me."

Romance Is the Main Course

Ever hear a frantic businessperson say, "My plate is full"? He or she is complaining about having too much to do. In a romantic life, it's nice to have a full plate. It means you load your days with as many meaningful moments as possible. You conspire and aspire to touch the feelings of your romantic partner. Many marriages would benefit from more plate loading and less bickering.

Romance Is a Topping

You can live without whipped cream. You can live without maple syrup. You can live without cream cheese, peanut butter, and jelly. It's physically possible, but would you want to? Romance is the same. You can live without it, but you probably don't want to. In some way, nearly everyone, from grade schoolers on up to senior citizens, is looking for love (and, we hope, not in all the wrong places). Romance makes life a little sweeter and a lot tastier.

Romance Is Dessert

There are many components to our definition of love: friendship, companionship, a spiritual soul-mate connection, passion, lust. Some are unique to a couple. At the end of the day (or the meal), dessert and romance add that little extra that turns a dinner into a feast, or a marriage into something much more glorious.

Romance Is the Icing on the Cake

One line that will never be heard from a person's deathbed is, "I sure wish I had spent more time at the office." But you may hear, "I sure wish I had spent more time telling you how much I love you." Romance is the glorious completion of a full life. It is the icing that can be spread over love, marriage, and many other interpersonal relationships that people enjoy as they travel through life. Enough said.

A Baker's Dozen

What He Can Do for Her

1. Hold the door, help her to her seat, take her arm; in general, be an old-fashioned gentleman.
2. Cook dinner and wash the dishes when she's exhausted.
3. Watch the kids when she's swamped with work and needs to catch up.

4. Let her sleep in.
5. Caress her feet at the end of a long day.
6. Give her an "extra-effort" good-bye kiss in the morning.
7. Give her a generous compliment in front of your parents.
8. Rub her neck and back while she's doing the dishes. Then dry the dishes.
9. Give her the remote. Say "You pick," and mean it.
10. Come home on Friday night with a chick flick in one hand and a pizza in the other.
11. Brush her hair.
12. Send her a small bouquet of flowers at work.
13. Sign your notes to her "I love you."

What She Can Do for Him

1. Serve him snacks and his favorite beverage in your sexiest nightie during the ball game. Then say, "Come and see me when the game's over."
2. Let him "decompress" after a long day of work before you talk about anything serious.
3. Tell him he's a stud, in front of his buddies.
4. Gently scratch his bare back with your fingernails.
5. Ask him a complicated football question, and act as if you really care about his expert answer.
6. Give him a hot towel fresh from the dryer as he steps out of his long wintertime shower.
7. Give him a butterfly kiss (flutter your eyelashes against his skin).
8. Compliment him when he dresses in something you really like.
9. On a long trip, rub his neck while he drives.
10. Do one of his regular chores without being asked (e.g., take out the trash, if he usually does it).
11. Meet him for lunch with a picnic.
12. Buy a boutonniere and surprise him with it on a day you know he'll be wearing a suit (even if it's for church).
13. Give him as a present something he wants but wouldn't buy for himself.

How to Get Started

Every once in awhile, you hear someone say, "Physician, heal thyself." Usually, the intention is to get a friend or family member to start some kind of self-improvement program. An element of healing can sometimes be part of the romantic process as well. Romance can help restore a heart broken in a previous relationship. Romance can help heal the wounds of an argument or an unfair criticism. Now, don't get us wrong, we're not telling you that romance is some kind of cure-all for life's problems. Romantic gestures are simply part of a happier, healthier relationship. And in the end, healing yourself means looking for ways to enhance the moment, whenever you feel inclined. To get started, take a look at how you view the world. After that, you'll be ready to take the right steps toward a more amorous life with the people who matter.

A romantic outing is a great antidote to loneliness.

If You're Lonely

Everyone gets lonely at some point in life, for one reason or another. Perhaps you haven't yet connected with a special person, or you just broke up with someone. Maybe you're widowed or separated by some other circumstance that creates a void that can only be filled by connecting with other people.

Many singles say that the worst part of being single is trying to find ways to meet interesting new partners. The bar scene can be depressing. Gyms are sweaty and you're not exactly looking your best there. It's tough trying to find a spot that isn't so trendy that the goal becomes "looking chic" or that is so isolated that no one is around. So what's a lonely person to do?

For openers, stop looking and start living! It's easy to cocoon yourself in your job, surf the Internet, or simply watch television for hours on end. This can build a cycle of loneliness that gets harder and harder to break. Instead, go to romantic places. Small cafés, museums, art galleries, and dozens of other venues offer a chance to get out, possibly socialize, and feel alive. Cafés, coffee shops, and symphonies are often attended by couples, but not exclusively. Besides, one of the greatest lessons you can learn from these experiences is that being alone isn't bad, as long as you enjoy your own company. If you do, you'll be seen as an even more attractive person when someone does come along.

When you are home, look at reading materials of all kinds. Study everything from the *Wall Street Journal* to *People* magazine. Absorb those little tidbits that give you something to contribute to every kind of conversation. Then add in some brainstorming materials, about how to be more sensuous, or look better, or grow spiritually. A well-rounded person who is growing and improving is attractive in any setting. More friends, more involvements, and more parties and social engagements reduce loneliness and increase the odds you will meet someone as interesting as the person you've become.

If You're Looking for a Spark

Married folks and other long-term partners in search of a romantic jolt can be divided into two general categories: (1) couples in which *one person* wants a hotter romantic fire, and (2) couples in which *both* are excited about turning things up a notch. Obviously, category two is the more desirable situation. However, it is possible to turn that fuddy-duddy you're living with into more of a Romeo or Juliet, even if he or she is resistant or disinterested at first. It's just a bigger hill to climb.

The biggest enemy of a listless marriage is probably a mind-numbing routine. Judging from the sales of time management books, lots of people wish they had more time, so they try to manage the time they do have more wisely. The lessons learned from those books may be limited simply to working more efficiently in order to get everything done.

A small romantic touch that only takes a moment can linger throughout the day. Think of it this way: It's possible for a scent or an aroma to completely change your mood by evoking strong memories or feelings. It could be the clean, fresh scent of the air following a spring rain, the tasty aroma of the barbecue grill firing up next door, the sweet fragrance of blooming lilacs, or the earthy smell of a freshly mowed lawn. In the same way, a romantic gesture can be the spring rain that reminds you of your youthful days of passion and intimacy. It may be something as small as an extra affectionate good-bye kiss as the day begins, or a small note placed in your loved one's briefcase to be discovered at just the right time. Or it may be a little more elaborate, like sending flowers to your partner's workplace "just because." Whatever the inspiration, no matter how small the effort seems, the outcome can be surprising and uplifting. It can change the whole nature of an afternoon or evening.

If You Have a Strong Foundation

What separates a good athlete from a great one? What is the difference between a skilled musician and an exceptional one? It's talent, of course, but more important, practice. And so it is with the romantic couple. If you think of being romantic as a talent, some people are clearly more "talented" than others. Some lovers know instinctively how to set a mood to tantalize and dazzle their partner. It may be an innate gift, or it may have developed over the years by watching and learning from others. Where it comes from is less important than the fact that it's there.

For those building on a strong foundation, new romantic moments provide lots of great memories that you can savor for years to come. For you devoted husbands, wives, and lovers, this book can serve as a resource and, we hope, an inspiration. Becoming a warmer, more loving, more romantic partner is a noble objective.

The Journey Begins

Being romantic is a pattern of living. It's a cycle that feeds itself. Remember being told as a child that when you pointed the finger of blame at someone, you had one finger aimed at the accused, and four others pointed at you? Romance is like that. One small gesture of affection comes back in many pleasant and unexpected ways. Before moving on, take a quick look at this checklist of the supplies you'll need as you begin your journey to become more romantic. Add your own touches. A true romantic expresses the very best part of his or her nature to a favored friend and partner. And there's no time like the present to take that first step!

A Checklist of Supplies

Supplies to Buy

- Blankets (in the trunk of the car)
- Bubble bath
- Candles
- Candy
- Champagne or wine (if so inclined)
- Favorite foods
- Flowers
- "Just-because" cards
- Oils and lotions
- Paper/sticky notes
- Perfume/cologne
- Planning calendar
- "Protection"
- Ribbon
- Silk sheets (if you like)
- Stereo, CD, or tape player
- Valentine's Day cards
- VCR
- Video camera or regular camera

Supplies You Have

- An adventurous spirit
- Creativity
- Curiosity
- Dedication
- Energy
- Experience
- Generosity
- Gentleness
- Honesty
- Intuition
- Optimism
- Passion
- Selflessness
- Sense of humor
- Sensuality
- Spontaneity
- Tenderness
- Thoughtfulness
- Whimsy

and . . .

- The object of your affection!

CHAPTER 2

What Leads to Romance?

F ar too much that is written about love and romance sets it up as some kind of competition or battle between the sexes. It seems the best we can do is to describe men as being from one planet (Mars) and women as being from another (Venus). Instead of focusing on what we have in common, we seem more interested in what makes us different. In the world of romance, that kind of viewpoint cuts two ways. On the one hand, you can celebrate and enjoy the differences that exist between you and your romantic partner. On the other hand, these differences can also drive people apart, especially when they become the focal points of arguments and disagreements. It is better to look first for the things you share rather than the things that separate you.

Your Ideal Partner

Do you believe in a "perfect fit" partner, some ideal person who is lingering out there somewhere? If you do, romance gets a little tricky. Instead of simply savoring the moment with the person you're with, you'll always have a lingering doubt. "Is he the one?" A strong case of "greener pastures" syndrome can develop if you're constantly keeping an eye out for your "true love." Probably the best way to solve this problem is never *assume* your dating partner is or is not "the one" until you have much more evidence. Of course, sometimes you know going in that someone isn't a great match, but that shouldn't stop you from seeing where a romantic road leads. There may be some great times along the way.

> Single people are not the only ones looking for romance. Many married folks find themselves wishing they could recapture some of that old magic. It doesn't hurt for single people to read about enhancing married romance, or for married people to read about single's romance. Everyone can learn a little bit by seeing other situations.

However, the path may get a little bumpy. Lots of little girls are warned, "You have to kiss a lot of toads before you find a prince." And although there is no comparable warning for little boys, the point remains the same. Finding the right person is fun, demanding, exasperating, risky, confusing, mind-boggling, and often time-consuming. So take a deep breath, stay alert, and savor the variety of people you will meet and the experiences you will have along the way.

Not "Ms./Mr. Right," but "Ms./Mr. Right Now"

There are plenty of good reasons to date someone who may not be your now-and-forever choice. When rebounding from a bad relationship or a broken heart, you may need something more casual in order to give yourself time to heal. You may be focusing your attention on some other aspect of your life (such as your career, education, or family) and not have time to devote to a serious relationship. Or you may simply want to spend time with someone because you share an interest or hobby. Don't limit your choices by labeling someone as "not my type." Meeting a variety of people can help you discover who "your type" really is.

What Women Encounter As They Meet Men

Remember what we said earlier about the difference between a romance (a serious involvement with someone) and being romantic? If you believe what you read in many magazine articles and books, most men have trouble with commitment *and* emotional interactions. We're not going to dispute that there are some guys who simply don't want to be tied down, but not all guys suffer this hangup. For single women, finding the right kind of guy may seem about as likely as finding a needle in a haystack. That's because there are so many to sort through. Let's talk about a few of the types you may want to avoid.

The Bragger/Stat-Keeper

Ask a male friend about this type. If he's a close friend, he'll warn you about the kind of guy who dates women primarily to build bragging fodder. These smooth-talking, tell-you-what-you-want-to-hear types are much more common in high school and college than at any other time in life. This type sees you as nothing more than a potential notch on the belt. Being used is never romantic, so keep your eyes open and remember the old marketing adage: "If it sounds too good to be true, it probably is."

The Gamma

Closely related to the Bragger is the Gamma. This fellow wants to mess with your head. He likes to keep you insecure and off balance. As a result, you'll never know if he means what he says or just says it to keep you around. A classic characteristic is his wandering eye. Also, he'll constantly work on your self-confidence by trying to make you question whether you're good enough for him. Feeling small or incompetent is not romantic. Tell him to get lost!

The Cynic or Woman Hater

Sooner or later, practically everyone is hurt by a romance. A Cynic or Woman Hater carries a grudge. Perhaps he didn't vent his anger toward the woman who caused his pain. So, guess who catches it? Cynics are more emotionally detached. Women Haters are going to use you as a whipping girl. Neither one is going to be very interested in candlelit dinners with real conversation. Both types are going to belittle you. If you discover either trait, move on.

The Man Who's Looking for Mom

Emotionally immature men are often looking for a new set of apron strings rather than an adult companion. A needy guy who constantly wants to be reassured or taken care of is substituting you for his mother. If you have a maternal instinct, this might seem appealing at first. Unfortunately, the initial emotional buzz quickly wears off and is replaced by an intense desire to say, "Oh, grow up!" When he doesn't grow up, you have a choice: keep playing mommy or find someone new.

Mr. Thunderbolt

Do you have any very dramatic friends? To these folks, everything is black or white. This type tells you it was love at first sight. When the lightning and thunder wane, however, he quickly becomes disenchanted and loses interest. Mr. Thunderbolt is a champion of the grand sweeping gesture. Overly elaborate gifts and dates are nice; but are they truly romantic? The answer is in your comfort level. If the presents and outings make you feel squeamish, you know something isn't quite right.

After a series of dates with these types, most women are pretty discouraged. Some are ready to give up. But just about then your luck may change, because, sooner or later, you'll meet the next type.

A Man Who Wants a Solid, Honest Relationship

When you meet this guy, there's a sense that you've reached some kind of Promised Land. So be careful. You don't want to scare him off by acting like Ms. Thunderbolt! Relationships with these "real men" get started in all kinds of ways. An acquaintance becomes a friend and a friend becomes something more, or sometimes an adversary becomes an ally. Mutual attraction develops out of dozens of scenarios. When it happens, remember this famous piece of advice: *Carpe diem* (Seize the day)!

Men who are excited about romance want pretty much the same things women want: honesty, effort, sincerity, and so forth. Their interests are as varied as the activities we'll describe throughout this book. Don't just assume every man likes sports and hates ballet. Take the time to find out, and let the fun begin!

For Women: Is He the Right Kind of Guy for You?

- He asks you how your day is going. Then he asks a follow-up question based on your answer.
- You notice he is considerate to everyone, but even more so to you.
- He makes eye contact (rather than looking lower).
- Even though you're smart enough to know he finds other women attractive, he doesn't ogle them when you're around.
- He passes the compliment–to–constructive criticism–ratio test: 10 to 1.
- He appreciates your small gestures of affection.
- He makes lots of small gestures of affection back.
- You feel special, noticed, and valued when he's around.
- You get the sense, and then he tells you, he would never deliberately hurt your feelings, even if you break up.

What Men Encounter As They Meet Women

Some men have been trained by their peers to always be suspicious around women. After all, they're told, women never reveal their true motives. Too many of them are bossy, clingy, and just want to change you. Their goal is to take away your freedom and fasten on the old "ball and chain." Believing these tales, some men stay guarded, always a little bit aloof and cautious in matters of the heart.

Sure, there are manipulators out there. But it's a safe bet that just as many women are looking for something genuine as men. So, while you don't want to wear your heart on your sleeve, you also don't want to be so defensive that no one can break through. It's a matter of common sense, intuition, and paying attention. Let's talk about a few of the types of women you might want to avoid.

The Man Hater

When a romantic involvement goes bad, the aftereffects linger with some people more than others. Like her male counterpart the Woman Hater, the Man Hater derives her bitterness and anger from bad relationships and advice from other wrathful women. Fortunately, this type is fairly easy to spot. They constantly use phrases such as, "Men are all alike" and "All men think with their (private parts)"—and *they believe them.* So, unless you're a masochist, steer clear and move on.

The Star

Have you ever been at a party where one woman demands to be the center of attention? She flirts with every guy in the room. These self-appointed local celebrities treat men as baubles or ornaments—window dressings designed to kowtow and fulfill whims. A Star is rarely serious about a man and will constantly work to make sure he never upstages her. The best advice: Let her take her act somewhere else.

The User

Closely related to the Star is the User. The User dates a smorgasbord of men, keeps as many as possible on a string, and always "takes." She is not emotionally available to any guy who has a bad day or is in a foul mood. To do so means the User would have to be a giving person, and she's not into that. Users want their suitors to lavish attention and gifts on them, but they provide little or nothing in return. Dating a User is a one-way street leading to self-contempt and usually to some kind of conclusion such as, "How could I have been so stupid?" Who needs that?

The Excessively Needy Woman

One of the most romantic things a man can do, in the proper circumstances, is to be the Prince Charming who solves a crisis. There's something special about being able to help someone. Sadly, some women immediately start to overrely on a guy. Needy is not romantic.

Ms. Thunderbolt

Like Mr. Thunderbolt, Ms. Thunderbolt is easy to spot, because one date leads to an overreaction that immediately makes you nervous. She may start planning a wedding and family in just a few short weeks. In college, this type used to be referred to as the co-ed trying to obtain an Mrs. degree. Desperation and freneticism are not attractive. "Careful" is the watchword here.

Just when you might be ready to give up, your luck may change and you'll meet the next type.

A Woman Who Wants a Solid, Honest Relationship

What leads to romance for men? Probably the same factors that lead to romance for women: chemistry, shared interests, maturity, and physical attraction. Discovering a woman who is sincere and interested in you is a great feeling. A common plot point in both popular romance novels and great classical works is that one special moment when a relationship changes. A kiss, a touch, a talk, or a look leads a guy to the realization that he's found someone very special. The feeling is a combination of relief, exhilaration, and fear. There may be no finer point in life.

For some men, the moment when they know they've met the right kind of woman jumps out unexpectedly. For others, the excitement builds slowly. There may be false starts and setbacks. But eventually, many of us manage to connect with one key romantic partner. It may take lots of looking, but the time does come. The trick is to try to enjoy the looking as much as the finding.

For Men: Is She the Right Kind of Lady for You?

- You don't spend all of your time trying to make a grand impression. Instead, you just enjoy her company.
- She notices the small things that make you unique.
- Being with her causes you to dream about being more than you are.
- She doesn't try to polish your rough edges or change you.
- She recognizes you have interests that she may not share, and she tries to accommodate your pursuit of those interests.
- When something good happens, she's the first person you want to tell.
- She recognizes your need for "guy time" and doesn't make you feel guilty for occasionally wanting to hang out with your friends. You want to reciprocate.
- When she compliments something you do or one of your traits, you know it's genuine.

The Role of Chance, Luck, or Fate

"Sometimes it's better to be lucky than good." This phrase is often associated with sports, but it is just as true in the world of romance. Stumbling across someone special is often a matter of chance.

Does that mean you should wander aimlessly, hoping fate will intervene? You could, but your odds of success would be pretty low. The alternative is something you could call *focused fumbling around.* Finding romance is often a combination of looking right under your nose and being in the right place at the right time. The secret is to stay optimistic, keep an open mind, and spend time in settings where there is a greater chance for luck to happen. Focused fumbling around gives fate a chance to occur. Go out. Do the things you like to do, by yourself and with friends; and maybe most important, send the right kinds of signals. They include:

- Appropriate dress
- Eye contact
- Good personal hygiene
- No rings on your wedding ring finger
- A smile and a pleasant demeanor

Use your time wisely. Don't go looking for a theater lover at a football game. Don't imagine you'll find a teetotaler in a bar. If you're in a gym, and the guy talking to you is muscle-bound, expect to do lots of weight-lifting. If she shows you a picture of her cat in the first ten minutes, especially if she refers to the feline (or any pet) as her "baby," know that animals are important to her. Religious people are more likely to find compatible dating partners in church. Those of you with lots of interests should probably spend time on a college campus or somewhere else where various activities take place, so that the odds will go up that you will "luckily" meet someone interesting. Although you can't be too obvious, you can put yourself in the right kinds of situations. From there, various kinds of gods probably take over.

Here are some signs that he or she is a romantic at heart: Remembers your birthday without a prompt; enjoys "cuddling" dates, in which not much else happens; knows your turnoffs and avoids them; constantly does nice things for you behind the scenes; gives you inexpensive, small, meaningful, and thoughtful gifts; puts romantic thoughts into words and shares them with you.

Be creative. Watching your niece or nephew at a Little League game or soccer match may help you run into someone else watching his or her niece or nephew. You'll know right away this person loves family, just as you do. If nothing else, you'll be able to spend some quality time with your niece or nephew.

Romantic Opportunities in Married Life

If you have taken courses in marketing or sociology, you've probably heard of the various stages of marriage. They generally include:

- Newlyweds
- Parents with young children
- Parents of teenagers
- Empty nesters
- Kids moving back home

Each stage of married life presents romantic opportunities. Building romantic episodes is different in each stage, but everyone can get on board when the romance express leaves the station, no matter what stage you're in. What leads to romance when you're newlyweds is somewhat different than what leads to romance when you're grandparents. The important thing to remember is that both *can* and *do* represent times in your life when it is possible to add to your romantic portfolio. So, let's take a quick look at each phase.

A pastor friend told us that if a newly married couple places a half-gallon jar beside their bed and puts a penny in the jar every time they make love, the jar will be full of pennies in a few years. Then, if they take one penny out every time they make love, they will probably never empty the jar. Newlywed passion, while somewhat temporary, can bond you in ways that are permanent and private.

Newlyweds and Romance

On the surface, it would seem that a recently married couple should have the easiest time staying romantic. In many ways, that's true. But, at the same time, obstacles do appear. First, there are all those negotiations. Toilet seat up—toilet seat down? Who cooks? Who does dishes? Who manages the checkbook? Whose parents do we visit for Christmas? The list of potential romance-busters is long.

Also, many newlyweds are as broke as they're ever going to be. They can treat their poverty as either a problem or an adventure. The same holds true for romance. You can't afford to go out for those exotic, expensive, and romantic meals that you might have enjoyed on your honeymoon. Chances are, as a newlywed, your primary form of entertainment is your television, maybe your car. The old bar scene isn't ideal anymore, because lots of those folks are single and rowdy. And besides, it's expensive, and you have to go to work in the morning.

On the other hand, romance at this stage can be intense, creating the kinds of memories you will cherish for the rest of your lives. We've had many friends tell us that their poor early years were as much fun as they've ever had because, for the first time, they were building something together.

To make the most out of the newlywed years, it's important to make excuses to stay romantic. Walks, talks, intimacy, quiet dinners, and dozens of other moments should be treasured. You can't repeat those first few years, so take a big drink from the newlywed cup.

At the same time, it's crucial to recognize you won't keep up this frenzied pace. Therefore, don't assume something is going wrong just because your level of emotional intensity diminishes. Think of romance using the "blind men describing the elephant" allegory. You may be holding the elephant's tail when you're first married, but over time, you'll see more of the romantic "big picture."

Romantic Activities for Newlyweds

- Have a picnic on your apartment floor.
- Guys, give her one rose for your one-month anniversary, two for the two-month, three for the three-month, and so forth, to the end of the first year.
- Ladies, after you shower, write "I love you" on the steamy mirror when you know he'll find it.
- Keep a journal of great moments from these early years, so you can share them in later life.
- Save water and money. Take showers and candlelit baths together, even if the tub is too small.
- Plan "one tank of gas" trips to nearby locations for times out together.

Parents of Young Children

Maybe we're weird, but we thought one of the most romantic things that ever happened to us was having a baby. Still, there are pitfalls to pregnancy and the early childhood years. Romance is diluted by fatigue, your level of activity, and the need to channel your energy away from your partner and toward your kids. There are dirty diapers, midnight feedings, potty training, fits, tantrums, and all sorts of other distracting aspects to parenting. Some times are great, like birthday parties, Christmas with

Santa, summer vacations, and the like. Still, it's an easy time to allow the romantic part of your married life to falter, or, at least, be put on hold.

Restoring romance in the early childhood-rearing years takes planning, patience, spontaneity, and, yes, extra effort. You have to learn to grab small moments, because many times that's all you get. Planning can be a major asset at this point. You need to set aside nights to be away from the kids and alone together. You can hire a sitter for an evening, swap baby-sitting nights with another couple in the same predicament, or ask Grandma and Grandpa to watch the youngsters (if they enjoy doing so). It also helps to arrange your day so after bedtime there is a period in which you can be together without chores, paperwork, Internet access, television, or other distractions. The secret is to not get lost in the sea of *Barney*, video games, parent/teacher conferences, lessons, recitals, and everything else oriented to the under-ten crowd.

Also, think about the flip side of this era. There's something tremendously romantic about wrapping Christmas presents at midnight and hiding them together. It is entirely possible—and desirable—to integrate kid-raising activities with feelings of passion and romance toward each other. Kids learn about love by watching their parents, so having kids and feeling love and romance toward each other should not be considered mutually exclusive things. They can work together to make your life richer, giving a greater sense of meaning and purpose to everyday activities such as working, shopping, cooking, and cleaning. When that happens, love blossoms and romance blooms in entirely new ways.

Romantic Activities for Parents with Young Children
- Schedule a date night (just for the two of you) every two weeks and stick to it.
- Ladies, set up a "spoil my husband" night. Indulge him, so he knows he's just as important as those ever-needy and demanding kids.
- Guys, set up a "Mom's night out." Shoo her out of the house to one of her favorite activities or hobbies that she's ignored since the baby was born.
- Set up dual holidays. Have one part for you and the kids, and one part for just the two of you, especially for New Year's Eve or other big celebrations.

- After the kids' bedtime, have dinner alone together on a regular basis.
- Give each other time alone for bubble baths, reading, tinkering, and other activities that help keep you sane.

Parents of Teenagers

The teenage years present a new kind of challenge to the married couple, as well as new opportunities. When the kids are small, you can simply put them to bed or hire a sitter to get some quiet time together. As they get older, they come and go in more random patterns; and the difficulties of everyday teenage life seem to grow a little worse each year. Among other things, this means you're going to be pressed to help in as many ways as you can, just as they become more resistant to your "meddling." How can this lead to romantic moments?

You can also be tremendously amused by your teens' viewpoint of your romantic life. They probably think you're a couple of old geezers who couldn't possibly be amorous. That in itself makes for a great inside joke.

The secret is to designate your times and places. Sure, some of the spontaneity is lost, but other things may crop up instead. There will come that one marvelous night when, for the first time, *you can leave them home alone, by themselves.* At that point, they love pizza. Buy them some, and the two of you can head off for your own night out.

Romantic Activities for Parents of Teenagers
- Have your own "prom" date on the same night as theirs.
- Schedule weekend retreats to romantic places as often as you can (see Chapter 5 for some ideas).
- Concentrate on the "random acts of kindness" part of your relationship. A little extra consideration during these years goes a long way.
- Gross out your kids by being really affectionate in front of them.
- Start a new hobby that gets you out of the house together. Dancing is a great one; just be sure to pick a style in which you're holding each

other. Ballroom, swing, salsa, and some of those other sexy Latin dances come to mind.

- Use your teens' romantic bumbling and stumbling through the dating years as inspiration by comparing it to your much more sophisticated, romantic program.
- Give regular tension-breaking back rubs to each other.
- Don't forget the flowers.

Empty Nesters

A sense of loss (the empty-nest syndrome) often descends when your children leave home for the first time. A great deal of your time and energy has been given to the day-to-day aspects of their lives, and, suddenly, they are taking care of themselves. For some devoted parents, one key part of life is over. Fortunately, the joys of parenting do not end with the empty nest. You can take pride in their college and work accomplishments, and a new role as grandparents lingers out there as well.

Empty nesters who take second honeymoons and work at restoring some of the private intimacy that first took place as newlyweds go a long way toward reducing and eliminating the postpartum of kids moving out.

To the rookie empty-nest family, some coaching is in order. A shift must take place. It involves taking active steps toward revitalizing and renewing the time you spend with your spouse. One thing that helps is that this stage of life is often your highest earning period. There are college costs to defray, but you can create a budget that includes lots more funding for your entertainment account.

With proper diet, exercise, and medical attention, the empty-nest stage can be a time of revitalized physical affection. You can take your time, knowing there will be fewer interruptions. And you have a level of familiarity that makes it possible to immerse yourselves in passion. Of course, you won't be the gymnasts you were in the early years of your marriage, but you may find yourselves setting other kinds of records.

Romantic Activities for Empty Nesters

- Close the curtains and become nudists for a night.
- Read those journals you wrote in as newlyweds, while reviewing old photos and videos.
- Take second honeymoon*s* (plural).
- Walk together for exercise early in the morning or around dusk.
- Have all of your kids come home at the same time, to remind yourselves why you're so glad you're now empty nesters. Go out for a romantic dinner the next night.
- Leave a rose on the bed as you depart on a business trip.
- Send a steamy message to greet your spouse as he or she arrives at the hotel on the business trip.
- Do one activity you used to do as newlyweds that you haven't done for years.
- Visit the place where you met.

Kids Moving Back Home

A new phenomenon has swept across the United States. It involves children of empty nesters moving back home. Many young people are not able to afford houses or have other difficulties that cause them to move back in with their parents. This can be a troublesome time on the romance front.

First, these twenty-somethings are independent and usually have some disposable income. So, while you think they should be saving up some kind of down payment, they're out partying, at least on the weekend. Second, they create at least a mild strain on your budget with increasing food costs, utility bills, and other expenses. And, of course, they don't even dream of reimbursing you.

Third, they're adults. They don't want you messing with their affairs, rendering advice, or telling them what to do. Dealing with disruptions to the tranquility of your home can be frustrating, but it's extremely important to avoid taking out your frustrations on your spouse!

An even more difficult complication occurs when your child brings grandchildren home to live with you. Although you may adore the little tykes, you're not used to the chaos anymore. Once again, romance can suffer, and fingers can easily be pointed at each other, rather than at the source of your aggravation.

The empty-nest feeling was the loss of a familiar pattern of living, which was, at least in part, focused on your family. The "kids moving back home" stage involves the loss of your newfound freedom. Still, romantic adventures are possible. You need to leave, or you need to get the kids out of your house, at least for a night or two. Then, it's a matter of negotiation. You have to come up with a plan you can all live with. It should also be a plan that forces your children to live independently as soon as possible.

When they finally do leave, enjoy the fact that your home is once again your own. During these golden years, you can return to romance in its fullest glory. Start by celebrating the small moments, and planning for the bigger ones (the fortieth, forty-fifth, and fiftieth anniversaries, for example). Use your time to revel in each other. Romantic memories can be supplemented nicely with new moments.

It's All in the Attitude

What should be apparent by now is that romance is a state of mind as much as a series of activities. You can turn any age into a romantic period. The best place to start is by assessing how you currently spend your time. Then take steps to add some spice to your love life. You'll be richer for it.

Attitude Adjustments in Long-Term Relationships

Many married folks and established couples want a little more heat and passion in their daily lives. Remember that the history you share throughout your adult lives—the good times and the bad—can bond you in a very special way, as nothing else ever will. Cherish this connection, and you will develop a deeper passion based on mutual love, trust, and respect. This special warmth helps you adjust your attitude during the leaner times and helps you appreciate your partner in the quiet moments when you're alone.

Attitude Adjustments for Single People

Culturally, it seems as though we've been trained to believe women are more naturally tuned to finding romance. Waiting patiently, like lighthouse keepers on the shore, women instinctively know when the man of their dreams comes into the harbor. If only it were so! In reality, women seeking real romance are in the same boat as men. There's lots of sifting and sorting to complete before a real "catch" appears.

It's easiest to find love when you stop looking.

Still, singles may be the most inclined just to be out looking for fun. Often, that's when romance pops up. Be open, receptive, and careful. In other words, open the door when opportunity knocks.

A Note of Caution

At the same time, there are those dangers associated with dating that we mentioned at the start of this chapter. Some of them are new, and others have been around for a while. All of them require caution. When you're out there circulating, be wary of the following situations:

- **Drugs.** Rufenol ("Ruffies") is sometimes known as the "date rape" drug. Colorless and odorless, it is easily slipped into a drink. Once the drug is ingested, the victim loses the ability to control his or her faculties and resist an attack. Afterward, the victim has trouble remembering the incident. Rules of common sense apply here. First, know as much as you can about the person you're seeing. Second, don't leave a drink unattended in a bar or dance club. Third, it's a good idea to have a friend check up on you on date nights, especially when you are getting to know someone. Finally, if something bad happens, call the police and file charges.

- **Date rape.** Date rape has been a problem for as long as there have been dates. Of course, it is impossible to know who will attack you and who will not. Again, common sense is the key. When you're first seeing someone, arrange to meet in safe public places instead of being picked up at your home. Observe how he reacts to the word *no.* A course in self-defense probably isn't a bad idea either. If he attacks, fight him off if you can and call the police.
- **Stalking.** Incidents of stalking have risen dramatically in the United States. Often, they follow a failed relationship. Other stalkers pick their victims at random. Both genders can be stalkers, although males are more likely to be the offenders. Take this problem seriously. Contact the authorities, get a restraining order, and be very aware of self-defense and home security. Many times stalking becomes part of a pattern that began with violence in the relationship. This kind of violence can easily escalate. If you become the victim of a stalker, expect to make dramatic changes in your life for your safety and peace of mind.
- **Dating and domestic violence.** There is no excuse for one person to hit, hurt, or verbally assault another. There is a great deal of evidence that many violent crimes go unreported. If you are the victim of a violent crime, it is vital that you stand up for yourself and your rights. Call the police. Get away from the offender and stay away.

Counseling is often helpful for those who are trapped in a violent relationship. Every day you wait is one more day in which something terrible could happen.

It is sad that we have to talk about such things in a book about romance. Unfortunately, modern life compels us to mention these tragic problems. We want you to experience the pleasant and positive side of dating, and, if at all possible, avoid the harm that exists in our world.

On that less-than-pleasant note, we're still going to remind you of the importance of being outgoing, optimistic, and enthusiastic. Don't be scared off by the dark side. Instead, try to construct the right atmosphere for your romantic life.

CHAPTER 3
Times in Your Life

In Chapter 2 we talked about how to make the most of romance during certain times in your life: when you are single, as newlyweds, as parents of small children, as parents of teenagers, and as empty nesters. In this chapter, we're going to look at these stages in a different way. Each stage can teach you something about romance, and these valuable lessons can help you become a more intimate romantic individual or couple. It never hurts to look back and see what there is to draw from your past as you encounter new experiences.

Puppy Love

Do you remember your first crush? Was it on a teacher, on one of your friend's parents, or on an older, wiser kid from your neighborhood? Many times we develop our first romantic feelings for a totally unrealistic prospect. There's something very innocent and endearing about those kinds of emotions. They set the very first boundaries in the field of love. And it doesn't take long to move on to something a little more tangible. Sooner or later, most kids develop romantic feelings for a peer, feelings they can't quite understand. When you're going through the process, the intensity of this passion is as strong and as real as anything you've ever encountered. Fistfights may break out, tears may be shed, hearts are broken, and your palms are undoubtedly sweaty when you're courting that first special sweetheart.

Puppy love has infinite value. It teaches us our first lessons in affection and courtship. You also learn about a new kind of pain, whether it's rejection, a breakup, or anger at yourself for being so shy. For a fortunate few, the attraction is mutual. Even these kinds of minor attachments can lead to warm memories of a first dance, first kiss, and more.

Once you become more sophisticated, those times may seem a little silly. They're not. It never hurts to recall the curiosity and excitement you experienced. It might even be fun to break out a pop bottle and play a retro game with your current sweetheart. Lighthearted play is great for a romance at any age.

Romantic Lessons from Puppy Love

- The other gender isn't "the enemy"
- The joy of holding hands
- What lips feel like
- Why you should take dance lessons
- How to deal with rivals
- Other ways to show a girl you like her (besides pulling her pigtails)
- People can be awfully mean
- Having a crush can be pretty cool

Coming of Age

Adolescence is a troubling time. For the most part, kids experience a combination of adult feelings with youthful insecurities. Trying to fit in or be popular and figuring out who you are and what the world is all about dominate adolescent thinking. In the midst of these jumbled emotions, romances ebb and flow. The language changes, but the mechanics are pretty much the same. Whether you're dating or going steady, for the most part, it's a battle against raging hormones, emotional confusion, and evolving bodies.

Many of you may think of this age and time as the period when you met your first love. And it's possible you still carry some kind of idealized torch for that person. Romantic feelings are more profound during these years. It's very painful when a relationship ends. Being rejected hurts even more.

There are two sides of the adolescent coin to cover. The first concerns dealing with this period as a parent.

Mom and Dad's Viewpoint

Whether you like it or not, first dates or romantic involvements seem to start a little younger with each generation. So, Mom and Dad, you walk a fine line between not taking them seriously and being overprotective. On the one hand, your kids' feelings are real and strong. On the other hand, you don't want them to become so overwhelmed by these new attachments that they lose sight of the other joys of childhood. Consequently, it's a good idea to keep them active in schoolwork, afterschool events, church or other spiritual activities, and other character- and confidence-building projects. Then, if they can fit in some time for flirting, good for them.

The Adolescent Perspective

The other side of the coin is what adolescent love can give to you. One of the best aspects of these attachments is youthful exuberance. You get your first taste of nonsexual romantic passion and often of sexual experimentation. You may also struggle with worries about being clumsy and unattractive and feeling like an outcast. These negative experiences can be great building blocks for your romantic repertoire. That's because it's a time to develop sensitivity, compassion, empathy, and consideration for the feelings of others.

Nothing makes a better lover than someone who truly cares about the needs of his or her partner.

The primary battle, on the romantic front, is to take the scars you earn during these years and set them aside. It's tough to forget the kind of pain young people can inflict on each other. But it's important to evolve. As adults, a whole new world opens up on the romance front. You don't want a few bad episodes from those early years to spoil what's coming next.

Romantic Lessons from Early Adolescence

- Some guys are just out to use you sexually.
- Other guys are so infatuated with you that they walk into walls as you pass by.
- Some girls love to taunt and tease.
- Other girls are so infatuated with you that they can't stop talking about you to their friends.
- Summoning up the courage to ask someone out can be really difficult.
- Breaking up is hard to do.
- It feels great to meet someone who is as enamored with you as you are with him or her.
- The telephone is a great gadget.
- E-mail is a great gadget.

The College Years

Ah, freedom! Going away to college adds a new dimension to life. Romance often changes with it. Lots of teenagers leave a high school sweetheart behind. They promise to be faithful and break up soon after. Long-distance relationships are hard at any age, but especially when there are so many new choices available. Besides, college life adds other aspects to your development as an individual. As a result, it's easy to drift apart.

Campus life is unique, with an abundance of new responsibilities and challenges. There are whole new sets of ground rules for everything from going to class (or not) to drinking to dating. It's easy for a cocky high school senior to turn into a cowering college freshman. Insecurity often resurfaces.

College romances can take many forms. Each one can be a nice instruction guide for later on. With the proper attitude, you can enjoy these years as much as any because many new romantic activities are possible. Jump in with both feet! But pay attention! Some of these new situations can be treacherous.

A Crush on a Professor

In high school, you may have gotten the warm fuzzies for a young teacher. In college, the same pitfall awaits. After all, many profs are slightly older, attractive, intelligent, established, and confident. You wouldn't be the first to feel intrigued by this seemingly older, wiser man or woman.

Remember this: You are in college to get an education. The instructor is there to pass along knowledge, not get dates. Most colleges have rules against professors getting involved with students. As a student, you're in a power relationship with that teacher, which is not a good way to start anything. An ethical professor will immediately back away from any kind of an advance; an unethical one will take advantage of you. Either way, you lose. So, what should you do if you find yourself fantasizing about one of your professors? Keep it as your own little secret; enjoy it for what it is, and move on.

A Freshman with a Crush on a Senior

Another man- or woman-of-the-world type is that sage senior you just met. Once again, the attraction stems, in part, from the perception that this person is more of an adult. Many romances blossom between these two age groups, so there must be something going on. Some succeed, and some don't.

Keep in mind what we said in Chapter 2 about Stat-Keepers, Gammas, Stars, and all of those other not-so-nice types. It's easy to get used when your heart is all aflutter because that senior is paying attention to you. This means you need to think with your head as much as with other parts. Are you attracted to the person or to the persona? Remember, this person is going to leave after graduation. You don't want to be forfeiting your education to chase what may or may not be your dream love.

Drinking and Dating

Probably the biggest hazard of college age is access to legal and illegal substances that can get you into a great deal of trouble. Alcohol use creates a number of problems on campuses, including binge drinking, drunk driving, losing control, and so forth. It's hard to avoid the social pressure that causes you to drink yourself silly, but drinking too much does not bode well for romance, grades, or your self-respect.

The typical college student thinks about sex at least once every ten minutes.

Instead of falling into these traps, try to deal with college as the free-flowing learning experience that it's supposed to be. Being romantic does not always mean being serious. The idea is to enjoy these moments without jeopardizing the rest of what you're doing.

Many times, love does emerge at college. From mixers to football games to all-night study sessions to spring break vacations, the potential is there to meet new people and find romance. If it's the real thing, a whole new chapter is opening up. Negotiating your way through a deeper relationship during the college years can be tricky, so approach the situation with your eyes wide open.

Senior Syndrome

Graduating from college means that you have to get a job and live in the real world. For most seniors, the prospect is pretty scary. As a result, many seniors start grabbing for some kind of security. What better way than marriage? That way you can enter your brave new world with someone by your side. Senior syndrome is a sticky wicket. It's nearly impossible to untangle feelings of insecurity about the future with love that feels so real. The net result is lots of June weddings following May graduations.

Senior syndrome weddings are second farewells for lots of new grads. They gather their college friends together for a good cry and good-bye, and a new life begins. A major shock to the system occurs as a whole new pattern of living emerges. If you are getting married right after college, reread the "Newlyweds and Romance" and "Parents of Young Children" sections in Chapter 2. If you're staying single, you'll be entering another interesting era in your romantic evolution.

Romantic Lessons from the College Years

- There are lots of attractive guys besides "lookers" and athletes.
- There are lots of attractive women besides cheerleaders and socialites.
- Hooking up with people who share the same interests can cause some major sparks on the attraction front.
- Just talking and sharing is romantic.
- You have to juggle work and play, class work and clowning around. A good potential partner recognizes your need for balance.
- Being blurry-eyed drunk doesn't do much for your love life.
- Feeling confident and accomplishing something like getting a college degree can make you feel very attractive.
- Smarts are sexy.
- You can have a great time on a budget.

Single and on Your Own

Uh-oh. Freedom *and* responsibilities—it's sure not as much fun as just plain old freedom. Young adults cope with all kinds of novel situations, such as finding a job, paying bills, living alone, and making their own way. Some move back home. Others get roommates. Most still don't know what they want to be when they grow up. It's another vulnerable time.

Romance when you're twenty-something and single is unique. For the first time, you may have some disposable income, even if it's not a great sum. You're probably tired, or soon will be, of the bar scene. Time pressures are more noticeable as well; job hours are far different from college hours. Most employees must get up first thing in the morning and go to work. Physically, men are still in their peak years, in terms of sexual drive. Women may be struggling with respect issues at work, pay differentials based on gender, and parental pressure to "get married and settle down."

Against this backdrop, the romantic possibilities are endless and exciting. You're not limited to campus life. A little bit of money can go a long way, when it comes to local entertainment and travel. Flowers, wine, and candles don't cost that much. If you have a nice apartment, you have privacy and can tailor your "nest" to fit your individual personality. It's a great time to be alive and working on your love life!

We spent quite a bit of time describing this stage in Chapter 2. For now, keep in mind that practically everything written in this book applies, in some way or other, to single people. Times change, you grow older, and levels of prosperity rise and fall, but the opportunity to build a great love life is ever-present.

The Mature Adult Years

Body image is a factor that probably isn't discussed as much as it should be when romance is being addressed. That's because it's a bit uncomfortable. In the United States, we are obsessed with having the perfect form, it seems, in ourselves and in the people we date or marry. And, of course, no one can live up to those expectations. What is even more disturbing, however, is how body image intrudes into our romantic world.

The average married couple spends fewer than twenty minutes each day talking. Is that enough?

As we age and become fully developed adults, things shift. Wrinkles form, parts sag, and stomachs expand. It seems as though we've been trained to believe this means we're less sexy and less romantically inclined. Not so!

Getting older has its advantages. You're much less clumsy, in every sense of the word. If you're in a long-term relationship, you know which physical buttons to push to make your partner feel great. Chances are you've developed a familiarity with your partner that's very comforting—there's nothing you have to prove; you can be yourself. In conversations, it's much easier to get along and to stay away from those touchy subjects, especially during amorous evenings. There can be a great mixture of security, trust, and new adventures left to share. You deal with others as adults. You also know who to avoid and why.

Single adults are much more aware of themselves and what they're looking for in someone from the opposite sex. They are established in jobs, and, hopefully, in their social lives. Dating is no longer a "do or die" issue. When someone intriguing comes along, you know how to entice and/or ask that person for a date. So what are a few varicose veins, wrinkles, or extra pounds in comparison?

There is an old beer commercial that says what all grown-ups should remember, both in daily living and when working on enhancing a relationship: "You only go around once in life, so grab for all the gusto you can." Stop worrying about getting older. It's a waste of time. Get on with the business of enriching every bond possible, with family, friends, and especially with the love of your life.

Ten Things to Stop Doing If You Want a Better Love Life

1. Watching television (The average family watches six and a half hours per day!)
2. Surfing the Internet (This new technology is a major time thief in many families.)
3. Bickering about the small stuff
4. Overindulging kids at the expense of your own lives
5. Engaging in obsessive holiday preparations that overshadow actually enjoying the season or the day
6. Indulging in a nightly cocktail/happy hour before dinner
7. Complaining about in-laws

8. Fighting over money
9. Thinking about sex as a commodity that you can trade in a relationship
10. Working a job that sucks the joy out of life without looking for alternatives

Suddenly Single

Lots of the things we've been talking about so far in this chapter are half biological and half stage-of-life. The "suddenly single" syndrome can happen at any time, at any age. After going through a divorce, the last thing you probably want to think about is romance. Divorce is tough. For some, new financial burdens take precedence. For others, kids endure the brunt of the breakup. Many divorced people feel distrust, anger, confusion, and other negative emotions.

The majority of divorced people in the United States eventually remarry.

Without a doubt, some time must pass for the healing process to begin. There will be some baggage to carry around. If infidelity was a problem, trusting someone new is difficult. When a career takes precedence over a marriage, it may be hard to believe someone values you more than his or her job. Each cause of a divorce leaves behind a trail of aftereffects. Moving forward to something new and better may be difficult at first.

At the same time, it may not be too long until a void appears. We're all social critters; we love to share; we love to love. Against this backdrop, you begin to rebuild a romantic life. It's probably going to seem odd and awkward at first. In many ways, this kind of single life is tougher than the first time around, especially if you have kids. You may feel inclined to set romance aside until your youngsters are grown. Each person adjusts in his or her own way and at an individual tempo.

A Quiz for the Divorced Romantic

Are you ready to get involved again?

1. Are you tired of dining alone?
2. Do you enjoy time with your kids but wish for something more?
3. Can you put your animosities toward your "ex" behind you, or will some poor soul you're dating have to deal with them?
4. Are you fretting that life is passing you by and you should be out there enjoying it?
5. Could you get past the weird feeling associated with kissing someone new?
6. Can you handle telling your children you're going out on a date?
7. Do your friends try to "set you up"?
8. Does meeting a new and intriguing person of the opposite sex interest you?
9. Is your confidence back?
10. Are you often lonely?

If you answered yes to fewer than five questions, you're probably not ready to date again. Give yourself more time to heal. If you answered yes to five to eight questions, you're close; try something on a small scale. If you answered yes to nine or ten questions, what are you waiting for?

Midlife Issues

No matter how you define it, midlife is a time when people start asking lots of tough questions: "Why am I here?" "Am I getting the most out of life, or am I just blowing it?"

Mortality seems much closer. After all, aging is more apparent when you look in the mirror. Physically, you may not be able to do the things you used to do. Even looking at a clock or a calendar may remind you there is much less time left. It's easy to get caught up in morbid thoughts and forget to live.

How should a person deal with midlife? Obviously the answer depends on life circumstances. People who are single or divorced deal with it differently than those who are married. Happily married couples are able to enjoy midlife in ways that unhappy couples can't. Those who started families late may have teenagers or even younger children still at home. Others are beginning the empty-nest stage of life.

In these situations, there are a few things you can do to enhance your romantic state of being. They include the following:

- Paying careful attention to your health
- Exercising regularly
- Keeping a strong focus on your love life, no matter what the obstacles
- Using as many resources as possible to try new adventures
- Shifting the focus away from kids and back onto each other
- Going to counseling if depression and negative thoughts are getting the better of you

Many married couples remain sexually active throughout their entire married lives.

One of the best countermeasures for feeling old and run-down is to feel young and in love. And it may very well be your spouse of the past twenty-five years who gives you that new surge of energy. At midlife, your children are old enough to take care of themselves, especially when they start driving. There is less pressure to be the "perfect" anything (parent, spouse, friend, career man or woman, and so on). Instead, it's possible to take some time for yourself. If you're a woman, your sex drive may reach an all-time high. You know by now what pleases you and are less afraid to ask for it. In general, you can approach life in a whole new way. This makes it much easier to enjoy romance.

The Golden Years

Do you remember a beer commercial that showed an older couple getting amorous, trying to make it look funny? The commercial didn't play well, because it seemed almost mean-spirited. It raises an interesting issue, however. Not many of us like to think of Grandma and Grandpa getting "hot and heavy," to use a euphemism. We're okay with them hugging and giving each other a nice little smooch, but anything more, and we've got little creepy crawlies just pondering the mere idea.

On the other hand, a whole generation of baby boomers is moving into the grandparent phase of life. In fact, their grandkids are known as "Echo boomers." And, lots of these fifty-plus types are still in good health and quite active. This means, friends, the old fire hasn't gone out yet!

If you are approaching the post-midlife stage, it's entirely possible that you are as interested in firing things up on the romantic front as any twenty-year-old. The great part is, you have a new and different kind of freedom to work with. Financially, many people in their fifties, sixties, and seventies are pretty well set. Travel is possible, nights out are manageable, and the number of possible places to go exploring grows. What a great time to rekindle what started a long time ago!

Romance and Retirement

Lots of senior citizens report that retirement is a crisis period. Several things happen at once. For openers, many seniors combat feelings of being "useless" or nonproductive. There is a transition from building a financial nest egg to learning how to enjoy the fruits of your labor. The time can make any new retiree a little cranky at first.

To complicate matters, if one spouse retires before the other, or if one has always stayed home while the other worked, there will be a post-retirement adjustment period. You may be "bumping into each other" quite a bit. Many retiring husbands are forced to cope with a tendency to become household micromanagers. They challenge long-standing cooking and cleaning patterns and basically wander around the house feeling lost. It's not unusual for some bickering to develop.

With this going on, it's sometimes harder to feel relaxed and affectionate. Quite honestly, both spouses have to work at redefining the relationship to accommodate these new circumstances. That means each one needs to give a little ground. Sharing projects works for some couples and causes fights for others. The idea should be to discover ventures that make you feel closer. Small road trips together, time apart for hobbies and interests, and careful planning of daily, weekly, and monthly activities really help. With any luck, you're going to be spending a long time in this new arrangement. Romance happens best when you get the other stuff sorted out first.

Remember, when one spouse retires, every member of the family is affected.

Precautions

There are a few limitations to this age. First, it's vitally important to stay as healthy as possible. You should have regular checkups and screenings for high-risk diseases (heart and blood pressure concerns, breast cancer for women, prostate problems for men, skin cancer for past or present sun worshipers, colon cancer for everyone). The trick is not to mistake an illness or problem for "old age." Lots of conditions can be detected and treated, including depression—a condition that regularly strikes seniors. Feeling well leaves you free to pursue romantic interests.

Another new issue for seniors is the use of Viagra, the drug that enhances sexual performance in older men. If you or your spouse is considering taking it, there are a few things you should know. First, there is no one-to-one connection between sex and romance. You can have great sex and it may not be all that romantic. And you can have an incredibly wonderful night of romance without sex. Be sure you're identifying the correct problem. Is there a lack of physical intimacy with your partner, or is there simply a more basic form of affection missing from your marriage?

Second, some men simply shouldn't take the drug for health reasons. It doesn't make sense to put yourself at risk (heart problems, high blood pressure) for one night of sex. Consult with your doctor first to get all the facts.

Many couples are truly frustrated by declining sexual desire or performance. For this group, the Viagra alternative may be a tremendous windfall. While it's true that sex and romance don't always go together, they sometimes do, in very wonderful ways. A night of wining and dining can be carefully constructed to help you enjoy "the old days" of passion. When that happens, you are truly enjoying the great benefits of this age of medical care. Go for it!

Another limiting factor associated with aging is energy. As you move into later life, you may need more rest or require a different pattern of rest. Some retirees find that the most romantic part of the day is first thing in the morning. Fortunately, nothing is stopping you from using that time to do all of your "couple" activities, from a round of golf to bowling, to some quality time in the bedroom. A little bit of flexibility and creative thinking can help you restructure your calendar and clock to arrange times to be together. For those who do, these truly become the Golden Years.

Old Age Alone

Probably the greatest tragedy in a person's life is losing a beloved spouse. This is true no matter what the age, from a newlywed to a ninety-year-old. It hurts, and the pain never really goes away. Memories help, but they also serve as reminders of what was lost. For many, one final issue remains on the romantic front: "Should I try to find someone again, or simply live out these final years without a partner?" This choice is never easy. For some, becoming involved with someone new can almost feel like a betrayal of the spouse who died. It's easy to feel guilty when that happens.

For others, the prospect of living alone is depressing, even with family and friends nearby. The ache of losing a spouse is made worse by the idea that you have no one with whom to share your life. Your former husband or wife may be gone, but your craving for romance and closeness remains. To make matters worse, single women greatly outnumber the men available. This makes it more difficult to connect with someone new.

Fortunately, a number of options exists in between living alone and becoming immersed in another full-fledged relationship. For openers, a wide variety of senior citizens groups sponsor everything from major sightseeing trips to small dances and dinners. You can enjoy the activities and circulate without needing to be with a partner. We also know of several widows and widowers who have very close friends of the opposite sex without taking the next step into marriage. Some live under the same roof in a platonic situation. Others are intimate, but live separately.

Here are some things you can leave behind for your kids that are romantic and will be truly treasured: diary or journal; favorite old music; funny stories and other memories; love notes and letters; mementos of your honeymoon; recipes for favorite meals; scrapbooks; things you saved from your dating years; wedding or anniversary gifts; wedding photos and other photo albums.

It seems the secret is to battle loneliness while finding a comfort level for your circumstances. It's not easy. Starting over takes confidence, because you are going to deal once again with the same fear of rejection you first felt back in that puppy-love stage. As an alternative, some seniors who have lost a spouse rely heavily on the love of family to get them through. Even these folks can still enjoy a form of romance. Old photos, movies, videos, and books can remind them of previous days and nights of passion and closeness. It's even possible to travel back to your favorite haunts to relive memories. A few tears may fall, but they help you know you're still alive and feeling affection for a special person. There's nothing wrong with that.

Perhaps the best thing you can do, if being widowed becomes your fate, is to think about a legacy. Part of the legacy is financial, part is interpersonal, and part can be romantic. Tell your children and grandchildren about the great fondness you have for them and for your departed spouse. Let them know the depth and breadth of your feelings. Write down things you wish to pass on, or put them on some kind of audiotape or videotape. Trust us, your kids will treasure the memories you share regarding their beloved dad or mom, grandma or grandpa. The circle of life is most complete when we give back as much as we can to those we love.

CHAPTER 4
Times of the Year

E ach year contains a set of built-in holidays that provide plenty of opportunities for romance. You can capture the moment by taking the lead in planning the way the day unfolds. Your spouse, lover, or romantic interest will be thrilled that you took the time and made the effort to make the day unique. From there, good things are bound to happen.

We're going to walk you through the calendar and show you how to spice up each holiday and season. We hope this chapter will spark lots of great ideas. After all, part of being a great romantic is tailoring your approach to fit the person of your dreams. We'll get you started, and from there, only the limits of your imagination can stop you from being a romantic wizard!

Nearly every holiday can turn into a day or night of romance.

New Year's Day

Some people really like making a fresh start. Each New Year offers the potential to mend your ways or to make some other kind of personal improvement, as well as the opportunity to take some time out for romance. Examine your romantic life carefully. Ask yourself questions like these:

- What are my biggest priorities?
- Am I balancing life, work, love, and the things that really matter?
- How many times last year did I tell my spouse or partner that I love him or her? Was it often enough?
- Am I giving enough time to my romantic relationship?

Or, if you're single:
- Am I still single because I haven't met the right person, or because I won't give anyone a chance?
- Where could I go, or what could I do, to improve my odds of meeting someone special? Why don't I go there or do that activity more often?
- Am I enjoying being single, or am I just enduring it?

The goal of this kind of self-evaluation is to make sure you're doing what you want to be doing. It's pretty easy to drift away from the things that really matter. Once that happens, all kinds of inconsequential distractions can take their place. The first day on a new calendar can be an annual reminder to keep your life and love on course.

After you take stock, be thankful. You've lived to see another year. Your significant other is still in your life. There is still time left to fix any problems you're having or to make what you currently enjoy better. We all become better lovers and romantic partners when gratitude is a major attitude we carry around. New Year's Day is a fine time to start practicing more gratefulness on a daily basis.

Some New Year's Day Romantic Activities

- Snuggle up and watch football.
- Go to a parade if there is one in your area.
- Promise each other that this year will be your best ever.
- Build a snowman together.
- Take down Christmas decorations as a team; then write down the one holiday memory that's most important to keep.
- Buy a calendar and start planning romantic getaways.
- Figure out one new activity to share during the upcoming year.

Some people regard New Year's Day as a new beginning. Make a list of some things you truly want to do and work hard to stick with the list. What more worthy goal could you choose than to do more sharing and caring with your spouse or lover?

Super Bowl Sunday

What? Football and romance? It's not as far-fetched as it may seem. Most of the United States manages to pause on Super Bowl Sunday for a national experience. It's not just the game. Many people tune in to see which company comes up with the neatest new commercial. The halftime show is another mega event. The entertainment both before and after the game turns a winter Sunday into something fun and exciting every year. But how is all this romantic?

To turn the Super Bowl into your own private love festival requires some planning. For starters, there are altruistic things you can do to feel a bit closer to each other. Many local charities have a "Souper Bowl" event, designed to raise money for the homeless and the hungry. Others deliver pizzas and snacks as a way to generate funds for their groups. So, one alternative to simply indulging in a daylong television-watching party is to do something for the less fortunate. This is a great approach for those of you who don't really like or care about the game.

At game time, have a little fun. Figure out some inside communication that only you and your partner know. It can be something as simple as exchanging a kiss for every point scored.

If you do plan to build your day around the game, remember that the festivities usually don't start until the afternoon. That gives you a morning that can be shared in all kinds of nice ways: going to church together, taking in a leisurely Sunday brunch somewhere, or even spending time in your bedroom, first doing what comes naturally and then reading the paper as you enjoy breakfast in bed. You can almost always get a romantic rise out of serving your partner while wearing pajamas.

The Football Hater's Guide to Super Bowl Sunday

- Go shopping—the mall is usually open and empty.
- Give up the day so your partner can watch the game in peace. It's great barter material to be stored for future use; think in terms of massages or foot rubs.
- Invite fellow football-hating friends over and have your own little party.
- Make a bet on the outcome of the game with your partner involving something sexy. Insist on being paid in full before you go to bed that night if you win, and be sure to pay off if you lose. Either way, you win.

Memorial Day

The first big weekend of the summer signifies several things. For one, you'll probably be wearing lighter and more revealing clothes. Also, most families and couples start thinking about summer travel plans and vacations. Parents consider what to do with kids who are home for the summer.

How do you turn a holiday like Memorial Day into romance? First, take the actual reason for the commemoration seriously. The point of Memorial Day is to remember the sacrifice others made for you and for their country. The idea of "doing for others" and working for the greater good is a reminder that is beneficial to a nation, but it is also helpful for a couple.

Second, this three-day weekend offers many possibilities. Beyond a visit to a local cemetery where loved ones rest, take some time for each other. Couples without children can take a day off to relax together:

- Have a barbecue or picnic together, even if it's just in your backyard or on a rooftop.
- Stay up and watch the stars come out.
- Go to a parade and hold hands while you watch.
- Go to one of those spring festivals that many small towns hold over the weekend.
- Rent romantic movies and watch them all night.

Couples with kids can divide the time between events for the whole family and activities with each other:

- Set up a campout for your kids in the backyard. Take advantage of your time alone inside.
- Swap watching kids overnight with your friends to get some time alone.
- Undertake a major spring cleaning project. Throw a pizza/video party for your kids when it's finished.
- Go on a road trip and get two rooms at a motel, one for them, one for you.
- Take them camping, complete with a campfire and cooking outdoors. Make out a little after they fall asleep.
- Leave the kids with Grandma and Grandpa for an afternoon; then have a family picnic when you come back relaxed and refreshed.

Fourth of July

Fireworks go naturally with feelings of love. People use the metaphor all the time. You'll have the best access to fireworks displays each year on or near the Fourth, unless, of course, you live next door to Disneyland. Naturally, then, one of the most romantic things you can do is to share some time watching as things light up and explode over your head. Just watch the next time you're at one of these displays. Couples huddle together affectionately as the show takes place. Go and do likewise.

Lots of families tack on a few extra days of vacation to the Fourth of July holiday. That's a great approach. If you have more days off to enjoy, your opportunities to get away as a couple increase. In Chapter 5, we mention some of the places that are great romantic getaways.

If the Independence Day celebration falls on a three-day weekend, you have a variety of potential activities to enjoy. Our advice is to consider your tolerance level for crowds and traffic before you make any plans. Pools, lakes, and beaches are going to be busy. So, if you're looking for quiet time alone, they don't make much sense. Also, long drives can leave you tired and tense. You may want to adjust your travel time to parts of the day when you expect to encounter less traffic.

Things to Remember As You Celebrate the Fourth of July

- Swimming together can be very sexy—so is rubbing suntan oil on your partner.
- Fireworks foolishness can turn a fun, romantic day into a trip to the hospital. Safety matters!
- Don't forget the bug spray. Itchy bites won't put you in the mood for romance.

- Crowds are exciting but not sensual. Match the number of people around you to your romantic objective for the day.
- Cooking outdoors is fun. Doing other things outdoors can be memorable and tremendously arousing. Watch for poison ivy and poison oak!

Labor Day

The fall festival season is a great time of the year. Pumpkin festivals, Oktoberfest, and dozens of harvest celebrations are on the horizon. Labor Day kicks off this period. The actual Labor Day holiday usually marks the end of the summer break. As parents, it's a day of great joy and relief, since the kids have probably been getting bored for the last few weeks and are driving you crazy! So, how to celebrate?

Once in your life, help out with the annual Jerry Lewis Muscular Dystrophy Telethon or some other charitable event. It feels great to pitch in, and you'll come out feeling closer as a couple and better as a person. Also, recall the intent of the holiday, to honor workers. Take a few moments to do that.

Next, figure out which activities you want to include in your extended weekend. The football season usually gets started, baseball pennant races are heating up, and stock car seasons are winding down. For the sports-minded, Labor Day presents the opportunity to make one more trip to see a game, match, set, or whatever. Some couples love that kind of excursion.

For parents with kids in school, remember that Monday night of Labor Day weekend is typically a very low traffic time for most restaurants. If you want a quiet dinner together, feed the kids early and enjoy the solitude at one of your favorite spots. Call first to make sure they're staying open.

Things to Remember on Labor Day

- It's still easy to get a sunburn, which isn't very romantic. Cover up.
- It's also easy to be really grumpy with your kids and each other, after a long hot summer. Try to be patient.

- Lots of people die on the highways this weekend. Either stay home or use extreme care on the roads.
- All the cool videos get rented early, so either plan ahead or do something else.
- A nice shower together can reduce a great deal of stress. Try to work one into the weekend.

Thanksgiving

If you're a couple, you may be lucky in many ways when it comes to family. If you and your partner have been together a long time, perhaps you have resolved the traditional "Where are we going this year?" question. Still, even after working out the rotation program, there are all of those other preholiday challenges to tackle. That often makes Thanksgiving week part of a work-in-progress.

Single folks have to battle through that "time with family versus time with friends or special romantic partner" problem. After all, most parents want all of their kids to come home for Thanksgiving. And maybe you've noticed that once the meal is over, Thanksgiving can get fairly boring pretty quickly, unless you are an avid football fan. So, if the single soul wants to sneak out for some fun, who can blame him or her?

The same holds true for young married couples without kids. Many have to go back to work the day after Thanksgiving, which means it's natural to want to get away for some quality time alone. Mom and Dad can get frustrated quickly if you try to leave too soon, and this problem gets exponentially worse if you try to skip dessert or fail to help with the dishes.

Those of you with kids face an additional complication. Not only do you have to go back to work on Friday, but the kids have the day off. This gives them ample time to trash the house and generally make you crazy going into the weekend.

How, then, do you turn the Thanksgiving holiday into a time of loving tranquility? It all begins with expectations. Don't expect much. Shoot for "nice" rather than "perfect." Avoid touchy subjects when talking with family. Try to turn the cooking/cleaning process into a cooperative venture. Simplify as much as you can. Remember, Mom shouldn't have to bear the brunt of this holiday alone! There is always the option of buying one of those already made meals that some stores and restaurants deliver, or simply dining out.

Next, figure out what you like to do. It's possible to stay in bed and watch the parades on television, which gives you some nice quiet time together before the festivities of the day begin. Since your kids have Friday off, this represents another great time to work out some kind of trade designed to give you an evening by yourselves.

Singles may enjoy a practice we used before we got married. Since we knew we'd be separated and with our own families, on the Wednesday night before the holiday, we cooked our own separate dinner. We enjoyed a nice quiet candlelit dinner together before the hubbub began with our own families. Later, we expanded the concept to Christmas, for the same reason.

For the most part, however, Thanksgiving just isn't much of a romantic holiday for lots of folks in terms of long-term memories. You can always snuggle up with your partner to watch *A Charlie Brown Thanksgiving* on TV. There's nothing better to make you feel all warm and fuzzy.

Thanksgiving Do's and Don'ts

- Do spend one of the two nights (Wednesday or Thursday) focused on your partner, rather than on your extended family or children.
- Do use the whipped cream you bought for the pumpkin pie in some creative way. Buy an extra can just for that purpose.
- Don't fill the holiday with travel time and too many activities. Use it to relax instead.
- Don't resurrect old arguments with family members.
- Don't watch a football game you're not interested in, just to keep peace. Take the kids outside and play with them or take a walk instead.

Christmas/Hanukkah

The month of December can be highly emotional in many ways. There's the frazzled feeling of holiday shopping, the proud-parent buzz that comes from watching your child perform in a holiday skit, and for many, spiritual stirrings are often at their peak. We sometimes look forward with great anticipation to spending time with family. Others dread the same thing. The time seems charged with an extra dose of every kind of sensation. Not the least of these should be thoughts of romance, passion, and love.

The trick to enjoying this time is to keep it as simple as possible. You can't completely simplify the month and the holiday, but you can take steps in that direction. For example, it's a lot less stressful to spread out your shopping over a couple of months, rather than jamming it in during the final two weeks of the season. Set aside a little bit of money each month or open a "Christmas Club" account at the bank so there isn't so much of a financial burden.

Another helpful idea is to prioritize things. You don't have to go to every reception and party that comes along. Pick the ones you like and skip the rest.

Each year, your goal should be to work ahead as much as you can. Then when those neat events roll around, you're free to enjoy them without feeling guilty about not being ready for the season. Turn gift-wrapping, tree decorating, and food preparation into family time, either with your spouse or significant other or with the whole family. Everyone should share in the load, and the fun. Having holiday music playing in the background is soothing and heartwarming. Visits to Santa with young children are delightful. In other words, you can immerse yourselves in the joy and fun of the holiday season, or you can bury yourselves in the anxiety of "How are we going to get everything finished?" It's mostly a matter of outlook combined with planning.

Many people tend to get depressed or anxious around the holidays. If that's the case, try to arrange something to look forward to as part of the holiday season—perhaps a trip to someplace warm right around New

Year's Day, a special dinner out, a drive to see holiday decorations, or some other ritual you and your partner can share.

Romantic Holiday Activities

- Hanging the mistletoe together—then trying it out afterward
- Sipping hot chocolate together, after the kids are in bed
- Putting on some holiday music in your car, driving around, and looking at the lights
- Spending the night in front of the fireplace, if you have one
- Sharing a candlelit dinner alone, a few days before the holiday madness sets in
- Exchanging sexy or intimate gifts after kids are asleep
- Holding each other quietly, with only the holiday lights on
- Watching cartoons and feeling like kids again
- Watching classic holiday movies or discovering new favorites
- Giving your partner flowers and a card that combines holiday greetings with romantic sentiments
- Decorating your home and yard together
- Unwrapping each other

For those of you who are unattached, this season can be pretty depressing. Whether it's because you've just broken up with someone, are divorced, or have only been casually dating, the end of the year is a reminder for many that they are alone. And, of course, some relatives don't help the situation, asking all those great questions about why you're still single. Others just make you feel bad, because they look so happy and you become jealous. Not a pretty picture.

Those of you who can't share the holidays in some romantic way need to be more ingenious. For many, a swirl of activities, family events, and special times with friends can really help. Getting out is lots better than sitting home alone. You can also take full advantage of mistletoe opportunities at parties and in other places.

When these activities aren't enough, it's time for more drastic measures. We have one friend who spends Christmas Eve and Day with his family and the rest of the week on vacation. He always goes somewhere exotic, like Hawaii. He is, of course, fortunate to have enough money to indulge himself each year. Those of you with smaller funds can still take road trips to get away. Whether it's to a nearby lake or to visit a favorite friend, a change of scenery never hurts.

Or you can go to the other extreme. Instead of self-indulgence, get involved in some kind of program to help others. You can serve meals to the homeless, fill in for workers so they can be home with their families over the holidays, and provide extra assistance at your place of worship. There are also Christmas parties for needy families and food drives for the homeless that can use your help. Giving at this time of year feels extra good. You may be surprised to find other single people working in those venues. Also, many married couples and families discover these kinds of outward-focused tasks are more enriching than any presents they receive.

Whatever you do, don't become morbid and self-absorbed. Avoid watching movies or television programs that make you feel like an outcast. In many ways, the secrets to single-person holiday success are the same as for those with partners: Enjoy the things that are fun; don't do the things that aren't. Hang around joyful folks rather than Grinches.

New Year's Eve

Well, it's the end of the year and we've come full circle. Some people call New Year's Eve "amateur night." They're not far from wrong. Getting sloppy drunk is a bad way to start off a new calendar. You spend the first day of the New Year feeling lousy and tired. Sure, once in awhile it's fun to just go a little nuts and let your hair down. And maybe New Year's is the only time you do. You can, however, use this final night of the passing year to look back and cherish fond memories. It can be a time to share with friends, and later with a special person.

Avoid making the one you love jealous or upset by getting overly enamored with the midnight-kiss scenario. This is one good time *not* to work the whole room!

Probably the critical thing on New Year's Eve is to be sure you are in the arms of the one you love at the stroke of midnight. A passionate kiss is a great way to end one year and begin the next.

Romantic New Year's Traditions

- Toasting with champagne
- Kissing at midnight
- Having breakfast before bed
- Slow dancing right before midnight
- Letting the kids stay up to share in the celebration
- Making a "bad habit" basket (Have everyone write down one bad habit they're going to try to break in the coming year. Toss the pieces of paper into the fireplace. Watch as the bad habit burns away!)

Oh, Did We Forget One?

We were just checking to see if you were paying attention. How can you talk about romantic times of the year without paying homage to Valentine's Day? Of course, we've observed many couples who observe the holiday in better and worse ways. Some feel "forced" to be romantic, and somehow that never quite works out right. Others are much better at letting it flow more naturally and get better results.

So, the first thing to remember is that Valentine's Day often takes place on a workday. If you've had a bad day at the office, it takes awhile to unwind. Unfortunately, somehow you're supposed to be able to "switch it on" on Valentine's Day, which can get things off to a bad start.

Second, everybody and their cousin want to dine out on Valentine's Day. This leads to crowds, waiting lines, slow service, tepid food, and a less-than-attractive restaurant experience. This should be the one day you do something else. Let all those folks with less imagination eat out. You stay home, go early, or do something else that keeps you away from the bustling crowd.

Third, too may people equate "big" events and magnanimous gifts with Valentine's Day. Romance shouldn't boil down to trying to outdo each other. It's an easy habit to fall into and one that's hard to break. We believe the alternative is better. Go for the small. Understate this day and emphasize others. Don't expect bells and whistles, violins and fireworks just because some card company decided that we need to flood the mail system once a year. So, what should you do to make Valentine's Day romantic? Simple—spend it with someone you love. Take some quiet time to share. Watch the loving couples around you and draw inspiration from them. Plot and scheme to surprise your lover with a great romantic night sometime in the near future. Then, do the small, obvious things. Cards, flowers, a nice dinner, some fine wine, and other appropriate gifts are plenty. Those of you who are single might be surprised by the mileage you'll get out of simply inviting a romantic prospect to your home for a nice meal.

Things to Say on Valentine's Day

- "I love you."
- "You are very special to me."
- "I can't imagine life without you."
- "I'm going rub your shoulders for a while."
- "You're a great cook. Let me clean up while you relax."
- "You look as beautiful [handsome] as the day I first met you."
- "Wanna get naked later?"
- "All these years, and you still make me as hot as a teenager."

Things *Not* to Say on Valentine's Day

- "I guess you'll do. Wanna have dinner?"
- "You really don't need those chocolates."
- "I forgot to get a card. How was I supposed to remember what day it was?"
- "I suppose you're going to say you want to go out somewhere."
- "The line at the flower shop was just too long."
- "We never seem to talk anymore."
- "I need some space."
- "Hey, there's a great game on tonight."

If you're married, share the day with your kids. Remember, they probably got their hearts broken today, when a classmate they really liked failed to send them a valentine. Being good parents at a time like that brings everyone closer together. Show your love to your kids. The impression lasts a long, long time.

Birthdays

Some people get depressed on their birthday. Others celebrate in grand fashion. Others prefer a small commemoration, but nothing major. Keynote birthdays (like sixteen, twenty-one, forty, fifty, and other round numbers) are usually noticed more. If you've had to endure one of those black balloon "surprise" parties, with the over-the-hill jokes, cards, and comments, you know some people don't handle that kind of kidding very well.

The first thing you should remember about birthdays is to celebrate them in the manner that your spouse or partner desires. Those who are sensitive about getting old should be handled with care. Those who really like having a big deal made about their birthday deserve the best party you can conjure up, at least during some of the years. Communicate your preferences to your spouse and family, and expect them to abide by your wishes. It's not too much to ask. On the other hand, when you do run into that surprise party that you really didn't want, be gracious. They are well-meaning people who like you and want you to have a good time.

Both single people and those with partners can turn a birthday into a romantic night. Usually this involves all of the usual trappings (flowers, wine, cards, restaurants, and so forth). Still, to make a birthday special means putting in some extra effort and thought. Anything from a theme party to a great present can make the day exciting and memorable.

No matter how you celebrate, it's always a good idea to include the people you love. Your kids want to please you on this day. Your parents like to share the occasion. Your friends are going to call or come by. After all that, there is still plenty of time left for extra amorous attention.

Romantic Birthday Ideas

- Give your spouse or partner a sexy birthday card privately.
- Serve breakfast in bed.
- Try giving an IOU of the racy variety as an additional no-cost gift.
- Prepare a special dinner and clean up afterward.
- Have flowers delivered to your lover's workplace.
- Leave happy birthday notes in unusual places, such as on the car seat, in a coat pocket, on the bathroom mirror, or in a wallet or purse.
- Give a whole series of small gifts that reflects your partner's personality and preferences.
- Call your lover at work and tell him or her, in specific detail, what gifts you plan to offer at the end of the day.

Many times you can get a present your partner will really enjoy without going broke. The trick is to pay attention. When he or she lingers over an item in a store but doesn't buy it because it seems a little extravagant, you have an opening. There is, of course, also the direct approach. Just ask.

Anniversaries

Anniversaries can be tough. They have quite a bit in common with Valentine's Day, if you think about it. You're *supposed* to be romantic, no matter what happened during the day. Sometimes that's not so easy. So, what should you do? There are four principles that may make things go more smoothly on your anniversary, whether you're a married couple celebrating number twenty-three or a dating couple celebrating one month together. They are sincerity, flexibility, simplicity, and fun. Let's take a closer look.

Sincerity

This one is tricky. If you're having problems in your relationship, sometimes an anniversary represents a tough moment in the year. Should you act as if everything is okay? Should you talk things out? Or is there some other strategy? The best approach is one you work out together. It never hurts to say, "You are important to me," even when things aren't going so well. An anniversary can be a time to recommit to each other, if that is what is in your heart.

Flexibility

The first thing to remember about an anniversary is that the day is not etched in granite. If it falls in the middle of the week, do something modest on the actual day, and schedule the big event for the preceding or following weekend. Those of you with kids may have additional weekday responsibilities on school nights, so plan something ahead of time. Then, if things work out so that you're feeling especially amorous on the night that your actual wedding took place, grab the moment and enjoy every minute. If not, wait until you can enjoy being with each other on a more relaxed day.

Simplicity

Don is a management professor. He tells his students that some companies put far too much effort into *making plans* and far too little into *following* those plans. The same is true for anniversaries. Sometimes we get so caught up in making sure every single thing is perfect—from the candles to the flowers to the card to the wine—that we forget to enjoy each other. So keep it simple. A great anniversary can be quiet, intimate, and very special. This is not to say that every once in awhile you shouldn't go all out. Going the extra mile on behalf of your spouse or partner is a great thing. Just don't feel as if you have to do it every year.

Fun!

The key thing about an anniversary is to enjoy it. Do whatever the two of you like to do the best. Those who like dining out should make their reservations early. Those who like horseback riding should go to the stable. Those who like sex . . . well, you know. The main thing to remember is that you don't have to do the "expected." Flowers, cards, and all those things are nice, but it's possible that the most romantic thing you can do is to look at old photos and videos, or watch a movie, complete with pop and popcorn instead.

If you're married, you made sure your wedding ceremony reflected your tastes and personalities. Those of you who are seeing someone special try to make sure you're doing things both of you can enjoy. So, it just makes sense to turn anniversary commemorations into things you'll treasure and remember.

Fun Anniversary Ideas

- Recreate the night you met in minute detail.
- Play the "pick up someone in the bar" game, in which you meet your partner at a bar and ask him or her to go on a date.
- Disappear for the whole day. Call in sick if you have to, but spend twenty-four hours indulging each other in whatever strikes your fancy.
- Play strip poker. Take your time.
- Go dancing. Try out some new steps you've never done before.
- Leave a trail of flower petals to the bedroom for when your spouse comes home.
- Write a love letter to your partner, spelling out the top ten reasons you fell in love.
- Reply to the love letter by listing the top ten reasons you're glad you're married.

Special Days

If you're like most folks, some of your most romantic moments are spontaneous. Even though there are all of those calendar-based days to be amorous, never forget the power of surprise. Everything from a simple touch to a grand gesture can say, "I love you." Acknowledge other days that are special to the two of you, such as the day you met, your first date, or the day you moved into your first house.

Sweet Seasons

Where we live, there is nothing quite like the splendor of the fall leaves. The colors are usually spectacular, and we make a point of taking drives to enjoy the sights and smells of autumn. For those who are paying attention, each season of the year offers different romantic opportunities. Here are a few ideas about romantic activities that are part of the seasons of the year.

Spring

Think rebirth, renewal, fresh starts, and great fragrances. The scents of spring are some of the most pleasant of the entire year. Spring rains can be dramatic and full of fury or quiet and peaceful. Both give you the chance to cuddle and enjoy nature's presence. It's no big surprise that spring break is a major national event, especially in many coastal regions. Clothes come off, bathing suits go on, and love (not to mention quite a bit of debauchery) blooms among college students.

It has been said that spring is the time when a young man's thoughts turn to love. That feeling certainly isn't limited to young men. The first warm spell of the year can be a great inspiration, if you let it. When winter's cold grip leaves, cabin fever ends. People get out and about. Spring should remind you that it is always important to re-energize a relationship. Take this time to renew the outdoor activities you enjoy with that special person, from gardening to golfing.

Summer

Heat and passion are words that go together. Summer goes with heat, so summer should go with passion. Clothes that were kind of skimpy in the spring are genuinely tiny in the summer. It's the season of oils, lotions, swims, sun, and fun. For many, family vacations are part of the activities. These things allow you time to relax and enjoy each other. They can also be times to touch all that bare skin that your partner is showing.

Summer events such as picnics and barbecues are great times for couples to share. The contrast of cool food with hot summer days can inspire you to feed your lover one grape at a time, while he or she rests in your lap. Strawberries go great with champagne. Sharing food can be a sensuous activity, and summer is a time when finger foods abound. And let's not forget that summer is also the season of skinny-dipping.

Quiet walks on a beach or by a lake can turn into moments of great passion!

Autumn

There are lots of things to do besides looking at leaves when fall arrives. Football games and tailgate parties abound, and there are hayrides, bonfires, apple-picking, and pumpkin-carving to enjoy. It's a time to give thanks for nature's harvest. Kids and adults alike enjoy the fun of Halloween. Wearing masks and dressing in costumes can be titillating. For many couples, it's a time to return to the college or high school where you first met. Reliving old times often reminds you of what was attractive about your partner from day one.

Depending on where you live, fall is when you light that first major fire in the stove or fireplace after a long summer break. Even for those who only use candles, autumn should be the season that reminds you of the connection between fire and love, flames and passion.

Winter

After spring has sprung and fall has fallen, if you live up north it turns cold as heck. What's romantic about that? That probably depends on your outlook. We don't get a whole lot of winter where we live, but we still know the value of warm water on a freezing day. Hot tubs and Jacuzzis are great when you're trying to get the old circulation going. Hot tub baths with someone you love often get even more going.

For everybody, winter is a time when the sun goes down earlier in the evening. If nothing else, that should remind you of the relationship between night and romance. Darkness provides cover. Candles can break the dark and warm your heart. A cold, quiet blanket of snow can be a time of peaceful, serene intimacy. Let the season do its worst with swirling snow and howling winds; you can find ways to do your best with the one you love.

The Seasonal Romantic Compatibility Quiz

Take this quiz first; then give it to your partner or the person you are dating.

1. My favorite feeling is:
   _____ Hot and sweaty   _____ Cold and crisp   _____ Normal
2. During the winter, I:
   _____ Get depressed with cabin fever
   _____ Get out and enjoy the snow
   _____ Get away and go south
3. During the summer, I:
   _____ Stay in air conditioning as much as possible
   _____ Love to go outdoors
   _____ Wish it were winter
4. Autumn makes me think of:
   _____ Things dying
   _____ Playing in the leaves as a child and other cozy memories
   _____ Winter coming; then I get depressed
5. Spring makes me think of:
   _____ Daylight Savings Time
   _____ New life and new love
   _____ Spring cleaning and other housework I hate
6. If there were one season I could eliminate, it would be:
   _____ Spring   _____ Summer   _____ Fall   _____ Winter
7. If there were only one season all year, I would want it to be:
   _____ Spring   _____ Summer   _____ Fall   _____ Winter

(continued)

Now, count the number of times your answer exactly matched your spouse or date:

If you have five to seven matches, you are seasonally compatible.

If you have three or four matches, you probably have seasonal "issues."

If you have two or fewer matches, you need to figure out how to work around how each season affects your moods, so you don't end up arguing or getting on each other's nerves.

CHAPTER 5

Places and Settings

One of the great romantic movies of all time is *Gone with the Wind*. And one of its most famous lines, asked by Scarlett O'Hara, is "Where shall I go? What shall I do?" Maybe you feel a little bit like Scarlett when you and your partner try to come up with ways to enhance your romance. We're going to try to help you out with that dilemma in this chapter. There are dozens of ways to make a few hours, days, or weeks radiate with romantic energy. At the same time, it's wise to remember the old adage, "Home is where the heart is." Couples who want to build a more exciting romantic life together need to start by putting their heart into the process. From there, the rest is easy. Romantic places are all around. (And be sure to check out Appendix A for a state-by-state listing of some wonderful romantic getaways.)

Beaches

Okay, we admit it, being beach bums is one of our favorite activities. A sandy shore is romantic for so many reasons. For example, there's that wonderful salty aroma that lets you know you're getting close to the ocean and then you hear the soothing rush of the waves. There are so many wonderful pastimes to share: sunbathing, beachcombing, rubbing suntan oil on each other, wading, tossing a Frisbee, holding hands, kissing, swimming, reading, sleeping, and picnicking. Mornings are calm and serene. Afternoons are filled with hustle, bustle, and excitement. Sunsets and nights practically demand that you hold each other. And if the beach is private enough, who knows where that might lead . . .

It's no wonder so many young people are drawn to the shoreline. Skin is everywhere and romance is on lots of minds. A campfire, a cool drink, someone playing a guitar, and some private space are just the thing for teenagers and college kids. But why let them have all the fun? Just remember the sunscreen, a floppy hat, and a beach umbrella, and off you go.

Mountains

For the most part, people tend to go to beaches when it's warm, even though they can be just as enjoyable on cold days. On the other hand, a trip to the mountains normally means you'll be running into cooler weather. Mountains are where they keep the snow, after all. Mountain ranges of all kinds are beautiful and spectacular. They are also tremendously romantic.

Mountains are usually associated with words like "inspiration." Certainly seeing them can give you that awestruck feeling. The power of nature can be overwhelming. Quiet moments with someone you love are special. Mountains lend themselves to that.

The kinds of activities vary by how physical you want to get. Hiking, skiing, biking, and climbing require quite a bit of exertion. Wining, dining, and sightseeing are alternatives if you don't want to build up a sweat. Both types of activities are excellent ways to spend time with each other. Also, many ski lodges and mountain resorts offer hot tubs as part of a vacation package. That way you can be cold first, then hot, then really steamy.

Forests and Campsites

You nature-loving romantics know all about the joys of outdoor life. Sleeping under the stars or under a canopy of trees can be an almost spiritual experience, especially when you share the evening with someone you love. Even during the daytime, a walk in the woods is a pleasant way to spend an hour or two. Hold hands while walking under magnificent towering trees (such as the redwoods, our favorites) and think about how long they've been around, as compared with our short time here on Earth. If that doesn't draw you closer, nothing will!

For those of you who really like to rough it, add campfires, outdoor cooking, hiking, and sleeping in a tent. Sharing these projects with a partner or spouse can be fun. Including your kids in the process is educational and enjoyable. You can always get a little quiet time later, when they're (safely) exploring or asleep.

There is a logical connection between nature and romance. Romance is natural and often leads to doing what comes naturally. Just make sure you pack the right kinds of things, like bug spray, nonperishable food, and items to make the hard ground a little more comfortable. When you're properly prepared, everything you've heard about "roughing it" is true: Food tastes better and the air smells sweeter. Feeling warm and fuzzy quickly follows.

Lakes

Drifting around in a canoe or small boat gives you some great time to rock and roll with the shifting waters. Boat rides by day are scenic and fun. Boat rides (carefully) by night are delightful and intimate. Sleeping on a houseboat or larger craft is unique and enjoyable. There are an endless variety of ways to enjoy the water.

A lake is a different experience from a beach. By day, you can share picnics along with cool refreshing dips in the water. Water-skiing and other water sports are great fun. (Don't forget the sunscreen—a bad sunburn won't put you in the mood for romance.) By night, you can hunt for your own private cove, fish, swim, or skinny-dip, depending on the time of night, the degree of privacy, and your willingness to be adventuresome.

Monuments

Scattered throughout this wonderful land are monuments of all sizes and shapes. Visiting them as a couple can combine a sense of history with feelings of closeness. You will probably always remember the first time you saw the Golden Gate Bridge. Every monument, from the Space Needle in Seattle to the Washington Monument in D.C., adds one more memory. Make a list of the monuments you want to explore. Then make a point of getting to them as your lives unfold. Part of a strong emotional attachment comes from shared memories and moments. Seeing the Mall of America in Minnesota, the Gettysburg battlefield in Pennsylvania, or the Arch in St. Louis creates a little mental video you'll probably replay time and again.

Special Places

Lots of couples have their own favorite spots to go to get away together. We have friends who had a dance floor built into their home because they enjoyed square-dancing so much! When they moved into their ideal living quarters, he beckoned her to share their first promenade to the tune, "Can I Have This Dance for the Rest of My Life?" Wow. Such a grand gesture makes us feel like romantic novices. Anyway, with some careful thought, we're pretty sure you can figure out where your partner likes to go for intimate moments. Here are a few of the more common places.

Cruises

When the two of you really need to get away from it all, one great way is to go on a cruise. Romance is easy to find—or rediscover—while you are drifting away to some foreign port. The dining opportunities are fantastic, and there are lots of activities, from gambling to dancing to live shows. Cruise bargains abound, with low off-season rates and two-for-one specials. Keep your eyes open. You may find a deal you just can't resist, especially if you're flexible and can leave on short notice. Finding a good deal will only enhance your enjoyment.

Cruises can still be romantic even if you don't have a significant other with whom to share the experience. There are several cruise vacations set up specifically for single people. You may just meet the partner of your dreams and get a great tan at the same time!

Sunrises

Okay, so you're not a morning person. You can work around that, at least every once in a while. Ladies, remember that most guys are fairly easily aroused in the morning. It's a peak time! There is something sensuous about dewdrops on the grass and the serenity of a sunrise. Most of the year, you'll notice lots of birds and insects chirping away as the sun peeps over the horizon. These are sounds you just don't hear the rest of the day, especially in the city.

Coffee lovers can take a little extra time to enjoy their favorite brew as they cuddle under a blanket. When you get up that early, there will be plenty of time to savor a more elaborate breakfast later. This time of day can be shared in quite a bit of privacy, even for those of you with kids.

There's also the other possibility, which is that you've stayed up all night. This bleary-eyed occasion represents another romantic opportunity. The first time you stay up all night talking with that special someone is a memory that tends to stick. Capping it off outdoors watching a new day begin is almost symbolic, or at least it can be. Something is dawning besides another day—a new phase in your life.

Either way (all-nighter or early riser), sunrises can be special. Walking together, having breakfast together, or simply sitting together as the sun comes up can create a nice time to bond with your partner. So, once in a while, set the alarm and get outside.

Sunsets

Being in the arms of someone you love as night begins to fall is an intimate way to end the day. Many times we're out and about when the sun sets and don't even really notice it. That can also happen with a romantic partner, when you take him or her too much for granted. The trick is to remember to take a few moments to enjoy each other and the brilliant sunset.

Think of the classic song "Night and Day" as you read this chapter. Love and romance take place at both times.

Sunsets make great viewing material when they are combined with some of the other romantic spots mentioned in this chapter. The beaches on the Atlantic coast of Florida and on the West Coast have especially breathtaking sunsets. Forests provide neat angles of shade as the evening draws near. There are many lakes throughout the United States where you can watch the sun sink into the water. The possibilities are nearly endless.

Although sunrises and sunsets can be quiet and inspirational for any couple, it seems as if we notice them most when we're first falling in love. Avoid falling into the trap of being "too busy" to enjoy them as the years go by.

Under the Stars

The link between stars and love is strong. Everyone from teenagers to seniors can enjoy the vastness of a starlit sky with someone special. And it's not just the stars that are synonymous with romance. Out there among them is the Moon, with each lunar phase, from full to new, adding another dimension to the great outdoors.

Whether you're lying on a blanket, sitting on a porch, or reclining in your car while parked on lovers' lane, the odds of something spectacular happening up in the sky are pretty strong. If you're trying to build or restore some romance in your relationship, take advantage of this free light show as often as you can, without the distractions of any other event. Hold hands, hug, and talk quietly. Allow the calmness of the night become part of a moment of solitude together. You never know where it may lead. If you have been intimate under the stars, you know it's a really different and enjoyable experience (unless it's at the height of mosquito season).

In Front of the Fireplace

As we've said, flames go with passion. Fireplaces fit with romance. There is something so cozy about the warmth of a burning log that just isn't the same as an electric furnace. When you've built up a raging inferno to heat a cold winter's night, there will be a full bed of embers glowing by the end of the evening. After the kids are in bed and the day's chores are finished, turn off all the lights and sit quietly as the fire crackles softly. As your eyes adjust to this one source of illumination in the room, you'll see what wonderful things it does to the features of the person you love. There is no other way to create this kind of glow. Soft conversation, romantic meals and snacks, and passion mesh easily with time spent by the fireplace.

If you don't have a fireplace, you can light several candles around the room for the same effect. Just don't leave them unattended!

Gardens and Gazebos

Those of you who have visited New Orleans, Louisiana, and Charleston, South Carolina, have probably seen some of the wonderful garden areas that fill in small spaces in the French Quarter and downtown areas. Lunches and beverages are available in some of these cozy nooks and make for nice little moments to appreciate with someone you love.

At the same time, you don't have to book a flight to the South to view nice gardens. They are everywhere. Different regions have earlier or later seasons where things bloom. Each offers wonderful fragrances and beautiful sights. It's easy to associate flowers with love. Visiting gardens can be a pleasant and romantic thing to do.

Gazebos can be found in many parks and in an increasing number of backyards throughout the country. They are spots to sit while having coffee on a lazy morning or dessert following an elaborate meal. Gazebos are traditionally romantic places.

Anywhere with Candles

Even a church can be a really romantic spot. Think about it. When a couple gets married, all the candles in the church are lighted. Candles produce scents and sights. They provide warmth with a flickering little flame. There is a special bond between candles and many aspects of our lives. They are used in many spiritual and religious ceremonies. Candlelit dinners are one of the most romantic activities, in most people's minds, whether they take place at home or in a restaurant.

We light candles to remember people and to let them know they're in our hearts and thoughts. We light candles to celebrate holidays. We light candles on birthday cakes. We give candles as gifts. It is almost as if we *need* candles to note the more important moments, even when the glare of florescent lights is all around.

A room filled with candles practically demands romance. Try it. Anywhere from a bathroom, to a living room, to a bedroom will work. Just remember safety. It's not romantic to watch a set of drapes ignite.

CHAPTER 6

Actions Speak
Louder than Words

There must be a million ways to say, "I love you" without uttering a single syllable. Being romantic requires all types of communication. Every couple can develop a series of silent signals to convey important messages. These connections form as you get to know each other and grow all through life. The unspoken language of love reaches two audiences. The first, of course, is a spouse or partner. The second (and equally important) target is other people. It's such a heartwarming feeling to know the one you love is willing to let everyone know he or she thinks you're the greatest. A really romantic lover delivers messages to both audiences regularly. How do you stack up? If you'd like to improve communication with your love, here are a few suggestions.

Start with Your Eyes

Eye contact is a key part of any romantic coupling, except possibly when you're kissing. The rest of the time, think of "loving looks." The eyes are the windows to the soul; so yours should express your affection in no uncertain terms. Use them to send all kinds of special messages to your partner:

- Catch your partner's attention in a crowded room. Raise your eyebrows to remind him you want to get together, the sooner the better.
- Winking enables you and your partner to share an inside joke or an intimate response that no one else may even notice.
- *Never* roll your eyes or look disgusted when your partner is talking. It's bad manners and makes you seem petty.
- Play "stare down," or have staring contests. They're lots of fun and can be arousing as well.
- When you're talking to someone, look at your partner out of the corner of your eye. It makes him or her feel included and important.

Pay attention to your partner's eyes. They tell lots of tales. Watch as they brighten when he or she smiles. Notice when they're full of tears. Find out why; then respond carefully. If your lover seems distracted (his or her eyes keep darting away), it may very well be that you've started a conversation at a bad time.

The first thing you should memorize about the person you're dating is the color of his or her eyes.

Finally, eyes can hurt feelings. Guys, when you ogle another woman in front of your spouse or partner—well, it's just not a good idea. Jealous types have an especially hard time with this. Do your girl-watching some other time, when you're not with *your* girl. It would be foolish (and unrealistic) to say you'll never notice an attractive person again after a romance is under way. Just let discretion be the better part of valor. Ladies, the same applies to you.

Lip Service

What a wonderful device the mouth is. Think of all the great things it does. It helps you breathe, eat, taste, talk, and sing. Your mouth is also a vital romantic tool. Take a good long look at your lover's mouth. It smiles at you, kisses you, and says all-important words such as, "No really, I don't mind if you go golfing this weekend. Just save some time for me later." Lots of things about your mouth are great little romantic devices. Lips and tongues are for kissing; teeth are for nibbling. And your voice contributes mightily to the well-being of your relationship when you use it just to talk. Some of you can even add something special to a night of passion by singing to your loved one.

Since we're talking more about actions that speak louder than words, remember the key role a moan plays. Getting loud while being passionate adds great intensity to the moment without the necessity of words.

Some people don't feel comfortable kissing and cuddling with their partner in a public place. If your partner feels that way, don't hold it against him or her. You might want to save the public mushy stuff for key times, like anniversary parties and birthdays.

It really helps to know your partner's likes and dislikes when it comes to all things oral. For example, some men really don't care for lipstick. They think natural bare lips are as sensuous as a woman can get. Another area to monitor is kissing. There are many styles of French kisses, and lots of women agree that having some guy try to reach your tonsils with his tongue is not very attractive. It's a tough thing to do, but don't be shy about showing your partner how you like to be kissed. Both of you will benefit greatly.

Then there are those other things you kiss. Some men really enjoy it when you kiss their fingers, for example. Some women really like it when you kiss their earlobes and neck. Others aren't impressed. It's a great sign of affection to give your partner a little peck on the forehead. One of the wonderful things about getting to know each other is finding out which areas work and which don't.

Special Smooches

Butterfly kiss. Flutter your eyelids across someone's skin.

Electronic kiss. This is the kind you send by e-mail. Go to *www.cyberkisses.com.*

Eskimo kiss. Rub noses (it's best when neither of you has a cold).

Gallant kiss. Kiss her hand as they did in the old days, but remember your lips touch only your own thumb when you do it right.

Grungy kiss. Try it first thing in the morning, before either of you brush your teeth.

Stop-and-go kiss. Kiss each other at each red light. Pray for a traffic jam.

Testing Your Romantic Skills

1. Do you mouth the words "I love you" to your partner when you can't talk to each other any other way?
2. Do you notice the way your partner purses his lips, because he wants to be kissing you?
3. Do you kiss at least five different times every day (not all at once and in totally separate settings)?
4. Does your mouth turn you into an exceptional lover?
5. Have you ever played the "tasting game," in which one of you is blindfolded and the other one feeds you "surprise" flavors?
6. Do you occasionally feed each other when sharing a meal?
7. Have you found that spot on your partner's neck where a small kiss will send shivers down her spine?
8. Has all your work at keeping your teeth in good shape and being aware of your breath paid off (that is, on a date)?
9. Do you know how to blow air on your partner to get his or her attention?
10. Have you built a nice long list of the tastes (food and otherwise) that your partner enjoys?

The answers to questions 1–3 and 5–10 are yes or no. Question 4 should probably be an essay—and a long one at that. In any case, if you can honestly answer yes to eight or more of these questions, you're doing great. If you answer yes to five to seven questions, your skills need a bit of work. If you answer yes to fewer than five questions, you're probably wondering why you spend so much time alone. That's what this book is for—so keep reading for tips on improving your romantic skills!

Using Your Hands

When you're trying to speak without words, your hands come in, well, handy. From the earliest days of puppy love until the golden years of retirement, handholding goes together with being affectionate. Sometimes you interlock your fingers. Other times you go palm to palm. Either way, this kind of connection can be a simple, unspoken way to enhance a romance. You can hold hands while sitting, walking, or even lying in bed at night before you doze off.

If you don't pay that much attention to holding hands in your romantic life, consider this: Many hospitals have a nurse or some other person hold a patient's hand while the individual is in surgery. This calming touch helps lower the person's blood pressure and may also reduce the pounding of a frightened heart. And this happens while the patient is asleep!

Taking your partner's hand is an outward show of affection. Whether it lasts for a brief moment or a longer time, we all need to keep touching each other. Try it some time, if you and your spouse have forgotten this kind of involvement. You'll probably immediately sense that you're filling a void that had been getting larger over time.

Romantic Hand Movements

- Learn how to spell out "I love you" in sign language.
- Caress your partner's hair with just a light touch.
- Scratch his back.
- Brush her cheek with the back of your hand.
- Rub his arm while he watches television.
- Massage everything on each other.
- Watch romantic couples. They almost always are in physical contact. Do likewise.
- Let your kids see you holding hands and touching each other every day. The message you're sending is vitally important.
- Give her a manicure and pedicure with lots of extra kneading.
- Place those hands where he likes them best, often.

More Physical Messages

A true romantic uses every body part available. A passionate lover keeps a mental notebook detailing every single thing you like and routinely goes through the whole list, just for your enjoyment. Romantic touches are limited only by the breadth of your imagination. Here are a few ideas just to get you started on your own personal physical media campaign:

- Lock pinkies instead of holding hands.
- Nuzzle each other.
- Play footsie.
- Nibble on ears.
- Brush your arm against your partner's while sitting together.
- Body paint each other.
- Write words on your partner's back, either dry-skinned or with lotions and oils.
- Give scalp massages to each other.
- Wash your partner's hair.
- Dance cheek-to-cheek.

Also, keep in mind the value of rubbing. Rubbing up against the one you love, when handled with care, is a great sign of affection. Bundling, cuddling, and all that other body-to-body contact are part of feeling close.

Other Actions That Deliver Strong Messages

Every new day brings another chance to show someone how much you care, not with lip service, but with actions. You can start with the smallest act of thoughtfulness, like bringing your spouse a cup of coffee in the morning, and watch your fondness for each other as it builds over time. Making a point to do the little things that make someone else's day better is investing in your love account. It will grow, with interest.

We've all heard the expression, "Do as I say, not as I do." It's easy to sermonize when the subjects are romance and love, without ever practicing what we preach. The end result is a series of missed opportunities. To avoid this pitfall, a good rule of thumb is, "It's impossible to kill someone with kindness!"

The rest of this chapter is devoted to romantic actions. Some may not seem directly linked to time in the bedroom or some other passionate moment. But if you think of a romantic life as one spent trying to create a stronger bond with the one you love, these items are cornerstones of great relationships. From there, the sparks fly more easily and a life in love is more likely.

Kindness

The late 1990s brought the phrase *random acts of kindness* into our national lingo. It's a great idea to do something nice just for the heck of it. In a marriage or loving relationship, random acts of kindness should be deliberate, routine, and practiced daily. There is no more powerful way to tell a lover he or she is important than to act lovingly without expecting anything in return, even if it's just remembering to put the toilet seat down.

Kindness says in no uncertain terms that you care. In a world where we often mistake bravado for masculinity, gestures of gentle affection are among the most masculine things a guy can do. Kindness is a spiritual virtue as well. Truthfully, there is no downside to being considerate of another human being, especially when it is someone you truly love. As a result, it's romantic to unload the dishwasher when it's not your turn, to volunteer to take the dog for a walk on a cold winter night, to pick up dirty clothes without giving it a second thought, and to help out whenever you can.

Show Your Love with Random (and Not-So-Random) Acts of Kindness

- Start her car and warm it up on a cold day.
- Field a phone call from someone he doesn't want to talk to.
- Bring her a bowl of hot soup when she has a cold.
- Listen to him without interrupting or giving advice.
- Offer to take the kids to school so she can sleep in.
- Draw her a bath. Bathe her and towel her dry. Use a warm towel that you heated while she was soaking in the tub.
- Do the laundry when you know your partner is worn out. Fold it and iron it.

Manners and Courtesy

Some manners should be observed as often as possible. Saying, "Excuse me" when you let out a little burp is always in good taste. Replying, "Bless you" when someone sneezes costs nothing and is a way of being pleasant. In general, exhibiting good manners when you're with your partner or spouse is simply showing respect.

Remember, manners go beyond the physical to include not asking inappropriate questions (such as, "How much do you earn?").

Dating manners are especially helpful as a romance blooms. You don't want to put up with someone who has impolite language or sloppy dining habits, do you? As you size up a potential partner, you're going to notice these things.

Meanwhile, it seems as if manners are a little more complicated in this generation. For instance, we struggle with questions like these:

1. On a date, who pays for what? How do you decide when you're going Dutch?
2. When a man asks out a woman who has children (divorced or widowed), is he also offering to pay for a baby-sitter?
3. How do you introduce someone you're living with to nosy people who should mind their own business?
4. What is the correct way to tell a guy his fly is unzipped when you're out on a date? How is it that you noticed in the first place?
5. What is the correct way to tell a woman you can see her breast because her shirt is open a little more than she intended, or should you just avert your eyes? How is it that you noticed in the first place?

These issues can be troubling. They make us glad we've been off the marketplace for over twenty years. Still, we want to be able to give quality advice to our kids, and to you. So, here goes:

- Talk about going Dutch before you actually meet on the night of the date. Go with what feels right. If the woman asks the man out, she should not be surprised if he asks, "Are you buying?" Guys who aren't comfortable with being that forward should bring along enough money, just in case, and then follow her lead.
- The guy should offer to pay for the sitter and the woman can accept, agree to split the cost, or decline, depending on her financial circumstances and what makes her comfortable.
- For introducing a live-in lover, we like, "This is my friend, Julie."
- For the guy with the open fly, just say, "Ummm . . ." and point shyly with a nice smile. How you discovered the problem is your business.

- For the lady whose breast is revealed, point to your own chest, say something like, "I think you're unbuttoned." Then smile and avert your eyes until the distraction is resolved. Once again, how you discovered the problem is your concern.

There are some manners that are just common courtesy. For instance, the man should walk on the outside, by the street, as you head down the sidewalk. "Please" and "thank you" should flow freely in any relationship. The man shouldn't always buy. The woman shouldn't always be the one to fetch the drinks and snacks. In other words, don't confuse manners with being nice. Don't get stuck in traditional gender roles, even though you may not abandon all of what they offer. Develop your own mix of doing pleasant favors for each other and remember the basics you learned as a child. If you didn't learn as a child, you can quickly pick up everything you need to know by watching classy adults.

Also, play the flip side. What does being discourteous say about your feelings? If someone can't take the time to behave appropriately, that person probably has little regard for you. It's certainly the opposite of being romantic. After all, there's nothing worse than inviting a man or woman to stay the night and have him or her sneak out before you wake up. When you don't want to face that person in the morning, he or she shouldn't be there in the first place.

Showing Your Love in Tough Situations

Perhaps the time when actions really speak louder than words is during a crisis. We all lose family members; suffer failures at work; and experience other, less traumatic problems. An understanding partner helps you battle through these situations with both words and deeds.

Part of being truly romantic involves knowing when to shut up and just hold your partner tight. It means knowing when to go way out of the way to be helpful. For instance, my father passed away right before Christmas. Don took it upon himself to do almost all of the holiday shopping and present wrapping so I could tend to my emotions and to other things that needed to be done. This was as romantic as any candlelit dinner could ever hope to be.

It is often said that you can judge a nation by how it treats its poorest citizens. The same is true of a lover. You can judge someone's true commitment and feelings by how he or she responds during a difficult period. Those who avoid the situation and retreat don't have your best interests at heart.

Silent Moments

Besides knowing when to be quiet and just hold someone because he or she is having a bad time, there are times when silent moments speak volumes. For example, there is the serene, unspoken sense of completion that follows making love. As you lie quietly together, the gentlest caress is a major message. Even on nights when you simply go to bed to sleep, there is a time in which you rest, without words, as the day ends.

Many couples can travel silently down the highway, confident that they don't have to speak to feel warmly about each other's presence. Those of you who attend religious services may touch each other softly as you ponder what is taking place. There is a special form of sharing in sitting or kneeling in a pew with someone you love.

Keeping silent means holding your tongue when a sarcastic comment is about to come out. Loving someone often includes keeping your mouth shut, whether it is letting your partner vent without interrupting or avoiding saying something critical or judgmental.

Part of being a great romantic partner is knowing when *not* to speak.

Unspoken connections take place in a wide variety of venues, from enjoying a film or video at home to watching your baby as he or she sleeps. Bonding happens in all sorts of ways. Knowing what to say is important, but so is knowing when to stay quiet.

One other way to let silence become part of your romantic portfolio occurs when you sit quietly and put the one you love directly in your thoughts. As you ponder his or her face, voice, touch, and endearing qualities, you'll be in a moment when there is affection in your heart even while you are separated. It can happen in a car, in your living room, or anywhere that it is possible to take a few minutes to savor the fact that someone has captured your heart. It's a great way to end the day or to calm down when you're troubled or angry. Try it sometime.

Grand Gestures

Toward the other extreme, every once in a while, you just want to shout out to everyone within hearing distance, "I love my _____," where _____ might be your husband, wife, lover, partner, or romantic friend. To make the statement in no uncertain terms, you design some major event. These can take all kinds of forms. There are surprise parties for birthdays and anniversaries. There are dinners and evenings out. Or, you can cook a major dinner at home, complete with candles and all the extras. On an even greater scale, trips and vacations, second honeymoons, weekend retreats, and other getaways that you take the initiative to arrange are grand gestures with lots of romantic potential. (See Appendix A for a state-by-state listing of some great getaways.)

Grand gestures usually generate two results: immediate passion and long-term memories. Immediate passion leads to fun, lust, romance, excitement, and other good stuff. There is also quite a bit to be gained in the long term. You can reinforce the positive feelings you received from being the beneficiary of a great gesture. How? Here are a few ideas to help savor the memory:

- Make a scrapbook with photos and other small items (ticket stubs, programs) as a remembrance of a great trip or visit.
- Buy a photo album and fill it with pictures of you and your partner doing special romantic things.
- Keep a collection of love letters sent by your favorite person. Have them bound like a book, so you can keep them forever.

- Edit a special videotape presentation of your key times alone together. Give it as a gift for a special occasion, such as the anniversary of the day you met.
- Keep a journal as a personal reminder of all the nice things your partner does for you. Reread it often.

Changing Personal Habits

We are all creatures of habit. Some habits are benign, like how we get ready for work in the morning and what we put on a hamburger. Other habits have dire consequences. As a society, we seem to be pretty good at doing all sorts of unhealthy things. It doesn't take much of a leap of faith to say that stopping a bad habit or starting a good one represents actions that speak louder than words, especially when they are based, in part, on trying to become a better romantic partner. Let's look at a few specifics.

Good habits are sometimes hard to start, but they have valuable lasting effects.

Eliminating Bad Habits

One ticklish problem that can serve as a roadblock to romance happens when you or your partner has a habit that the other finds repugnant. Some simple examples include smoking, nail-biting, cursing, and various personal hygiene issues. If you really want to show that you care, and that you are trying, stopping a bad habit is a big signal.

Other bad habits can lead to huge fights and marital problems, and can cause the demise of even the most romantic, loving relationship. We're talking about alcohol and drug abuse, as well as other self-destructive acts. Although we can't devote space here to discuss the problem, suffice it to say that showing your love can be one motive for stopping a bad habit. It probably won't be the only motive. You have to *want* to change first.

That leads to another troublesome topic: weight. It is so easy to tangle body-image concerns with feelings about your spouse or partner, sex, and other important issues. When it comes to weight and romance, many women become frustrated if they feel they're carrying around too many pounds. The same can be said for many men. The question is: How do you deal with the issue in a romantic relationship? We suggest using kindness and empathy as guides, but you also have to know the value of what is truly important in a partnership. Then, if your spouse or partner tries to lose weight, make sure he or she is going about it safely, be supportive, and don't be critical if the attempt fails. If it succeeds, compliments should flow like a river after a downpour. (Of course, compliments should flow like a river any time.) Someone you love has made a major life change. You should appreciate it and render your total support. But never—and we mean *never*—evaluate your feelings toward someone based on something as trivial as weight. If the person feels as if he or she has a problem, that is a big enough burden on its own.

Kissing and making love will help a person who is trying to quit smoking get past the craving, at least for a while.

On a much brighter note, there are lots of smaller, silly habits that you can quit as a sign of affection. For example, it is possible to learn how to refrain from dropping your underwear on the floor and leaving it there all night. People can be trained to throw away the empty milk jug instead of putting it back in the refrigerator. Some folks can even train themselves to stop nail-biting, knuckle-cracking, and other distracting habits. When these habits are changed in the name of love, it's a good sign about how a person truly feels about his or her significant other.

Forming Good Habits

Other actions have to do with starting good habits. For instance, what if you suddenly decide it would be great to get in shape? You can easily turn this new habit into something you share with the person you love. The two of you can join an exercise class together. Lots of couples walk or jog together. Building positive habits with each other can be a bonding experience and add more fun to life.

Along the same lines, think of all the possibilities that learning a foreign language, taking music lessons, or going to an art appreciation class offer. Everything from cooking to gardening is taught in special classes throughout the country, and you can attend together to start a positive new habit (such as dining at home more often to save money instead of going out all the time). There are dozens of ways to enrich and enhance your personal experience while creating a stronger connection with someone you love. Just remember: Never try to put up wallpaper together. There are some things even a fantastic relationship just can't handle!

Never say, "I love you" if you don't mean it. Always say, "I love you" with both words and deeds.

The Unspoken Language of Love

Some folks think it's common for people to have pets that match either the owner's looks or personality. Others will tell you that over time married couples look more and more alike. Why? Because they interact so much that they take on each other's facial expressions and gestures. This means wrinkles form in the same place, or some such thing.

Whatever the case, we're pretty sure that many actions couples share take the place of words. Knowing when to leave a lover alone is a real gift. Reminding your partner that his favorite television program is about to come on says you know what he likes and that you want him to enjoy those things. Packing a small lunch for a spouse who is running late for an airplane means she will be thinking of you all through the flight.

It's fun to watch the silent love language of people at different stages of life. Kids walk arm-in-arm as they head down the hallway in junior high and high school. Many young couples still drive down the highway side-by-side in the front seat, even though it's not the safest thing in the world. Middle-aged married couples seem to just react to each other. The husband knows to drop the wife by the door when they go somewhere (one of those gentlemanly, not sexist, things to do). Old-timers have their patterns worked out so well that it would take a linguistics expert to unravel the silent messages that travel back and forth.

What does this mean to you? Maybe it means you should take a little more time to work on your romantic skills. Start by engaging in one action each day. Then, over time, let it come naturally. Soon your partner will be bragging to everyone about how nice you are.

Actions That Show You Care

- Send flowers
- Fill the car with gas, because you have some free time and your partner has a full plate
- Light candles, just for atmosphere, on an evening not headed for sex
- Take the phone off the hook so your partner won't be bothered while working on a key project
- Buy his or her favorite snack food and leave it out on a night you won't be home
- Check out the following Web sites for some cyber sweetness:
  www.whodoyoulove.com
  www.lovingyou.com
  www.adoringyou.com

CHAPTER 7

Music and Romance

Every person has different romantic buttons. Some people are most powerfully affected by words, others by touch, and others by what they hear. There is a strong connection between music and romance. Part of this connection may be due to the age in which we live. With radio, television, tape players, CD players, and the Internet, you can listen to a wide variety of music twenty-four hours a day. You can heighten the impact music has on your love life in two ways: by sharing a special musical event with your spouse or partner, or by adding musical touches to the romantic events and memories you're trying to build. Think of it this way: Music can help put you in the mood for romance and make your time together even more special.

The Musical Compatibility Quiz

But first, it may be a good idea to see if you and your partner are on the same page when it comes to music. Take a look at our Musical Compatibility Quiz to see how well your musical interests mesh. From there, you can build your romantic world with the songs and styles that make the most sense.

Pick the answer that comes closest to how you feel, then ask your partner to do the same.

1. Country music makes me want to:
   _____ Hurl
   _____ Dance and sing
   _____ Get drunk and cry
2. Taking my lover to the symphony would probably make me want to:
   _____ Come down with the flu
   _____ Bring along a radio, so I can hear the game
   _____ Get all dressed up to enjoy a great evening
3. Watching a ballet is like being:
   _____ Hypnotized by beauty
   _____ Tortured slowly
   _____ Bored to tears
4. Tony Bennett's or Nat King Cole's songs make me feel:
   _____ Warm, tingly, and kissable
   _____ Old
   _____ As if I need an excuse to leave
5. High-energy rock-and-roll of all sorts:
   _____ Makes for a great concert
   _____ Is good when I'm in my car by myself
   _____ Is related to the moral decline of the nation
6. Hip-hop makes me feel:
   _____ Clueless
   _____ As if I'm on the cutting edge and cool
   _____ As if I need earplugs

7. Christmas music:

_____ Puts me in the holiday spirit

_____ Makes me mad, because they start playing it in October

_____ Is a necessary evil

8. Rhythm and blues or soul music:

_____ Energizes me

_____ Annoys me

_____ Is sometimes enjoyable; sometimes not

9. Alanis Morissette:

_____ Moves me

_____ Is from a generation I don't understand

_____ Never heard of her

10. Grunge music:

_____ Shaped my formative years

_____ Sounds like a bunch of whining kids bellyaching

_____ What's grunge music?

11. I'd play a KISS, Iggy Pop, or Ozzy Osbourne album or CD:

_____ At a party

_____ When I know no one can hear

_____ When hell freezes over

12. My reaction to music in general is mostly:

_____ Emotional

_____ Not very strong

_____ Intellectual

Add up the number of times your answers match those of your spouse.

If you have ten to twelve matches, you're a musical marriage made in heaven.

If you have six to nine matches, you need to make sure you're working around your partner's musical tastes. Give and take a little.

If you have five or fewer matches, you probably fight over the radio and CD player all the time! We hope there are other areas in which you're more compatible.

Sharing Music

There are many ways to turn music into a shared experience. Musically compatible couples find lots of ways to enjoy each other's company while they listen to their favorite tunes. Some of these moments are powerful; others are quiet and intimate; others are just old-fashioned fun. Here are a few ideas about how to savor music together.

Here are a few romantic places to sing together: around a campfire, in the car, beside the Christmas tree, on the dance floor, on a hike, at a party, at the piano, or in the shower.

Singing

It wasn't that many years ago that families enjoyed a tradition of gathering at the piano for a songfest. One gifted member would play, and the rest of the family and friends would chime in. Many households still enjoy this activity, mostly around the holidays. Singing together can be a wonderful time to bond. If you don't believe us, watch a young couple singing to their first child. Affection is probably dripping off them. For some, harmonizing is a way to attach music to romance.

You can sing a cappella, with a radio, or with an instrument if one or both of you plays. Romance and fun often go together when you are belting out a favorite tune with a special partner.

Singing to Your Spouse

For those of you who feel vocally challenged but still love the singing concept, think about your lover singing to you. Images of a serenade floating up to you as you gaze lovingly from the balcony should immediately come to mind. When one spouse prepares the gift of a song for another, lots of good things seem to follow. Those who are able to "receive" a song get a great one-on-one out of the deal, whether it's in front of an audience or at home alone.

Musical performances are a unique form of romantic communication. Musical ability is often attractive. A singer can seem to be "in control" of a room and an audience. The song itself may be seductive or have some kind of special meaning. It just seems as though musical people have an edge when it comes to making an impression.

Still, even if you're not Whitney Houston or Garth Brooks, you may find a way to touch a romantic nerve in someone you love simply by making the effort. Or, you can go the safe route and dedicate a song to your partner on the radio, in a club, or somewhere else.

Attending Concerts and Symphonies

Watch couples who go to concerts together. They always seem to be attached somewhere, either holding hands or draping an arm around the back of the chair. Others hug as they listen in venues such as outdoor rock concerts. Music does bring people together. People go to concerts to feel as if they're part of something larger. These shared experiences are great romance builders.

You can hire a local college group to serenade your partner in your home. They'll love the gig and you won't have to pay too much to create a memorable occasion.

Taking Musical Vacations

Music lovers with different tastes can travel to New York or Las Vegas to share some great musical moments. For blues, New Orleans, Kansas City, and Chicago are a few of the more famous possibilities. California has great jazz festivals, as well as places where you can find energetic salsa music. In Hawaii, you can enjoy some great island songs. In Florida, listen as Jimmy Buffet sings "Margaritaville." Just about every region has a local flavor to enjoy.

In general, music can make an evening both exciting and romantic, from trips to a local tavern that features your favorite bar band to vacations that are more elaborate.

Mood Music

We can't write a chapter about music and romance without mentioning Barry White. He belongs to a class of crooners who specialize in providing great background music for dining, lounging, kissing, and seduction. Each generation produces a few wonderful voices that make practically everyone feel like getting a little closer. Maybe your favorite is Frank Sinatra, or perhaps you prefer Celine Dion singing the theme song from the movie *Titanic*.

It may not be vocal music that makes you feel amorous. Classical music inspires passion in some folks. New age and atmospheric music tantalizes others. The secret is to know what you like and what your partner likes. Then find the common musical ground that creates the proper mood for the evening.

Different kinds of tunes inspire different kinds of moods. Some songs are playful, some are energetic, and some are for more serious romance. You may even discover that playing one of your children's records creates a special moment. A great part of growing together is discovering just the right style for your relationship.

Some Great Romantic Tunes

"Ain't No Mountain High Enough" by Diana Ross and the Supremes
"A Kiss to Build a Dream On" by Louis Armstrong
"A Wink and a Smile" by Harry Connick Jr.
"Come Rain or Come Shine" by Ray Charles
"I Honestly Love You" by Olivia Newton-John
"If I Fell" by the Beatles
"Love Is a Many Splendored Thing" by the Four Aces
"Make Someone Happy" by Jimmy Durante
"The Rose" by Bette Midler
"Through the Years" by Kenny Rogers
"Unchained Melody" by the Righteous Brothers
"Unforgettable" by Nat King Cole

"When a Man Loves a Woman" by Percy Sledge
"When I Fall In Love" by Celine Dion and Clive Griffin
"You and I" by Eddie Rabbitt and Crystal Gayle

Spur-of-the-Moment Inspiration

You can use music as a tool to inspire or to touch your partner in many different ways. Take the time to create a "mix" of his or her favorite tunes to use during travel time. Buy your partner a CD or tape that you know he or she will love. Give it as a surprise gift that isn't connected with any birthday or holiday. Put on a beloved old song when he or she comes home from work. Tape a concert of one of his or her favorite performers to give at a key moment.

"Our Song"

Most couples have a romantic song that they call their own. Some magical moment had a musical element in it, and from there a memory was built. These feelings can last a long, long time. Music brings out powerful emotions in lots of folks, especially when it's attached to something else with meaning.

If you share a song (or maybe more than one), do something to enhance it. Keep a copy of the words in your scrapbook. Buy the CD or tape and listen to it every once in a while, as part of a special occasion or just to relive an old mood. These nostalgic tunes inspire great memories and warm feelings, so take advantage of them.

Your song may come from a first date. It may be a song you shared often as the relationship first started. It may be one you listened to when you weren't together. Radio personality Casey Casem has built a tradition of "long-distance dedications" for just those circumstances.

Dance and Romance

Closely connected to "your song" may be the dance you shared while hearing the music. Dancing gives you and your partner the chance to become more intimate and sensual. We dance for all kinds of reasons and at all times of our lives. Some of us are nimble and graceful; others are stiff and awkward. But we all can enjoy the moment when we hold our loved ones in a dancing embrace. Think about the times dancing came into play as part of your romantic development.

As a Child

One wonderful way to spend some affectionate time with your children is teaching them the value of a dance. From the dad who lets his daughter stand on his feet as they waltz together to the mom who enthusiastically shows her kids the Hokie Pokie, there is a wonderful, uninhibited quality to teaching rhythm and movement. Most children intuitively know they're doing something special when a parent includes them in this form of musical celebration. It's as important to teach your kids dancing as it is their ABCs and multiplication tables. Musical learning is linked to intellect and reasoning skills as well as creativity. Besides, it's a blast. We'll bet lots of you have very fond memories of dancing with your folks. So, do the same thing with your own kids. Odds are you'll feel closer to them, and to each other, at the end of the song.

Men who can dance well are in a similar category as musicians—women flock to them.

As You Grow Up

Do you remember the nervous anxiety that accompanied your first dance? Did it take place at a school dance or was it a "boy-girl" party at someone's house? Dances are part of growing up for many young people, and they significantly enhance romantic development along the way.

If you're a teenager, let us give you one piece of unsolicited advice: Make sure you go to at least one homecoming or prom dance. It happens once in a lifetime. You get to dress up and be formal. The memories last a long, long time. Even before that time, junior high events and other high school mixers are great chances to practice your dancing skills and some of your early romantic moves. Take advantage of them.

In many parts of the country, a Sadie Hawkins event gives a girl the chance to ask a guy who may not have even known she was interested. Turnaround dances, sock hops, and other forms of retro dance parties are great training grounds. It never hurts to work on a few steps before you hit the big event.

The great part about early-year dances is that they give you the opportunity to learn how to mingle with folks from the opposite sex. You actually get to touch each other in a courtly fashion. Never underestimate the value of these early romance training sessions, and never forget what you learned as you went through them. The key lesson to absorb is that being courteous, pleasant, and well-mannered allows the other person to be the same. Good stuff, that.

As You Date

Dancing rituals are often similar to mating rituals. You circle each other, watching closely, and then move in. During the early stages of a romance, however, dancing can include other ingredients, besides showing your prospective partner what a great lover you're going to be, if the relationship progresses that far. For instance, you can dance just for fun. There's a great release that goes with booty shaking. In the early stages of a romance, you may go out with a group of friends where everybody dances with everybody. That gives you a chance to spy on each other and show off your moves while the other watches with appreciation. All the while, people are laughing, singing, sweating, and generally enjoying themselves. Later, as things become a bit more intense, you get to hold each other as you slowly sway to the music. No matter how you practice the art, it's a great way to share some time as you learn more about each other in a romantic involvement.

During Marriage or Long-Term Involvements

One of the great ways to spice up a marriage is to keep on dancing. In some cultures, dancing is an integral part of the social makeup of the community. It takes place regularly and on a variety of occasions. Sadly, many folks are so tied up with daily routines and extracurricular activities with their kids that they don't take the time to get away together for some quality moving and shaking.

For some couples, dancing can become a major social activity. For example, go to a square dancing party some time. It may take a while to learn the ropes, but it can be a great deal of fun. The same is true for line dancing, ballroom dancing, and lots of other forms. You can build friendships with others while you strengthen your personal attachment and attraction to each other.

For many married folks, dancing is going to be part of events such as weddings or New Year's Eve. But it's a shame to limit yourselves to only those occasions. To dance, all you need is a record, tape, or CD player and a little room. That means you can softly sway to your favorite tune right in your own living room.

A Time for Dancing

Ancient Native American and African tribes are not the only groups to use music to express cultural and religious values. You may even envy the rich heritage these dances express. But if you think about it, practically every community integrates dancing into its ceremonies. Some common examples include the following:

- **Weddings.** Most receptions feature a dance where the bride and groom take over the floor. Everyone "oohs" and "aahs" as the couple gets together for the first time following their nuptials. Then, the bride dances with Dad and the groom dances with the new mother-in-law. Wedding celebrations often include music that fits the tastes and the heritage of the couple and their families. Some of these can be quite unique. We have friends who received a "belly dancing" performance as a wedding gift. Soon after, everyone was invited to the dance floor for a very unusual musical festival that followed the wedding. No matter what the form, joy and merriment mix with romance at many wedding dances.

- **Anniversaries.** Lots of anniversary parties feature a band playing tunes from the era in which the couple was united. The special couple takes the floor and renews their partnership in the form of a nice, slow, romantic dance. It's easy to feel your romantic fire rekindling as you watch another couple celebrate their anniversary. Dancing can quickly add to the power of the moment.
- **Holidays.** Besides New Year's Eve, there are other great moments to go dancing. The Fourth of July is a great time to hold a casual outdoor party using a dance floor. After all, many folks our age tend to think in terms of groups like the Beach Boys when celebrating such an all-American moment. Why not add a little butt-jiggling to make the night more fun?

Building a Dance Portfolio

A great way to entertain yourselves is to do some research on dancing. You can rent movies to watch the various styles, attend dance contests, and watch television programs featuring various cultures. What you'll learn is that dancing is a universal language of love, romance, and, yes, sexual excitement.

But, be warned, the grace and sensual softness of many modern dances may cause you to pull over to the side of the road just to do a little smooching before you even get home.

If you have been fortunate enough to see some version of *The Lord of the Dance,* which features Irish step dancers and traditional Irish music, you are aware of the sensual power a dance can provide, even when you are just sitting in the audience. Dance troupes of all types routinely tour the country, often performing on college campuses and other places at very reasonable prices. Observing these performances can provide some great dancing inspiration.

We even believe you macho guys ought to try going to the ballet, at least once. If you have any kind of softer side at all, you may be surprised. Sitting in a darkened theater watching the exquisite movements of these talented individuals may give you pause. Taking your kids to see *The Nutcracker* is a great holiday event to share. Romantic moments with your spouse may quickly follow.

Other Musical Moments

Music can also come into play in other ways. For example, when birds sing, they are performing songs in their language in part as mating calls. Think about that the next time you hear a flock singing for each other on the first warm day of spring.

Most of you probably routinely get a song stuck in your head for a while. Some of these are clearly connected to thoughts about the one you love. Take the inspiration and run with it. Other tunes simply make you feel romantic.

When you think about it, music can be a background, a focus, a spectator sport, something you enjoy together, or a way to pass the time and think about the one you love; or it can serve as part of something larger, like a dance, wedding ceremony, dinner, or movie. At the end of the day, a life filled with love is probably also filled with musical memories. So, as the Immortal Bard once wrote: "If music be the food of love, play on!"

CHAPTER 8

Food and Romance

Although it might not seem like it on the surface, food plays a powerful, lifelong role in loving relationships. If you think about it, food has many important features. We eat to survive, to celebrate, to have fun, and just because it tastes good. Meals are one aspect of daily living that can easily be incorporated into a romantic program. We've organized this chapter using the classic journalistic approach: who, what, when, where, why, and how. It's a good way to spell out, in no uncertain terms, how to use food to enhance and enrich your romantic life. We're getting hungry just thinking about it, so let's get started!

Who?

Everyone! There are as many rituals surrounding eating as there are cultures and subcultures around the world. Each one expresses a sense of family, familiarity, religious belief, or community. If you focus on the rituals associated with romance and partnership, you'll find that there are long-standing traditions of meeting people and getting to know them better while taking in a few calories.

Using food as part of a relationship starts with young children having "tea parties" with parents and friends. Not long after, schoolchildren in lunchrooms around the world are trading snacks and treats, sharing meals, and learning the first elements of making friends and puppy love. Recess follows, giving them a chance to run off some of that bonding tension that may have started to build. Soon, these elementary food operations become a bit more sophisticated.

Just a generation or two ago, the place to meet was the local hamburger stand or malt shop. Inside the establishment and in the parking lot, youngsters mingled, flirted, and hung out while eating. Not much has changed, as you'll see if you visit the food court of any mall. Those with enough courage make the first move and sit with their most recent prospect. From there, the adventure begins.

Dining and Dating

Is there any more traditional date than dinner and a movie? Couples at all levels of involvement go to restaurants and snack bars to share meals. These dining moments range from the most casual to the most formal, depending on the occasion. There are so many details to work out in these early encounters. For example:

- Do we sit side by side or facing each other?
- What kind of food should I order (the same as my date, or something different)?
- Who pays?
- Should I order a cocktail or wine?
- How can I tell him he has something in the corner of his mouth?
- If it tastes awful, should I tell the chef or waitperson?

Most kids progress fairly quickly from hamburger-stand dates to that first formal night out. Often, a prom night begins with a trip to a fancy restaurant (after Mom and Dad embarrass you to tears by taking pictures and videos and calling the whole thing "sweet," "cute," or "adorable"). The prom night tradition starts years of evenings filled with sexual tension across a plate of appetizers.

> When you're going out on a dinner date, always carry breath mints for later!

As a relationship progresses, food takes on added meaning. You feed each other morsels and share tastes from each other's order. You develop favorite haunts. Discovering your partner's eating habits enriches your time together by giving you a common memory and bonding experience. Not long after, many couples progress from worrying about how dinner went to sharing breakfast. At that point, things start changing quickly.

Why Table Manners Are So Important
- Seating a woman at a dinner table is gentlemanly, noble, and romantic.
- Guys who eat like Attila the Hun aren't very good dinner dates.
- Chewing with your mouth open is disgusting and reduces the chances that someone will want to kiss that mouth later.
- The person across from you may have second thoughts about greater involvement if you can't get through a meal without crumbs, gravy stains, and other miscues showing up on your clothes.
- Many people find knowing how to order and sample wine sexy.

Newlywed Dining
After dozens of dinners designed to dazzle and entice, couples settle down to live together or marry. In both cases, dining changes. Part of the issue, of course, is wrangling about who cooks and who cleans up, which can be full of land mines. Once meals become part of the routine of daily living, you have to work at keeping the fire burning, so to speak.

Fortunately, many couples that have recently started cohabiting are free to come and go without the encumbrance of young children. That means it's possible to continue dining out as if you're still dating and add in the occasional special dinner at home. Newlyweds are able to take advantage of the full range of places to go and ways to make dining special that we'll talk about in the "where" and "how" parts of this chapter.

When someone cooks for you, bring a gift as a "thank you." Offer to fix dessert and help with the dishes.

If you're like most couples who are first living together, more than one meal may not even get finished until after you've made a quick trip to the bedroom. Also, late-night snacking presents an opportunity to do something extra nice for your partner. Making a trip to the convenience store for your sweetie, who has a strong craving for a Snickers bar or some ice cream, is a generous, loving display of affection. And, of course, you can make a point of bringing home your lover's favorite junk food, just because.

Family Dining

Are family dinners romantic? Probably not, unless you use some creativity along the way. Invent little games for each other. Play the classic flirting-under-the-table games, like playing footsie while you talk about Little League, lessons, and school stuff. At larger family gatherings, make it a point to share some small "insider" language or message that says, "I'm going to ravish you later, when we get home."

What?

The key question here is: Are certain foods sexy and romantic? And, of course, the answer is a resounding yes! There is a distinction, however, between foods that are romantic and foods that are "sexy" or sexual. For example, bringing your wife hot soup in bed on a day when she's down with a cold is a loving, romantic thing to do. Fixing your husband hot oatmeal on a cold winter day just to be nice is romantic. At the same time, some foods may fall into both categories. Most of the time, it depends on your attitudes and intentions while consumption is taking place.

Romantic Food and Drink

We did a little study on the subject just to see what others had to say. One source said the four sexiest foods are caviar, oysters, chocolate, and whipped cream. Another said the two most romantic drinks are wine and champagne. Are you getting hungry yet? Let's take a closer look!

Caviar

Caviar, the roe or eggs of fish, comes from the sea—as does Aphrodite, the goddess of love. We figure that must be caviar's connection to romance. Most experts agree Russian caviar has the best flavor. To enhance its flavor, serve it with chopped hard-boiled eggs, onions, lemon, and sour cream. It's a popular party favorite.

Caviar is also linked to fertility (since it is, after all, eggs). Supposedly, as long as the caviar is chilled properly, you can keep eating it for ten days after the tin has been opened. This means, among other things, it's easy to keep on hand for a spontaneous romantic moment. To keep caviar tasting its best, don't use a silver or metal spoon; the metal taints the flavor. Instead, use a mother-of-pearl, gold, bone, or even plastic spoon.

Oysters

Oysters are associated with libido. The legendary lover Casanova ate sixty oysters every day, according to some writers. Roman emperors viewed oysters as a means to gain and sustain sexual energy during orgies. Of course, there's no scientific backing for this claim, but since sex is mostly in the head anyway, maybe the illusion helps.

Oysters seem sensuous because of the way they slide down your throat when eaten raw. Just be careful to avoid ones that come from polluted seabeds. The sauces and beers that go with oysters help make them a fun and frivolous part of a night out with someone you intend to seduce. What's the harm in that?

Chocolate, Chocolate, CHOCOLATE!

Giving chocolates is one of our most valued romantic traditions. Every year around Valentine's Day, candy stores go crazy trying to keep up with orders. Chocolate is also a major part of other holiday celebrations. Chocolate gifts accompany birthdays, anniversaries, and other special moments. You can't go wrong with a nice box of chocolates.

Think of the many forms chocolate takes: bars, kisses, chunks, fudges, syrups, malts, ice creams, cakes, shakes, pies, icings, and toppings for strawberries. Recent research tells us there is more to chocolate than just the sugar buzz. Chocolate actually has mood-enhancing properties. So, while you just can't stuff yourself with chocolates all day long, they can make a great contribution to a night of passion.

Chocolate is made from the beans of a cacao tree, and people have been enjoying it for centuries. There are lots of ways to savor chocolate, starting with using it in cooking. Unsweetened chocolate is the pure ingredient; by itself, it tastes lousy. Bittersweet chocolate has a little sweetener added, and semisweet has more. Each recipe using chocolate asks for a certain kind, so make sure you're using the right one to get the best results out of your baking efforts.

Meanwhile, the chocolate you eat right out of the package is usually milk chocolate or white chocolate. There are different blends and levels of sweetness. And, of course, there are chocolate connoisseurs who insist our Americanized versions just don't measure up to Swiss and French chocolates. The key is simply figuring out which you like best, and then letting your lover know so he or she can buy you the right kind.

Try these chocolate-coated suggestions to share a little sweetness with your partner:

- Break a Hershey's Milk Chocolate Bar into its individual squares and feed your lover the little morsels one at a time.
- Chocolate syrup tastes great on ice cream *and* body parts.
- In New Orleans, some restaurants add a hint of chocolate to pecan pie. Try it if you want to taste a small part of heaven.

- Hershey's Kisses are always a nice addition to a date or night out.
- For a great retro date, go to a malt shop and share a chocolate shake.
- Fixing a cup of hot chocolate for someone you love is a terrific way to finish off an evening, especially on a cold winter night.
- Guys, if you want to score brownie points with your mother-in-law, make her brownies!

For those of you who are a little more adventurous, go to the bookstore or library and look up recipes for edible body paints. You'll soon see that art meets romance in some very unusual ways.

You can even enjoy chocolate without actually munching on food. Check your local department store and try these on for size:

- Demeter Fragrances Chocolate Mint Pick-Me-Up Cologne Spray
- St. Ives Chocolate Almond Body Scrub
- Tommy's Chocolate Cream Pie Body Hydrator by Tommy Hilfiger

When it comes to chocolate, the possibilities are endless. Use your creativity, your imagination, and your access to the Web to find more at:
www.HersheyChocolateWorld.com
www.nestle.com
www.SwissPlan.com

Whipped Cream

In the early sixties, Herb Alpert and the Tijuana Brass had one of the most scandalous album covers ever. The photo of a beautiful woman strategically covered with whipped cream probably sold more than a few copies of the album all by itself. It's easy to associate whipped cream with lust. This is a good thing, when used properly.

Whipped cream is sweet, spreadable, sexy, and fun. You can put it on desserts or on each other, or eat it right out of the container. And, of course, whipped cream can be brought to completion with a cherry on top. Keep some on hand. You never know when you'll want some merriment to break out.

> Sweet things are often associated with romance. Be creative in the sweet ways you say, "I love you."

Wine, Champagne, and Other Drinks

Wine is associated with Bacchus and Dionysus, gods of ecstasy and eroticism. It can be served separately or as part of a meal. Wine gives you a nice warm glow that can inspire necking, stroking, and more.

Wine is served in the finest restaurants and at the simplest picnics. The price and quality varies greatly, and the tastes available are as different as the number of enthusiasts who enjoy them. Teetotalers can simulate the wine experience with fruit drinks and nonalcoholic grape drinks. Some of these drinks even have bubbles, like champagne. The point is not (or shouldn't be) the buzz, but how it goes with whatever else you're doing, from snacking on cheese to a seven-course meal.

Here is a brief list of wines, a description of their flavor, and recommendations for some foods to serve with them. Don't feel compelled to stick to the list; these are just suggestions:

Barbera: fruity, tart, high in acid; serve with seasoned red meats, red pastas, wild game, hearty stews

Cabernet Sauvignon: complex, herbaceous flavor; serve with meat and game dishes, rabbit, seasoned chicken, duck

Carignan: basic red jug wine; serve with red meats and stews

Chardonnay: a little "oaky," says one source; serve with fish, shellfish, crackers, and cheese snacks

Chenin Blanc: a dry white wine (at least drier than Chardonnay); serve with steamed or sautéed fish, subtly to mildly spicy foods

Chianti: medium-bodied; serve with spaghetti and other Italian dishes

Claret: red table wine; serve with whatever you like

French Colombard: dry and crisp; serve with lightly spiced shellfish, not-too-spicy pastas

Fume Blanc: a little "smoky," as opposed to oaky; serve with mild fish and shellfish, poultry, pork

Gamay Beaujolais: light and fruity with raspberries; serve with poultry, lamb, ham, mild game, fish in sauce

Gewürztraminer: fruity and spicy; serve with fish in cream sauce, poultry, lightly seasoned pork

Gray Riesling: more spicy than fruity; serve with moderately seasoned fish and shellfish, subtly seasoned poultry, pasta

Johannisberg Riesling: fruity; serve with moderately seasoned fish and shellfish

Merlot: lush, soft, fruit aroma; serve with red meat, game, seasoned poultry, pork, ham, red-sauce pastas

Pinot Noir: silkier and lighter than Cabernet; serve with meats, pastas in red sauce, game, rabbit, veal, pork

Ruby Cabernet: red jug wine; serve with red meat, spaghetti, stew

Sauvignon Blanc: crisp, complex, fruity, light touch of spice; serve with mild fish and shellfish, saucy fish, poultry, pork

Sémillon: flowery, bland to bitter, sipping wine; serve with mild fish and shellfish (dry versions), dessert (sweet versions)

Zinfandel: berrylike with tannic nip; serve with red meat, veal, pork, rabbit, game, seasoned poultry, red-sauce pasta

There are also dessert wines and liqueurs, such as cognac or Irish Cream. These can be a nice way to top off a meal. Remember, however, you don't want to get so tipsy that you impede the reason for drinking them in the first place.

One of our sources called champagne the "queen of wines." No argument here. Ordinarily champagne is made from Chardonnay grapes, but others are often added. The carbonation process creates the bubbles and the fizz that everyone enjoys after they pop the cork.

Champagne implies celebration and romance as much as anything else you drink. It's served at weddings, anniversaries, on New Year's Eve, and at other meaningful times. Champagne is festive and normally goes straight to your brain, so think moderation.

The lingo of champagne goes like this: Demi-sec means semisweet to sweet. Sec is medium to medium-sweet, and brut is the driest kind. You can toast with all three forms, sip each type, and get carried away if you want to. Remember the scene where the man pours the champagne into the shoe of his celebrated lover and then drinks it? To each his own, as they say.

Never drink and drive! It's bad form that could lead to tragedy.

Milk and cookies can be every bit as romantic as champagne and strawberries when you share them with someone you love. A nice glass of hot apple cider following all of the Halloween festivities can be an invitation to amour. Another nice blast from the past drink is an ice-cream float, if you haven't had one for a while. They're twice as tasty when you share the same glass (use two straws so you can gaze into each other's eyes while you sip).

Lots of couples enjoy coffee together, from seniors who sip quietly in the morning to younger folks who head out to the trendy coffee shops. The whole Starbucks craze gave rise to people enjoying designer coffees, which is great fodder for an inexpensive date. In other cultures, tea is king. Those who don't like coffee or tea can head over to a smoothie place for something healthy and tasty. Other health-food types can go to juice bars.

At the heart of the matter is this nugget of wisdom: No one libation has an advantage over any other when you're being romantic. Alcohol may reduce inhibitions and increase interest, but it can lessen performance and sensation, and lead to trouble in other ways. Besides, with the prevalence of alcoholism in our society, it's fair to say you should save the wine and the bubbly for special occasions, and enjoy other things the rest of the time. If you're truly in love, just seeing your special someone's smile is enough to get the old juices going. All of those drinks are just window dressing for your feelings.

When?

We've already talked quite a bit about holidays and other special occasions, such as birthdays and anniversaries that include food. So, now, let's think about the ways to share food on a daily basis. Each time of day gives you one more chance to be romantic and generous, and to do one small favor for the love of your life.

Breakfast

Breakfast in bed has to be near the top of the list of romantic things to do. Surprising your lover with a meal garnished with a rose is a classic move. Sharing breakfast together in a hotel following an evening of passion adds to the memories of a night together. Bringing your partner a hot meal when he or she is sick is a kind and thoughtful gesture. Everything from a full meal to a simple piece of fruit or a glass of juice can be served in a horizontal position to someone you love. It's a great way to start the day.

Many nighttime seductions begin with a morning compliment.

Still, there can be more to the first meal of the day than breakfast in bed. If you think in terms of building and bonding, sharing the morning meal is a wonderful habit to start. Families who manage to spend this quality time together are often better off. Later in life, an empty nest seems a little less empty when you take the time to begin a morning with someone you love. You can talk politics, gossip, or make idle chatter. Remember to put the paper down and look at each other instead.

Brunch

Some people like to eat halfway between breakfast and lunch. Sunday brunch is very popular in hotels and restaurants. Going out for a leisurely midmorning meal on a day off or holiday is another way to turn simple eating into something more special. Dual-career couples without kids

(DINKS, as they are sometimes called) seem to be especially good candidates for regular brunches. It gives them the opportunity to share a meal and spend some extra time together on the weekend following a hectic workweek. Brunch gives you a relatively inexpensive meal, time together, and no one has to cook or clean up!

Lunch

Lunch often conjures up the idea of a "quickie." This can either be the food you devour or something else. Working couples can rendezvous at restaurants to relax, visit, and make plans. While you're there, you can also flirt and plant the seed for what you would like to have happen that night. The pace of lunch is often a little more rushed, but it's still a good idea to get together every once in a while anyway.

Dinner

Since we've already talked about dinner dates and meals for each other, there isn't much more to say about the nightly meal. Except for these ideas:

- Have a "fantasy" meal where you dress up like Antony and Cleopatra or some other famous couple.
- Feed your partner an entire meal. The rule is, he or she can't touch any food but can touch everything else.
- Teach your lover how to fix your favorite recipe.
- Learn to cook something new together.

Dinner is close to bedtime. Heavy meals may slow you down, so dine light when the next course is going to be intimate. Or, fool around first; then take your time savoring a candlelit dinner afterward. Rather than letting the clock set your dining schedule, let your heart lead the way.

Midnight Snacks

At the end of the evening, there's nothing nicer than sharing a piece of cake, a few bites of pie, some chips, or whatever your favorite snack happens to be with your partner. It's a small moment to interact and share your tastes. Sometimes it's the simple things that stand out.

Where?

Once you figure out what and when to eat and with whom you're dining, the next major question is where will this meal take place? Of course, there's always restaurants, your place, your date's place, outdoors, or places that are special to you. Each location offers great possibilities for making a night into something pleasant, sensuous, or memorable.

Restaurants

Dining out can take several forms. Let's start with something simple, like fast food in your car. How is that romantic? It depends. If you're looking for stuff to just slam down and keep moving, not so much. On the other hand, we've developed a long-standing dating tradition of hitting a fast-food joint for an ice-cream cone. It's light, simple, and you can catch up on the day's events or other topics while taking a relaxing drive. More than a few of those have led us back to the days of heavy-duty smooching. It's a good way to act younger as you're getting older. Besides, you can make a real show out of the sensuous consumption of an ice-cream cone, which does, after all, involve lots of licking.

The great part about dinner dates is that every night you're hungry again, so they're always an option for an evening of romance. Just take the time to go. If you're on a tighter budget, choose less expensive places.

Beyond fast food, trips to restaurants as a couple tend to take two forms. The first is going there to make the meal the evening's only or main event. The whole point is to take your time and indulge yourselves in a sumptuous menu. The second form occurs when dinner is a precursor to another activity such as a movie, play, or musical performance. Many couples dine after, rather than before, the show. Either way, food is only part of the evening's story.

When the meal is the whole point of the outing, the pace is usually a little slower. Taking the time to savor and share your food makes for a wonderful evening. As the meal progresses, you can talk, flirt, touch, taste, and gaze into your lover's eyes. Feed appetizers to your partner, try each other's entrées, and pay special attention to sharing your desserts. Love can blossom anywhere, whether it's at an inexpensive buffet or a fancy candlelit restaurant.

Things to Consider When Dining Out

- Try a new type of cuisine with your partner. Sharing a culinary adventure is romantic!
- Try to go during quieter periods, unless you like crowds and waiting.
- Don't stuff yourselves until you just want to go home and take a nap.
- For dating purposes, split the tab and "treat" each other regularly.
- If you're on a budget, keep the cost down by choosing a more moderately priced place or by skipping a few of the extras such as appetizers and drinks.
- After the waiter takes your order, whisper to your partner that you aren't wearing underwear. Then see which is hotter, the food or your partner.

There is another way to incorporate the restaurant experience into an evening. Just go for dessert. We already mentioned our drive-around ice-cream cone dates. You can take the concept further by getting dressed up and going to a nice place just for coffee and a slice of pie, or whatever the house features. Couples with money worries can use the approach to get out, circulate, and still not spend a fortune. Besides, many desserts have those sexy components in them: whipped cream, sauces, and chocolate.

Fixing Food for Your Partner

Do you remember the first time you prepared a meal for your partner? You probably do, since it's always a little nerve-racking and exciting. Cooking dinner to be shared by candlelight somehow represents the "next step" in many relationships. For one, the person is now coming into your home, which may be a first. At the least, the context of the date becomes the living room and dining room rather than some neutral site like a restaurant or movie theater. That adds worries about the appearance of your place, from how clean it is to whether he or she will like your taste in furniture and wall ornaments. In other words, your partner is going to learn something about you.

To create a softly lit, romantic scene, drape a colored scarf or handkerchief over a lamp. Just don't leave the lamp unattended in case the scarf ignites. Starting a fire of passion is one thing, starting a fire in your home is quite another.

Then, there's the food itself. The smart approach here, of course, is to ask your partner what he or she likes. You can also make suggestions, such as, "I make a pretty mean pot roast." When you receive a dinner invitation, be diplomatic but honest when asked about your food preferences. For example, "Well, I really like the idea of having dinner with you, but I'm a vegetarian, so maybe we could try something other than pot roast?"

There is also that dreaded moment when you try someone's cooking and it's awful. It's tough to not spoil the whole evening. Once again, diplomacy must come into play. Do your best to eat a little bit. The goal is to avoid hurting the cook's feelings; remember the effort he or she has made on your behalf.

To help avoid a bad-meal disaster date, teach your kids how to cook (even those males who are totally resistant). Point out that many of the world's great chefs are men. Also, remind them that some day Mom or Dad won't be around to fix stuff. Besides, men who cook for women are probably in the same category as men who can dance and men who can sing. They seem to fare pretty well when it comes to enchanting potential partners.

Fixing food for someone you are dating is one of those ventures in which you'll almost always get an A for effort, regardless of the actual quality of the meal. The great part is that as the cook, you have so much control over the setting. You can make it dimly lit and intimate, or bright and festive. The music you choose can be soft and seductive or energetic. In other words, you can reveal a great deal about yourself and how you want the night to go simply by how you set up the situation.

Make sure you have everything you need for the meal, including all of the utensils and cooking equipment. It never hurts to invite a friend over for a dress rehearsal before you try a new recipe out on a date.

Key Items to Have on Hand When Cooking for a Date

- Candles
- Cloth napkins
- Corkscrew for wine or champagne
- Entertainment for the time when you're in the kitchen and your date is waiting
- Favorite beverage (ask in advance)
- Flowers
- Lots of food (don't make your date go hungry)
- Mood music
- Prearranged menu (make sure you know what he or she likes!)
- Tablecloth
- Table decorations (make them creative and special)

Picnics

The picnic tradition goes way back in our culture. It's another way to be alone and intimate without going to a restaurant and without inviting someone to your home. Many of us grew up with family picnics. They also make nice dates. All you need is a cooler, a basket, a blanket, and some free time. You can sit in the shade or venture out into the sunshine on a cooler day. Sometimes you can use a picnic table and sometimes you can just find a spot.

Eating Outdoors: Love It or Leave It?

Is it true that everything tastes better outdoors? It depends on your perspective. Many couples love to fix light foods, grab a bottle of wine or soda, some chips or cheese chunks, and head to a park or beach. How many movies have featured romantic picnic scenes, with the man's head in his lady's lap, being fed grapes while they talk about love? On the other hand, some people don't believe that there is a great advantage to dining outside. You have to deal with the wind, temperatures that are too hot or too cold, insects, and all the messing around with carrying stuff out.

Why?

A couple who has been married for fifty years has probably shared many thousands of meals, even if they only eat together once a day. Since we all need fuel, and dining is where we get it, it just makes sense to learn how to share and enjoy meals together. They allow us to know each other better, treat each other, have fun, build family ties, catch up on the day's events, and share at least one part of every day

Besides, there is plenty of evidence that married men live longer than single men. They are more inclined to stop bad habits (smoking, drinking too much, and so on) and start good ones. In addition, cooking healthy meals for a couple or a larger family means you'll be getting vitamins and other key nutrients. Several of our single friends tell us they eat "sink" dinners; that is, they stand over the kitchen sink, gulp something down, and move on.

So, besides all of the loving, bonding, romantic things meals can do for you individually and as a couple, you are also more likely to eat right. Talk about a win-win situation!

How?

When you think of "how" to dine together, start with presentation. Romantic meals don't often involve setting pots and pans on the table. You have to make an extra effort to make things look nice. Keep in mind lots of foods can be shaped into hearts, from pizzas to cakes, cookies, pancakes, and whatever else you can imagine. You can also write with food and on food. A creative, fun-loving chef can arrange ketchup, mustard, frosting, candy, berries, and veggies to say, "I love you." Some flowers are edible or make appealing garnishes.

Then, there's the process itself. Serve a meal to your lover dressed as a waitress, maid, butler, chef, or servant at a Roman festival (think toga!). Start by seating your partner; pull out the chair and then help him or her settle in. Next, carefully place a cloth napkin on his or her lap. Serve the food from behind your lover's left shoulder, softly touching him or her as you present each course. This kind of formal dining is pampering at its best. To create even more of an atmosphere, make a ceremony out of lighting the candles and starting the music. Keep your partner as the center of attention throughout the meal. On rare occasions, like a birthday or after a big accomplishment, you might even want to feed your lover without actually eating the meal yourself. Won't he or she feel special then!

The question of "how" may also include "how long." Take the time to linger over a meal someone has taken great pains to prepare. Dining and romance take time. Enjoy, savor, and relish the time together.

A different way to serve food is by blindfolding your partner and having him or her guess what the food is. Think of the sensation of dipping your finger into chocolate syrup, whipped cream, or melted cheese. Figuring out the flavors is a sensuous adventure. Textures, aromas, and flavors can be combined for quite an evening. Take turns engaging in this kind of tasting ritual.

Other "how" issues involve intentions. Early in a relationship, you're getting to know each other while sharing a meal. As the relationship progresses, everything from fun to seduction becomes part of how you dine. For added fun, try dining in the manner of other cultures. For example, think of how the Japanese share meals. Go to the library or the Internet and look up various cultures. See what they do that you might enjoy. Try out cuisines from other places. It's one more way to share something new together, either in a restaurant or at home. Better yet, go there in person.

Later on in your love life, romance often burns brightly after a quiet meal together, whether at home or out on the town. Food is a great accessory for the couple who knows how to inspire passion through a simple everyday activity.

Flirting with Food

- Comment on the great aroma as you arrive at a restaurant or your date's home, if he or she is cooking for you
- Purse your lips into a kiss as you chew a morsel
- Put a taste on your finger and let your lover remove it
- Maintain constant eye contact as the meal progresses
- Do the old "one-drink-two-straws" bit
- Make a real show out of licking a spoon

So, there you have it. Our short course in the many courses meals can take. Romance can be part of everything from bacon and eggs to start the day to that special cake you whip up to celebrate a birthday or anniversary. We all eat. Romantics take the time to add just that little extra spice to meals. Next payday, do it up right. Everyone can use a night out away from the stress of the day.

A little flirting, a long tablecloth that hides all of your under-the-table fun, and who knows what the real dessert will be? *Bon appétit!*

CHAPTER 9

The Language of Love

How many times have you heard this dialogue in a television program or movie, "I know you love me. But you never *say* it." This problem must happen quite often, since it shows up in so many stories. If that's the case, it's a real shame. Although "I love you" may be easy to say, sometimes the words just aren't enough. You want to embellish. We're going to spend this chapter describing the wide variety of ways to link words to romance. Let's take a long look at the language of love and the romantic, sexual, and loving ties between words and emotions. But for it to truly be the language of love, the words must be spoken with sincerity; otherwise, they can be interpreted as merely lines.

The Romantic Read

People read for all kinds of reasons. Reading helps you relax, gain information, become inspired. Many women love to relax with a romance novel at the end of the day. Lots of people read articles in everything from *Redbook* to *People* magazine to pick up a few pointers about how to be more seductive, passionate, and affectionate. We've all been inspired by something in print that turned up a little romantic heat. Romantic words can also comfort, arouse, and generate new ideas. Practically everyone has been touched by something they've read, at one point or another.

Many of us also learned quite a bit about sex from those early manuscripts. Little boys circulated books like *Valley of the Dolls* in Don's time. Once again, it wasn't long until everyone discovered that reality isn't the same as fantasy, but the learning process was under way.

At the earliest age, many young girls read about the latest pop idol. The stories are always written in a style that idealizes and glamorizes just a single kiss from the heartthrob of the moment. This stuff is great training for romance in later years, even though you soon discover that the reality is a little different than the fantasy.

Books

Love stories are told in lots of different ways. More often than not, a great piece of fiction contains a romantic involvement between the protagonist and another major character. For example, the classic *Gone with the Wind* is first a novel about the Civil War that also presents an epic love affair between Rhett and Scarlett. Through the years, many tales have been told about war, peace, life, death, and everything in between; and love is the thread that holds the narrative together.

Reading books with romantic subplots can give even the most seasoned reader a new sense of passion. It's a great idea to turn off the television, log off the Internet, and take some time to pick up a great book on a regular basis. Lots of folks have discovered that reading together builds bonds and brings people closer, whether you're in a reading club discussing *Tuesdays with Morrie,* or simply sitting quietly together over a few carefully chosen pages.

Great Books with Classic Love Stories

- *The Age of Innocence* by Edith Wharton
- *Anna Karenina* by Leo Tolstoy
- *Cyrano de Bergerac* by Edmond Rostand
- *The Deerslayer* by James Fenimore Cooper
- *Doctor Zhivago* by Boris Pasternak
- *Forrest Gump* by Winston Groom
- *Franny and Zooey* by J. D. Salinger
- *Gone with the Wind* by Margaret Mitchell
- *The Heart Is a Lonely Hunter* by Carson McCullers
- *Howards End* by E. M. Forster
- *Jane Eyre* by Charlotte Brontë
- *Love Story* by Erich Segal
- *Madame Bovary* by Gustave Flaubert
- *The Postman Always Rings Twice* by James M. Cain
- *Pride and Prejudice* by Jane Austin
- *The Scarlet Letter* by Nathaniel Hawthorne
- *Sons and Lovers* by D. H. Lawrence
- *A Streetcar Named Desire* by Tennessee Williams
- *Wuthering Heights* by Emily Brontë

Romance Novels

A more specialized version of romantic writing is the romance novel. These books constitute a major portion of today's publishing industry. In fact, romance novels were projected to make up roughly half of the mass-market paperbacks sold by 1998! Romance books regularly appear on bestseller lists. The typical reader buys between four and twenty books *per month.* Women are more likely to read romance novels, because they speak in a voice that is "by women, for women," according to one expert.

In general, there are three levels of sexuality in romance novels. Sweet romances have pastel covers and sketchy descriptions of sex. About one-fifth conclude with a rapturous kiss in the marital bed. One specialty area in sweet romances, the so-called Christian romances, are sold in both regular bookstores and Christian bookstores.

Sensual romances are for middle-of-the-road readers. The hero and heroine have mutually satisfying sex. Lots of code words are used to describe body parts and the actual act. Terms like "peaks of ecstasy" dominate sensual romances.

Spicy titles contain more graphic descriptions. Anything goes in these novels, so long as the sex is consensual and occurs in the context of a committed relationship. Even bondage and whipping make it into these spicy novels.

Curling up with a romance novel on a cold winter night is a great outlet. Although mostly women read them, these novels do offer insights for men who want to know essentially what "turns a woman on" or puts her in a more romantic mood. Guys, think of reading a romance novel as a form of romantic espionage: You can learn something about what appeals to many females besides Fabio, the long-haired romance icon who appears on many of the covers. It may very well be that lots of readers would gladly have the real thing (a more passionate and romantic man) instead of a book.

Great Romance Novels
- *The Aristocrat* by Catherine Coulter
- *Best Kept Secrets* by Sandra Brown
- *The Cowboy* by Joan Johnston
- *Eye of the Beholder* by Jayne Ann Krentz
- *Fools Rush In* by Gwynne Forster
- *A Great Catch* by Michelle Jerott
- *A Night to Remember* by Adrienne Basso
- *One Tough Texan* by Jan Freed
- *An Original Sin* by Nina Bangs
- *Passion Flower* by Dianna Palmer

- *Pearl Cove* by Elizabeth Lowell
- *The Perfect Neighbor* by Nora Roberts
- *Rodeo Hearts* by Patricia Ellis
- *Silent Honor* by Danielle Steele
- *Starlight, Starbright* by Saranne Dawson
- *Twice Kissed* by Lisa Jackson
- *Wicked* by Jill Barnett
- *Wild to Wed* by Muriel Jensen and Jule McBride

Some critics complain that romance novels are essentially trash or soft-core porn, with tragically poor levels of writing. And it's true many use a standard 200-page formula in which the heroine first rejects the suitor, and then, by page 100, discovers he was indeed Mr. Right.

Poetry

Poetry holds an interesting place in the world of romantic writing. On the one hand, you could say it's just not as popular anymore. Poetry may not be as widely read as it was a hundred years ago. Still, the popular singer Jewel managed to release a very successful book of poems just a few short years ago. More important, however, is that poems are still part of our romantic lives. Everything from the poem that becomes the lyrics of a song to the poem that appears in a Hallmark card suggests many of us still like to see verse in one form or another.

The history of poetry and romance is rich and deep. William Shakespeare was, among other things, a great poet. Just as a reminder, how many of you know at least part of Shakespeare's "Sonnet 18"?

Shall I compare thee to a summer's day?
Thou art more lovely and more temperate:
Rough winds do shake the darling buds of May,
And summer's lease hath all too short a date . . .

Another great love poem is Elizabeth Barrett Browning's "How Do I Love Thee?":

How do I love thee? Let me count the ways.
I love thee to the depth and breadth and height
My soul can reach.

Guys, if you can't find your own words, words from poets like these are always great to include in letters, cards, and recitations. Here's part of "She Walks in Beauty" by Lord Byron, a poem that is likely to make her think fond thoughts about you:

She walks in beauty, like the night
Of cloudless climes and starry skies;
And all that's best of dark and bright
Meet in her aspect and her eyes:
Thus mellow'd to that tender light
Which heaven to gaudy day denies.

Good stuff. And this powerful poem, "To Althea, from Prison," was written by a fellow named Richard Lovelace. These words add power to any statement of affection:

Stone walls do not a prison make,
Nor iron bars a cage;
Minds innocent and quiet take
That for an hermitage;
If I have freedom in my love,
And in my soul am free;
Angels alone that soar above
Enjoy such liberty.

Now, we know that many of you are not going to sit down for a night with a book of poetry. And very few of you are going to take pen in hand to compose a verse. Still, you can think of poetry as a nice little extra in a romantic relationship. Just a little sprinkle here and there, and you've added some zest. Even noted maudlin writer Edgar Allan Poe recognized the value of a well-placed poem. His poem "To Helen" was written for his wife:

Helen, thy beauty is to me
Like those Nicean barks of yore,
That gently, o'er a perfumed sea,
The weary, way-worn wanderer bore
To his own native shore.
On desperate seas long wont to roam,
Thy hyacinth hair, thy classic face
Thy Naiad airs have brought me home
To the glory that was Greece
And grandeur that was Rome.

Poems can be sent and read as part of a courtship, as a message of ongoing love, or as an expression of thanks for a lifetime together. Take a look at this wonderful work by Anne Bradstreet, titled "To My Dear and Loving Husband":

If ever two were one, then surely we.
If ever man were lov'd by wife, then thee;
If ever wife was happy in a man,
Compare with me ye women if you can.
I prize thy love more than whole Mines of gold,
Or all the riches that the East doth hold.
My love is such that Rivers cannot quench,
Not ought but love from thee, give recompense.
Thy love is such I can no way repay,
The heavens reward thee manifold, I pray.
Then while we live, in love let's so persevere,
That when we live no more, we may live ever.

In the end, remember two things about poetry. First, if you try to write a poem for someone you love and it's halfway decent, you're probably going to make a big impression. Guys, lots of women will appreciate your attempt to get in touch with your more creative and personal side. Sending a poem is like sending a love letter: Odds are it will be well-received, if only because you tried. Simply quoting poetry may have a similar effect, because you took the time to find something that fit your situation.

Very few truly romantic poems start with, "There was an old man from Nantucket . . ."

Second, reading poetry may seem pretty dry. But, as with everything else in the range of romantic possibilities, you'll never know if you like it until you try it. Once in your life, take the person of your dreams to a poetry reading or agree to read some poetry together. If it works, great; if not, you'll know you've widened your horizons, if nothing else.

Magazines and Newspapers

Not every great idea you read will come out of a book. Lots of magazines contain articles and tidbits about how to be a better spouse or lover. You can even find those "Secrets of a Better Marriage" articles in publications like *Reader's Digest.* The best way to view these words of wisdom is with interest and caution. Often these articles generalize a bit too much with statements such as, "All men love . . ." or "Middle-age women all have these symptoms . . ." when, of course, they don't. Also, remember that the writer was probably able to sell the piece by offering something unusual or counterintuitive. So, keep in mind that if you see a piece with the title, "Be a Better Husband: Act Like a Jerk," it may be meant to sell magazines, not offer great advice!

Magazines are great for finding new activities, new recipes to cook for the one you love, and ideas about how to enjoy a night out. Many tell you about bargain vacations and other things a romantic couple can enjoy.

Magazines also do a good job of telling stories about love. You can read about a loving spouse going the extra mile or some other profound act of affection. These stories may inspire you to try just a little harder to be a better person and better partner. That's just as romantic as any candlelit dinner.

Just Say It

We talked at length about how actions speak louder than words in Chapter 6. At the same time, words do speak at great volume. It's crucial to keep reminding yourselves that very few people ever tire of being told they are loved. In a romantic relationship, doing all the small and big things is a vital ingredient to a vibrant love life, but saying the small and big things also makes a difference. For example, think of how potent the following phrases are in a partnership:

- "Please"
- "Thank you"
- "You're welcome"
- "I'm sorry"

- "I noticed what you did"
- "You look great"
- "I'm proud of you"
- "We make a great team"

These and many other little signals say, "I love you and you're important to me." We all love to hear them. We all need to say them. Besides simple conversation, there are lots of times, places, and ways to pick out the perfect *bon mot* and spring it on the one you love.

The time to say something special should happen in powerful moments as well as in daily life. Your routine, as a loving couple, should include a few words of affection every morning, as one or both of you head out the door. Saying good-bye with just a bit of extra effort is a great way to start the day.

The right words can also spice up the rest of a regular day. Some spouses and lovers exchange e-mail. Others make phone calls. Clever couples exchange notes, which they stealthily leave in a briefcase or purse. The occasional small interruption to the drudgery of the day that a partner can make with a few pleasant words can really lift the spirits. Try it sometime.

Then, there's the all-important dinner hour. Recent research suggests that families who have dinner together enjoy healthier lifestyles, because they take the time to prepare and eat things like vegetables. There's also a mental health aspect to a meal. Pleasant company and positive communication help food digest and melts away the troubles of the day.

Stress management experts have known for years that a supportive family can reduce the impact of the hectic lifestyle. Young married couples and seniors alike should make a point to share the day's events during the evening meal. We need to talk in order to stay connected. When it's done right, an enjoyable dining experience can be like the first step of an evening-long foreplay.

A sticky note is a romantic word quickie just waiting to happen!

Still, the most important time of the day to say something romantic is right before you fall asleep. We can't emphasize this enough. Whether it's after a round of rousing sex or just the end of a routine day, you should make one more contact with each other as night falls. Even those of you who have different bedtimes should make sure you say, "Good night" and "I love you" regularly. Anytime and anyplace are great times to say a few words of love and comfort.

Ways to Show You Care

Messages can be verbal and written. In the last section, we mentioned some verbal approaches, except for the idea of tucking a note somewhere for your partner to discover at work. There are several other ways to express your love. Romantic Romeos and Juliets are just as willing to say it in print. Here's how.

Cards

We live in a great time. Several outstanding companies think up new greeting cards each day. These cards can be funny, sentimental, poignant, or somewhere in between. This means a vast number of choices are available at practically any card shop, drugstore, or discount retail store. So you can take lots of time and pick out the one that perfectly expresses how you feel.

Everyone loves getting cards. You can even create your own card on a home computer or by using one of those in-store card-designing machines.

A card is a quick, thoughtful way of telling someone they mean so much that you were willing to take some time to send a message of romance, interest, passion, or love.

Love Letters

The past few years have witnessed a renewed interest in the idea of love letters. Three movies came out (*You've Got Mail, Message in a Bottle,* and *The Love Letter*) with love-letter themes. Several books are also available. Don coauthored one in 2001 with author Barrie Dolnick called *How to Write a Love Letter: Putting What's in Your Heart on Paper*. Here are a few of the highlights from that book:

- A love letter can be written using paper and pencil or e-mail, or it can be typed out. The most romantic is undoubtedly handwritten prose. The message is that you were willing to take the time to say something special in an old-fashioned way. Writing things down gives you the time to carefully consider what you want to say and gives you the chance to say it clearly.
- Anyone can write a great love letter. The key is to say what is in your heart. If you need help, there are aides in print and on the Web. You don't have to be a polished writer to eloquently say, "I love you."
- A love letter doesn't have to be long. A few sentences and paragraphs can say many things. A great letter gets to the point, whether it's flattery, a thank-you, or something more intimate.

Remember, you can write a letter for just about any occasion, from asking if someone is interested in dating to saying thank you for a lifetime of love. Putting your thoughts on paper commits you to something more lasting than a casual comment on the phone or while lying in bed.

More than one loving couple has stored love letters in a safe place to be read and reread at their leisure.

You don't have to be a writer or a scholar to send a nice note. Any husband in the world is going to enjoy the message, "I'm in the other room, naked," if it's placed properly under the right circumstances. From there, longer and more meaningful thoughts get easier to share. Writing is a wonderful way to add a new ingredient to a love life.

Anatomy of a Love Letter

- **The Introduction**
  Greet your lover with one of these phrases:
  - Dear ***,
  - My dearest,
- **The Body**
  This is the main section, in which you say what you want to say.
  Here are some examples:
  - I had a great time last night.
  - I want to get to know you better.
  - I appreciate your thoughtfulness (or some other characteristic).
  - You are terrific and here's why (brains, looks, talents, and so on).
  - I'm going to miss you while I'm gone.
  - Making love for the first time was very special.
  - I think I'm falling in love with you.
  - Should we think about getting married?
  - Happy anniversary.
- **The Conclusion**
  Think carefully about how you want to sign off.
  - See you soon.
  - Thanks again.
  - I love you.
  - Until we meet again.
- **Special Touches**
  Use pretty stationery rather than plain notebook paper.
  - Ladies, spray a hint of perfume on the letter.
  - Guys, use your cologne.
  - Add an embellishment like a Hershey's Kiss or a rose.
  - Wrap the letter with ribbon, as if it's a present.

Remember, many people keep love letters for a lifetime. In the past few years, the love letters Ronald Reagan wrote to his wife Nancy have been published. Many great historical figures have written love letters that now appear in books and articles. This happened because the letters made such a big impression that the recipient kept them. They are keepsakes to savor for many years.

As much as words can create ties, they can cut them apart. Biting, mean language should never enter into a romantic relationship.

Love Talk

Talk is the glue that binds a romantic love life. Keeping in constant communication allows you to share, prevents you from growing apart, and bonds you in ways that nothing else can. Notice how important talking is early in a relationship. Lots of you probably share a story about the time you "stayed up all night, just talking." As you and that special someone get to know each other, you open up and talk about things that are more and more intimate.

Unfortunately, once a marriage or partnership bond is in place, talking may be one of the easiest things to fall by the wayside. Lives get busy and kids and work occupy what used to be those more serene moments when you would visit calmly and quietly at the end of the day.

We have some advice for re-establishing the lines of communication. First, turn off the television. The average set stays on over six hours per day, while the average couple spends less than one hour talking to each other. It's no wonder intimacy breaks down when you know more about Regis than about how your lover's day played out. Second, log off the Internet. Articles are just now showing how isolated we're becoming as a culture, preferring a self-indulgent surfing expedition to actual contact with a human being. And third, as a couple you need to figure out when "quiet time" is better than either television, the Internet, or a conversation. Sometimes the most romantic thing you can do is to leave your loved one alone to sort things out. Watch for and learn the signals your partner sends when he or she needs to have some "space."

Never forget how small words lead to big love over time. A compliment is an ego-hug. As often as you can, let your partner know that he or she is important, loved, sexy, smart, fun, exciting, and great. Affection is a self-building cycle. Less leads to less, while more leads to more. It's equally important to say sweet things as it is to do nice things.

Saying What You Mean

Some people have a way with words. Eloquent men and women deliver loving phrases with the greatest of ease. They know how to whisper those "sweet little nothings." Verbal people have many advantages in life, not the least of which is that people around them assume they're really smart. And, truthfully, in some ways they are.

There's an upside and a downside to someone who is that polished. The upside is he or she can compliment you, talk to you, and advise you with words and phrases that are easy to understand and pleasing to hear. The downside may be that the person seems too slick, as if he or she were handing you a line.

Either way, most of us aren't quite that skilled. Consequently, it takes a little effort to learn how to say the right thing. Here are a few suggestions:

- Don't be afraid to pause before you speak. Consider carefully what you're about to say.
- Make sure that what you wanted to say is what the person actually heard.
- Be aware of differences between you and your lover. You may have entirely different ideas about what "relaxing" means. Speak in the language of your lover as best you can.
- Watch your body language. Sometimes your nonverbal communication speaks much louder than your words.
- Be more articulate by learning new words and phrases. Practice them.
- Remember, it never hurts to rehearse a speech to someone you love, especially when you want to say, "I love you" or, "I'm angry about something you did."

- Be careful with the words *always* and *never.* They will often start an argument, as in:

    "You never help me around the house!"

    "You never want to have sex."

    "You're always late."

    "You always have to get in the last word!"

In general, to get better at expressing yourself, read more and write more. Practice may not make perfect, but you can improve your communication skills.

If you really want help, take a speech or a drama class at a local junior college or college. As you become more comfortable with expression, you'll also find that you're becoming a better romantic partner. That makes it worth the effort.

So, What Should We Talk About?

If you're willing to set aside the time to talk, you're well on your way to a romantic evening. Many subjects make you feel closer as a couple. Topics can range from dreamy flights of fancy to stuff that is sexy and raunchy. Here are just a few ideas.

The Future

One of the most romantic topics is the future you're going to spend together. Dating couples and those close to an engagement may talk about the possibilities to come. Young couples entertain ideas about having children. Couples with kids talk about saving for college and building toward retirement. Older couples discuss how they want to spend their golden years.

Thinking about your future together connects you in a unique way. The only image that comes to mind is how you want to share what happens next. The message comes through loud and clear: No matter what, we'll be together. Now that's romantic. It also leads to a closely related subject.

Your Dreams

Years ago, Don did some research on the Social Penetration Theory. This theory suggests that many of us are very careful about what we'll reveal to others. It tends to come out in "layers." That's why the theory is also known as the "onion theory." At first, you are only willing to tell someone about peripheral matters, such as your favorite color, food, and type of music. Later, as you get to know and accept the person, you become more willing to tell him or her about more intimate things, such as embarrassing moments or private fantasies. The core of your personality is where all your deep dark secrets are hidden, and only a few highly trusted souls ever find out about them.

Somewhere in the "onion" that is your personality rests your dreams. Many people are pretty open about them. Others don't want to talk about their dreams. They're afraid of being laughed at or told that the dream is impossible. Any two people can open up and share their dreams. Sharing a dream and reaching for that dream is the stuff of love. It's romantic and intimate to share your ambitions.

The Past

Reliving memories of all kinds creates another unique connection. In a sense, we are what we've done and what we recall. We will become what we do next. So, we "are" all of the episodes and escapades that unfold in our time together.

For romantic couples, everything from the wedding night and honeymoon to the birth of a child is part of their unique story. You can embellish talks about the past with photos, videos, and other memorabilia.

Sex

We have a chapter coming up on sex and we don't want to steal our own thunder, so we'll just mention that one very romantic topic is intimacy. In the calmer moments of a quiet evening, you can reveal what your partner does that really gets you "hot." You can tell him or her some of your favorite sexual memories. Some couples like to "talk dirty." Lighthearted sex talk often ends up in some serious time in the bedroom, or, on the real lusty nights, right there on the living room floor.

One variation of sex talk you should try is phone sex. Now, we're not suggesting one of those 900 numbers or Internet sites. We mean that you can say some really sensuous things to the person you love while on the phone. Think of the possibilities: He is at work and you tell him just how you're going to ravish him when he gets home. She is away on a business trip, and you talk her through what's going to happen when she comes back. The more modest readers of this book can try phone sex without resorting to "naughty" words. Those of you with more familiarity and fewer inhibitions can really cut loose. Either way, it can be fun, romantic, exciting, and it can lead to some terrific passion after you hang up and meet in person.

Words of Comfort

Life is full of ups and downs. Everyone has bad days. Romantic partners know how to offer support. Some of life's rotten moments are pretty small. For example, a speeding ticket is frustrating but not the end of the world. Still, just about everyone comes home after encountering one of these nuisances needing to blow off some steam.

The key to responding the right way to a frustrated partner is empathy. Walk a mile in your partner's shoes. Remember, if it's happening to him or her, some day it might happen to you. A combination of sympathy and humor may help diffuse some of the anger and frustration. The real secret is to pay enough attention to discover what works best in your marriage or romantic relationship.

Then, there are the more serious times of tragedy. Losing a loved one or enduring a major illness creates a real emotional hardship. It's always better to be able to lean on someone who cares when disaster strikes. Being there for your partner often starts without words. Holding him or her speaks volumes. Then, as time passes, your partner may want to talk about the loss. It's never easy, but this is a time when romance and love must be shown with all the energy and thought you can muster. Love means lending support during the tough times as much as relishing the good times. A few words about faith may be helpful as well. Later, when the fog lifts, your spouse will emerge with a greater appreciation for you and what you mean to each other. Nothing builds lifelong romantic connection anymore than that.

Playful Talk and Pet Names

There's a fine line between teasing and being mean. Loving couples tease and play without ever coming close to crossing that line. The ability to laugh at yourself is a wonderful characteristic. Couples who can poke a little fun at their own foibles are better off. Life is serious enough. So, if you're a little absent-minded, you can either be tense about it or just shrug it off. People who are "neat freaks" may have to live with a few comments about the joys of messiness. When you laugh together, love tends to grow.

It can be fun to create names for each other's private parts, so long as the names are complimentary. After all, romance and love aren't supposed to be starstruck and serious. A little giggle now and then is just what the love doctor ordered.

Along the same lines, newlyweds and others enjoying blooming romances often develop pet names for each other. Over time these seem to fade, but they can become part of the memories you share.

Keep Talking

Talk is cheap. That's a good thing and a bad thing. It's a good thing when you and your lover are broke and bored. A rousing conversation on any subject means the night will be more interesting and fun. It's a bad thing when you choose words poorly or forget to talk at all.

Words can inspire arousal. Words also reinforce the deeds that shout, in the loudest possible voice, "I love you!" Words build the friendship that should be the foundation of romantic love. Words get us through the tough times and make the good times better.

Here's one piece of romantic advice to take to heart: "Keep talking." Open lines of communication supply the lifeblood of love and romance. It's that simple. And, while we're on the subject, remember one more thing. The human mind works at about four times the speed of normal conversation. Your brain is abuzz with activity as you go about the day's activities, even when you're talking to someone else. So, when your partner speaks, *listen carefully* and don't interrupt! It's a sign of respect you need to show. Besides, what is more important than clearly hearing what your partner has to say? Words only matter when they reach their final destination. In this case, that's the mind and heart of the one you love.

CHAPTER 10

The Arts and Romance

How many romances began in a dark movie theater? Slowly, carefully, some shy fellow summons the courage to do the old "yawn" move to get his arm around the shoulder of an excited young lady. Or, in a bolder attempt, he goes straight to handholding. The relationship between the media and romance is undeniable. Movies, videos, DVDs, television programs, museums, galleries, and playhouse stages should all be used to build love connections. The arts can be part of romantic life as it begins and grows, and they can embellish and enrich a long-standing romance. In this chapter, we'll describe some of our favorite art forms. We hope that you'll pick out a few to enjoy.

Movies

Without a doubt, motion pictures are still the staple of most dating diets. We use movies to carry us away from our everyday lives and enjoy adventure, fun, laughter, intrigue, drama, and, yes, romance. Sitting in a darkened room watching larger-than-life figures telling their tales makes for a great evening.

Keep a diary of great movies you've watched together. Looking back will remind you of how each affected you and how much fun you had.

Every few years another romantic classic emerges. Men, it's a good idea to resist the temptation to dismiss these films as "chick flicks." While we recognize that it is possible females like these movies better than men, nothing quite builds the mood as well as *When Harry Met Sally* or *Sleepless in Seattle*.

Ladies, the flip side is also true. If the man in your life loves a good action film and you don't, every so often you may want to bite the bullet and watch one anyway. It helps if you can work out genres you both enjoy as well as ones you don't. In general, we're in agreement that they don't make enough comedies. Laughter lightens the mood of the day and often leads to romance. No matter what your tastes, getting to know what your partner prefers in the world of cinema is just one way to strengthen a relationship by learning more about each other.

Some Great Ways to Watch Movies Together

- Go to a horror film. Grab each other for comfort and security.
- Watch a foreign film with subtitles. Then pretend as though you speak the film's language afterward.
- Smooch instead of watching the film. (Sit in the back so you don't distract others.)
- Go see a comedy after a rough week on the job. Let it help you unwind for the weekend.

- Attend a matinee and have dinner afterward for a great evening out on a weekday that still ends early enough to get a good night's sleep.
- Take your kids to a drive-in, just so they'll have the experience. Have them wear their pajamas and take along pillows, sleeping bags, and popcorn.
- Go to a really romantic film. Afterward, drive to a secluded spot and neck.

Videos

Technology has made movie-watching easier than ever. Whether by renting a film from a local store, watching a movie channel, or taping a show for later, couples are now able to share movies at home, where things can get much more intimate. A "dinner and a movie" date can just as easily take place in your living room as out on the town. For those who need to unwind from the hustle and bustle of life, that's a great advantage.

Home videos offer lots of benefits, such as:

- You don't have to get all dressed up. In fact, you can watch in your PJs.
- You can snack all you want while you watch.
- If you need to take a bathroom break, you can stop the film and not miss anything.
- When the movie is terrible, you don't feel as bad, because it didn't cost as much to rent it as it would have to see it in a movie theater.
- You and your partner can do a lot of cuddling as you view the movie. One of the best times to "spoon" with your partner on the couch is while watching television.

Take the phone off the hook when you put on a video. No sense being interrupted unnecessarily. Prepare your favorite snacks and treats in advance so you can happily munch while you watch. If you imbibe, you can enjoy a cocktail or glass of wine as the movie progresses. What makes this all romantic is that you can relax and enjoy a quiet evening together, with or without kids. You watch on your timetable rather than the one set up by the theater. For big-time movie lovers, those Surround Sound devices with big-screen TVs make your home feel much more like the real thing.

Television

Far too often people use television as they would Novocaine. It simply numbs the mind. Life is too short for that. So much of what you see on television makes no lasting impression and doesn't enrich you in any meaningful way. Further, the TV can steal you away from time spent as lovers. Besides, many critics point out that the unsavory lifestyles, violence, and other bad habits that are glorified on various programs have strong negative effects on children.

Several times research has been conducted in which a family agrees to turn off the TV for a month. What they discover is more talking, increased reading, better study habits, and, yes, greater intimacy among husbands and wives. What this suggests is that television can be a crutch that makes you worse instead of better. Chronic TV watchers are likely to be less creative and may have fewer social skills. It certainly merits caution.

Meanwhile, to use television to perk up your romantic life involves being careful, being selective, and getting to know what your partner likes. Pick a program or two to watch, and when there's nothing on, turn it off!

Fellows, recognize when you're making your woman crazy while you're channel surfing and put the remote down! She'll love you for it.

Art Galleries

Okay, it's likely that a great number of people who pick up this book aren't going to think that visiting an art gallery is very exciting or romantic. Lots of men just aren't interested. At the same time, it's never a good idea to dismiss something without giving it a try. You may be surprised by what you see.

To make an art gallery trip more romantic, invest some time and energy in the trip. Either check out some books from a local library or buy a few. Figure out what kinds of artists you think you might enjoy and then track them down. Remember, lots of great art uses nudes for models. That in itself may provide inspiration.

Also, keep in mind that a visit to an art gallery as part of a vacation may add a nice wrinkle to your trip. If you've been at the beach, a gallery offers an air-conditioned break from the sun along with some completely different kinds of sights. Besides, it can't hurt to expand your children's horizons by taking them along.

Museums

There are several reasons you should go to a museum. First, they can be fun. Second, touring a museum together can be educational. What's romantic about that? Smarts are sexy. Learning builds common memories and makes you more interesting to each other and to those around you. Third, museums display our culture and our heritage. As a couple, trips to museums while on vacation or business trips are engaging, giving you something new to discuss and remember. In our view, that's romantic.

Single folks can gain every bit as much from trips to museums. As you learn about something new (or old), you become more interesting to potential suitors or lady friends. Also, a visit to a museum means you're out circulating, not sitting home in front of an impersonal television set or computer screen. Finding a dating partner while in a museum may be a long shot, but as the word gets around through your friends, the odds increase they'll introduce you to someone who might be compatible.

Opera

Going to the opera can be very romantic. You get all dressed up for each other, which is always a good start. Attending an opera is one of the more formal nights out you can enjoy. When you combine it with a fancy dinner before and dessert or drinks afterward, a great night is in store.

Most men will probably report they'd rather step in front of a moving bus than go to an opera. That is a shame, because they don't know what they're missing. The music is live and powerful, the vocalists perform in a way you can't fully appreciate until you've seen it in person, and the stories range from funny to highly dramatic. Not only that, but taking a lady friend or spouse to the opera says, in no uncertain terms, "I don't care how much ribbing I take from the guys, I'm doing something new and different just to please you." That's romantic. Doing so generates tons of brownie points and gratitude. And the odds are she's going to go to great lengths to look beautiful. So, try it a few times. If it doesn't click, you are still better off.

The Ballet and Dance Troupes

Once in your life, you need to see *Swan Lake* and *The Nutcracker*. Go by yourselves or take your kids. *The Nutcracker* is a wonderful Christmas tradition. *Swan Lake* is mesmerizing in its beauty. Ballet has many of the same features as opera. You dress up, enjoy live entertainment, and see incredibly talented dancers. Once again, we know men tend to resist these kinds of shows. We still think you should give it a try.

For some added entertainment value, go to a performance of a dance troupe. Although you may be shocked by how sensuous some of these movements are, you'll certainly be impressed by the grace and power displayed by professional (and amateur) dancers.

Ladies, if you have one of those stick-in-the-mud types of lovers, make a trade. Go to one boxing match or football game in exchange for a performance of a ballet or a dance troupe. He may have a hard time actually saying it was enjoyable, but you'll be able to tell.

Plays

There are many kinds of theater. No one is going to like every version. There are the mainstream Broadway-type standards that are designed to reach a broad-based audience. Experimental theater (off-Broadway) is vibrant, challenging, and different. Some are quite powerful; some are terrible. Then, there are community theaters, college theaters, and high school plays.

To get last-minute tickets to performances, or to purchase tickets in advance to get better quality seats, check out one of the many ticket distribution centers in New York City.

Lots of couples attend plays as part of their dating experience. After all, you get to sit in a dark room brushing up against the person of your affection for several hours. People are usually more dressed up and the break between acts gives you a chance to visit and comment on what you're watching. Early on in your dating program you'll probably stick with fairly "safe" plays, like comedies and musicals. Students can attend plays on campus because they don't cost much and they may include performances by friends. Later, when you venture out to professional plays, the excitement of the program may build. Holding hands quietly as the performance unfolds is spine-tingling romance at its best.

Longer-term partners can take an excursion to New York to see a Broadway play or two while sharing a weekend of big city excitement. You'll get the chance to see personalities who have appeared in film and on television. The actual staging is more dramatic and larger than life.

Some of you may be willing to try even more experimental stuff. If so, give a performance artist a whirl. These shows are unique and run the gauntlet from funny to just bizarre. At the least, you'll come away with something to talk about.

Festivals and Fairs

There are more festivals and fairs than there are regions in the country. Most of these gatherings offers food, fun, rides, music, and other types of celebrations of local art and culture. A romantic couple out for a day can easily take advantage of these festivities. Most are inexpensive and offer lots of variety.

The same is true for county and state fairs. You can enjoy everything from pie baking contests, to rodeos, livestock displays, and rides. A trip to the state fair may remind you of your younger days, only now you're sharing the same activities with someone you love. A great retro moment may result.

Going to a carnival, fair, or community festival immerses you in the culture of the area. You'll meet some really interesting folks as you walk hand-in-hand through the best a town has to offer. Those of you with specialized tastes can even make a special sojourn to an event such as a regional bluegrass or blues festival. These events are fun memories in the making. They're also romantic adventures for many couples.

The Other Way to Enjoy the Arts: Participate!

This chapter wouldn't be complete if we failed to mention the great joy that can accompany being involved in the arts. There are lots of ways to become active. For example, you can be a patron of a local performing arts council. This means you'll help raise money to bring in talented performers, sell tickets, or help out in some other way. Among other things, it means you'll get to personally meet some of these folks.

Some of you may prefer to be more directly included without actually being in the spotlight. Community theaters and other volunteer organizations are always looking for people to help prepare programs, paint scenery, move sets during shows, sew costumes, and help with lighting and sound. If you have those kinds of skills, or are just interested, it's easy to find some group that will be thrilled that you want to assist. If you're single and are looking for a new way to meet people, this is a great outlet. Couples can get involved together.

If you have a little more nerve, you can actually get up on the stage. Singles may very well find romance in some type of performing troupe. You already know you share an interest with others in the cast or group. That old business about falling in love with a leading man or lady plays out more often than you might guess. Even if you don't find a romantic interest, you will have a great kind of camaraderie that's hard to match. There is a spirit that comes from this kind of team effort.

We also believe that getting involved as a performer or supporter makes you a more interesting person. This makes a single person more attractive to potential mates and helps a married couple diversify their interests. For those with mundane jobs or who are bored with endless nights sitting home watching television, becoming active is a great use of your time and energy.

Romantic people go and do—they enjoy all kinds of activities. Sharing new things and revisiting old favorites is lively, loving, and fun. Make it a point to try something out as soon as you put down this book. Then, prepare to be pleasantly surprised!

When it comes to using the arts to spice up your love life, we have one final piece of advice to give: Don't be shy! Ladies, your lover may not know how much you would enjoy a symphony or trip to an art gallery unless you tell him. Guys, it's important to resist the urge to think of the opera or museum visits as something for "wimps" or artsy types. Doing so means you're caving in to some ridiculous stereotypes.

We were once lucky enough to attend a speaking engagement by the late entertainer Steve Allen. In the question-and-answer session, he was asked about growing old. He said that the worst part, in his mind, was the realization that he wouldn't be able to read every great book, see every classic film, view every great painting, and watch every noble performance. His point was that life is so short that it's possible to let it pass by without being engaged by all there is to experience, which is probably where the idea of "wasting time" originated.

CHAPTER 11
Romantic Chemistry

Romantic chemistry takes many forms. Mood, atmosphere, interpersonal attraction, and other natural forces can work to your advantage when building a love relationship. When you think of chemistry, you may recall that tough class you took in high school or college or envision the chemicals used in science labs. That's not we're talking about here. Chemistry consists of everything that alerts you to the idea that someone is interested. It may be found in that small whiff of fragrance as the person walks by. It may be the unmistakable feeling that you've found someone you "click" with. Chemistry is the right combination of entertainment and intimacy that makes for a great night together. In other words, it's a vast array of input that creates the impression that things are just right.

The Power of Fragrance

Here's an interesting question: Can love truly be "in the air"? Do flavors and smells create love, or just spice up the love that is already present? More important, does it matter? Of course, it does. When you think about the tools of romance, one major tool is as plain as the nose on your face!

Part of interpersonal attraction is based on scent. When you're dating, you—and we're talking men and women here—tend to make a pretty big point of making sure you smell good. Everything from covering perspiration odor to having fresh breath to choosing the right perfume or cologne plays into the mix. It's not surprising, because you're trying to make the best impression possible. Over time, we've come to associate various fragrances with romance.

Since everyone has different preferences, choice of a perfume or cologne can be a major factor in how well a date plays out and also how the other person reacts. Someone who is wearing too much fragrance can turn you off pretty quickly. Someone wearing just the right amount can turn you on even quicker.

One word of caution for both sexes: Make sure your partner isn't allergic to a scent. Some people can't tolerate any fragrance. And remember to apply it lightly. You want to tantalize your lover with a hint of scent, not send him or her into a fit of sneezing.

As your relationship evolves, you tend to make a special point of wearing your lover's favorite scent on special nights, like anniversaries and dinner dates. The strong link between memories of fragrances combined with memories of passion means the evening gets off to a good start before you head out of the house. It may even mean your night out gets off to a late start!

Ladies, if you want to make sure the perfume you're wearing is sending the right signal, here's a tip: Go to a local store and try two or three perfumes on different parts of your body. Write down which went where. Then, let them interact with your own chemistry for a few hours because they will change a little during that time. Finally, ask your lover to smell each one and report which one he likes best. This little "dry run" can be very seductive and provide great information at the same time.

To get the perfume where you want it to go, spray a fine mist in the air and then walk through it. The mist will reach you all over in the right amount. To get that favorite fellow to find the scent in your hair, spray some on a brush right before you use it. The scent makes a nice impression.

Other key places to put perfume include:

- On your neck
- On his collar
- Between your breasts
- On your hair
- On your sheets
- On a love letter or card
- On his pillow when you're out of town
- On the back side of your knee
- In a closet
- On your PJs or in your underwear drawer
- On something you place in his briefcase

Some guys aren't all that interested in how they smell, but they should be. Why? Take a look at these statistics. One recent study of 332 college students revealed that the women consistently rated how a guy smelled as being more important than how he looked when it came to attractiveness. Married and single fellows, take note!

If you're married to a man who has lost interest in things like cologne, try a few subtle approaches. Buy him some scented soap or shampoo to see how he likes it. Or, put your favorite scent on your hands and gently touch his face as you kiss him. He'll carry that slight hint around for several hours and the impression may last even longer.

There is a strong connection between scents and memories. Old ones trigger recollections of past loving episodes. New ones can be created all the time. If you want to try something new, fill a tub with hot water and a few drops of lavender, chamomile, and sage. (You can buy these essential oils at a cosmetics or department store, or try a product like AromaFloria Stress Less Ocean Mineral Bath Salts, which contains all three.) Then get into the tub with your partner. The net effect of encountering these odors while soaking with your love will be a great "now" and a great memory later!

It's not just perfume and cologne that create romantic images. It can be a shampoo that leaves a delicate scent of fruit or flowers in her hair. Some of the most irresistible hair products are Aveda Shampure, Sebastian Collection Slinky Conditioner, and Donna Karan Cashmere Mist Conditioner. These are more potent when heated with a hair dryer, so ask your man to run his fingers through your hair right after you finish.

For women, it may be his aftershave or the hint of shaving cream that stays on his skin. Even kissing someone with freshly brushed teeth or newly gargled mouthwash may send out a minty scent that is attractive and seductive. Over time, romantic couples develop all kinds of connections based on how they "sense" each other.

One of the easiest gifts to give is a perfume or cologne that you like your lover to wear. Many fragrance lines also include body lotion, body splash, dusting powder, and shower gel, so your partner can "layer" on the fragrance.

More Romantic Scents

Besides the products we use on our bodies to smell better, there are other ways to spice up a night of romance. The most obvious is fresh flowers, which add a wonderful fragrance to a room. (Lots of guys also like getting flowers as gifts; they're not just for ladies!) A freshly cut Christmas tree leaves a distinct aroma that most people love. Scented candles are part of nights of seduction and passion in many homes. The secret is to be creative in using all of these tools to make the right connection. After all, the smell of a cup of hot chocolate may make the perfect impression when you want to cuddle on a cold winter's night.

Fragrances can have a powerful effect on a male's libido. One expert suggests that both fruity and floral aromas are attractive to men. A few drops of orange or grapefruit essential oil in a ceramic light bulb ring fills a bedroom with a seductive scent. Placing flowers into warm water causes them to bloom faster and emit a more intense odor, which also puts everyone in the right mood.

Let's also consider those scents that are less attractive and less romantic. For instance, cigarette, cigar, and pipe smoke fit into this category. Bad breath as well as the smell of liquor and heavy perspiration normally reduce the chances of romance. And remember that although you may be used to the smell of your pet, your dating partner may be more sensitive. Tidy up before inviting someone to your home and make sure that he or she does not have pet-related allergies.

Aromatherapy for Love

There are times when you want scents to fire you up and get you ready for passion. Fragrances can cause your brain to produce endorphins, which help calm you and improve your mood. At other times, you may just want to be soothed. If you're tense or stressed, you may be calmed by the scent of vanilla, lavender, mint, eucalyptus, or citrus. The aroma of freshly baked cookies or cake can relax an entire family.

Aromatherapy includes using drops of essential oils as well as containers of potpourri. Just for fun, try a few to see how they affect your mood and love life. One product contains an aroma dispenser with four distinct scents designed for individual moods. You can take advantage of one that is supposed to be calming one day and another that is sensual the next.

If nothing else, we hope we have convinced you that the nose is a major love instrument. What is especially great is that these suggestions are low-cost ways to add a little zing to your love life. When you combine them with other aspects of romantic chemistry, great things can happen!

Combining Scents with Other Senses

There's an important connection between the sense of smell and the sense of touch. Rubbing lotions and oils onto your lover's body often starts a major romantic and sensual event. There are many choices, from scented soaps to suntan lotions to specially designed oils for massage.

When you think about it a little more carefully, you'll quickly realize that applying a lotion or cream goes beyond feeling and smelling to seeing. So, fellows, the next time your wife or lover starts to "lotion up" her legs and feet after a shower to prevent drying and chafing, quickly volunteer for that duty. You'll get to inspect her firsthand while she relaxes and savors your masculine touch. Don't be surprised if more good things quickly follow.

Women can use similar tactics. Most guys we know love it when a wife or lover offers to join her man in the shower to give him a thorough scrubbing. Don't be shy about getting to every nook and cranny. From there, both of you can think of ways to incorporate the other senses, hearing and tasting. The possibilities are endless!

Both the giver and the receiver of this special love touch should greatly enjoy the moment. Massage causes the brain to secrete endorphins, which are calming mental chemicals. A firm touch is relaxing and soothing as it releases muscle tension. A lighter touch may make the hairs on his or her arm stand up with excitement.

Pheromones

Male pheromones are odorless substances that are secreted from the underarm and groin areas. When they reach a female's olfactory area, they may stimulate romantic and sexual interest. In a study conducted in England, thirty-two women were shown male faces in plain photos and male faces in photos treated with pheromones. All of the women rated the males in the pheromone-treated pictures as being more attractive.

This leads us to ponder two issues regarding pheromones and attraction: natural secretion and artificial use. These are two entirely separate processes.

Natural pheromones are secreted when a fellow encounters a woman who arouses his interest, or vice versa. Each responds by sensing the other and reacting based on a combination of thoughts. Is he interesting to her? Is she available? Is it the right time? Then, following the calculation of all of these ideas and variables, the two people react.

On the other hand, artificially produced pheromones are probably just a high-tech attempt at creating an aphrodisiac. Some stores sell a product called Philosophy's Falling in Love formula. (If you're interested, go to *www.philosophy.com* to find an outlet near you.) For around $60, you can purchase synthesized pheromones designed for women. They are supposed to make you feel like a sex siren and build the interest levels of the men you encounter. At that point, there are philosophical and practical issues.

On the practical side, you wonder if they really work. If they do, you may be turning on someone totally by accident. If this stuff just sort of randomly makes you sexually arousing, you could be tempting the entire room. Philosophically, you wonder if you really want to get a man interested through such artificial means. If no one can resist these chemicals, this may be the new millennium's version of getting him drunk and taking advantage.

We think it's better to let nature take its course. It might be fun for a night to buy some and try them out in the privacy of your home to see what happens. Still, the day may come when we're all sprinkling each other with synthetic love chemicals. That doesn't sound too romantic to an old-fashioned couple like us.

You may feel something very powerful happen when hugging or kissing someone that you can't explain, as if destiny or some other force were knocking on your brain telling you this is going to be a very special person in your life. That's chemistry.

Interpersonal Chemistry

Beyond all of these scents for your senses, there are many other factors that create and inhibit romantic attraction. After you've showered, bathed, splashed on cologne, brushed your teeth, put on a nice outfit, and filled the room with flower petals, there is still plenty of chemistry left. There will never be a precise formula telling us how to pick a perfect match. Luck of the draw interferes, along with lots of other quirks and circumstances. Still, we can see how romance builds based on some basic interpersonal features. We all use them to help us find love. They may also come into play as a romance grows and thrives over time. Here are a few ideas.

How People Identify Romantic Prospects

During the early stages of dating, most folks tend to have some "criteria" in mind as they sift through potential partners. Clearly physical appearance plays a role. All those anthropological studies point out that physical attractiveness depends on the culture, the region, and the time. Even in the United States, the era of the super-skinny, sexy model stage may be winding down. It's being replaced by healthier, more athletic women. Undoubtedly the same type of shifts in what makes a man physically appealing regularly takes place.

Also, what makes someone physically interesting in high school may not matter much later in life. By then, we judge people based on humor, kindness, intellect, and dozens of other observations. When a relatively decent match occurs, the odds for romance increase.

One thing we found interesting in doing research for this book is a process called "successive approximation." This means that it doesn't take long for either sex to figure out what he or she wants in a partner. Then, it has to be fine-tuned. So, a great number of people end up dating and even marrying a series of people with similar characteristics, from how they look to deeper personality traits. Only subtle differences are present. What that tells us is that we have a good idea of what we're looking for. It takes a little more work and weeding out to figure out what we don't want. Only a real disaster causes a person to seek out someone who is totally different.

At the same time, remember that romance and love are based on more than attraction. True, early on in a dating relationship, the first intimate moment sends major shivers down your spine, but after a while that dissipates. That's because the nervous tension of being with someone new and interesting eventually diminishes. You're less likely to giggle nervously or rely on whatever device you use to control those early butterflies.

Soon, something else replaces those early responses. For one, you start to notice the anticipation that builds up between the times you see each other. You spend time thinking about new ways to make an impression. You want to know more about this increasingly special person. At this stage, the chemistry of the relationship is changing dramatically.

Watch an older couple having dinner or shopping. Observe how they treat each other. There is respect combined with readily noticeable patterns and habits. Those are the kind of romantic connections that evolve over a lifetime.

After you've been together for a long time, a different kind of chemistry evolves. You start using the same phrases and even begin thinking more alike. The patterns of interaction become habits, in the good sense. That's because a loving husband or wife knows just how to make a partner feel better after a bad day, or to send a signal that he or she wants more attention. At the extreme, couples that have been married for years are said to start looking more alike, because they make the same facial expressions. If it's true that we turn over all new cells in our bodies every seven years, it's not surprising that interpersonal chemistry will increase the similarities between two people in love.

What Causes Us to Be Attracted?

Rate these items honestly in three different situations: (1) when you were in high school, (2) as a young unmarried adult, and (3) now (even if you're happily married). Notice how your answers change. Ask your lover for his or her answers to see what you might learn.

1. Physical features:
   _____ Chest   _____ Face   _____ Hair   _____ Hands
   _____ Legs   _____ Overall build   _____ Smile

(continued)

2. Mental characteristics:

_____ Aggressiveness _____ Creativity _____ Curiosity

_____ Integrity _____ Intelligence _____ Sense of humor

_____ Steadfastness

3. Personality:

_____ Attitudes _____ Disposition (that is, happy versus depressed)

_____ Honesty _____ Kindness _____ Values

4. Other:

_____ Is ambitious _____ Is intuitive _____ Likes family time

_____ Likes kids _____ Likes power

Other Kinds of Chemistry

As we go through life, many different friends will come and go. How we entertain ourselves changes. The manner in which we define "fun" and "romance" may also take a different path. To finish off this chapter, let's take a look at the "miscellaneous" categories of chemistry that affect our love lives.

Double-Dating and Groups of Friends

Most of you probably had experiences similar to ours when you were younger. The ways in which dating relationships are constructed as kids and young teenagers are much different than at any other time in life. At these ages, kids tend to run in groups. Many times a few guys become entangled with a few girls as various love interests develop. When the chemistry clicks, a group forms that goes to the coffee shop or mall together and sets up parties so everyone can be with everyone else, all the while building up the nerve to develop more solo love relationships.

Romance can bloom within sets of friends. While you are trying to discover exactly what you're looking for in a lover, you may find one convenient way to learn is by dating friends. Sooner or later, these things tend to resolve themselves, giving us memories and teaching us lessons for the years to follow.

Another kind of romantic chemistry takes place when double-dating comes into play, especially when two of the four people involved are friends. So, two guys who are buddies take their girlfriends to the movies, or two girls who are close invite their boyfriends out to a dance. Double-dating chemistry is unique. It relies on all four people liking, or at least being able to tolerate, one another. When it works, the fun grows exponentially.

As people marry and settle down, double-dating usually changes into "doing things with other couples." The point is the same: to share an evening of dining, dancing, or whatever with two friends. The same-sex and cross-sex patterns of interaction make these kinds of nights truly delightful, when they work.

Most marriage counselors would probably suggest that it's healthy for each member of a couple to have their own friends. Sometimes women just need "girl talk" and men need a "night out with the guys." The longer you've been together and the more powerful your romantic life, the more likely it becomes that you'll end up spending at least part of the time bragging about your partner.

Friction and Attraction

Do opposites attract? Probably the best answer is a resounding "maybe." On one level, no two people are exactly the same. The differences can be exciting to discover. They also keep things interesting. There are many couples in which one spouse is shy and the other is outgoing. Or a husband may love the spotlight while his wife loves being in the audience. This suggests that opposites may attract when one compliments the other.

There is also a difference between a disagreement about whether a movie was good and disagreements about how to spend money or discipline kids. Romantic friction tends to work best when the subject is relatively trivial.

Some couples seem to argue with a great deal of energy, but at the same time are drawn to each other. These folks like to feel engaged with each other, so a lively debate becomes an expression of interest and attraction. This friction works for some and not for others. Some couples carefully avoid any kind of confrontation. Neither method is right or wrong. The secret is to make sure you work things out in your romantic lives.

Serendipity, Premonitions, and Déjà Vu

Serendipity—the idea that a sequence of events must occur at the right place and in the right time, to someone's good fortune—probably plays out more often than we realize. Sometimes things just fall into your lap. The chemistry involved is partly based on your ability to recognize that fortune is smiling at you. So, when someone who complains that she never meets anyone who can make her laugh suddenly bumps into a person filled with great one-liners, that's serendipity.

Closely related are all of those other sixth-sense phenomena. Everyone has probably said at one time or another, "I just *knew* something good was going to happen today." Whether that "something good" is simply a self-fulfilling prophecy based on trying a little harder to find something positive in the day doesn't really matter. The point is the premonition played out.

Who knows, maybe there will be some serendipity in your purchase of this book, because the one you love has been wishing you would make an effort to be more romantic. If so, go with the flow. Love comes out in all kinds of ways.

These premonitions become more frequent the longer you stay together. That's because as you become closer, you start to think more like each other. Consequently, on the day you find yourself wishing to dine out, your spouse will come home and say, "I'm in the mood for Chinese food," or some such. That's one of the neatest parts of a long-term loving relationship. These quaint moments tend to happen more often, which serves to make a strong partnership even stronger.

Maybe the weirdest experience is déjà vu, in which you suddenly find yourself thinking, "I've been here before." These kinds of mental images do give us pause. Maybe there is more to destiny than we think. Maybe some things are supposed to happen.

An Interpersonal Chemistry Test

How good is your interpersonal chemistry? Can you pick the answer your lover would choose to these questions?

1. My lover likes sex best:
   _____ In the morning
   _____ In the afternoon
   _____ Last thing at night

2. My lover's favorite food is:
   _____ Something you can only buy in a restaurant
   _____ Something we cook at home
   _____ Couldn't say

3. I know my lover's favorite kind of entertainment.
   _____ Yes   _____ No

4. If I were offered a promotion that involved moving to another city, I know my lover's reaction would be:
   _____ To become angry
   _____ To be supportive and work toward the best decision for both of us
   _____ To rely on an agreement we'd worked out earlier about these kinds of decisions

5. I know if my lover likes it when I kiss him or her in public.
   _____ Yes   _____ No

6. My lover prefers:
   _____ Nights home alone together
   _____ Nights out with our friends
   _____ Entertaining people at our house

7. My lover prefers:
   _____ Going to visit family
   _____ Having family to our house
   _____ Seeing family without me being present

8. I know when my lover wants to have sex without a word being spoken.
   _____ Yes   _____ No

(continued)

9. When we go to a restaurant, my lover prefers:

_____ Having his or her back to the wall

_____ Sitting side by side

_____ Having me with my back against the wall

10. My lover prefers:

_____ Shopping together

_____ Shopping separately

_____ To let me do the shopping

11. My lover prefers:

_____ Handling the finances

_____ Sharing responsibility for the finances

_____ Letting me take care of the finances

12. I can tell when my lover is about to start an argument.

_____ Yes _____ No

13. I know what my lover would say is my most attractive feature.

_____ Yes _____ No

14. We tend to like the same kinds of movies and television programs.

_____ Yes _____ No

15. I know when it's time to give my lover some time alone.

_____ Yes _____ No

16. I know my lover's deepest, darkest secrets.

_____ Yes, for sure _____ I think I do _____ I'm sure I don't

17. We tend to like the same kinds of people.

_____ Yes _____ No

18. I like most of my lover's friends.

_____ Yes _____ No, but I haven't told him or her

_____ No, and he or she knows it

19. When we travel somewhere, I know if my lover wants me to be the passenger or the driver.

_____ Normally _____ Sometimes _____ Never

20. We have the same sense of humor.

_____ Yes _____ No

The more often you can find agreement on these issues, the better your chemistry. Discuss your answers to see what you learn about each other and your relationship.

Better Loving Through Chemistry

When Don teaches his students about research, he says that scientists work on three goals: (1) to understand, (2) to predict, and (3) to control. Romantic couples can share these same three goals. Doing so makes romantic chemistry work to your advantage in several wonderful ways.

First, understand how chemistry works. Your love relationship should be one of the most important parts of life, so it makes sense to work hard to try to improve it. This means getting to know how the chemistry of your marriage or dating situation works. For example, if you know your partner likes perfume, but in limited doses, apply just a small amount.

Understanding couple chemistry involves one key word: communication. Talk about things you like and don't like. Explain what turns you on and off. Tell this key person in your life when his friends are making you nuts. Build relationships with friends and couples that make your life more pleasant, so you look forward to going out together and sharing some new adventure. A meeting of the minds is the key to understanding romantic chemistry.

Predicting then gets much easier. Can you tell when your partner is preoccupied with work, angry about something, or needs your reassurance? This stuff isn't rocket science. It's just a matter of paying attention.

Control shouldn't be construed as a negative word in this context. It just means using all of your knowledge about your partner's preferences to make life better. It also means insisting on your own issues. Being a doormat in a relationship is a bad idea. Tell your lover, "I love it when you kiss me right before I go to bed," or "I'm thrilled when you tell your mother you love my cooking." Sending signals is part of chemistry. Receiving them is the other part. Together you can share a richer, more meaningful life on a daily, even on a moment-by-moment, basis. The rest is up to you.

CHAPTER 12

Romance Busters (and What to Do about Them)

he lion's share of this book has focused on "doing positives": how to use food, music, words, and deeds to improve your love relationships. To present a more complete picture, however, there should be a discussion about how to "eliminate negatives." We call these negatives "romance busters." A talented, creative, romantic person is just as tuned in to avoiding problems as he or she is to doing romantic things. Eliminating these romance busters goes beyond being a better husband, wife, or lover. Many of these tactics can help you become a better person. That's because the same things that damage romance also hurt friendships and family relationships.

Romance-Busting People

Love comes naturally to some folks. The world is filled with special people who make you feel better when you're with them. Maybe it's a gift, or maybe the individual works hard to be pleasant all the time. Either way, one of the great truths about love is that the more you give, the more you get. And those who are "givers" aren't even trying to be "receivers."

At the other extreme are the people who are just tough to love. They are so mean, negative, and nasty that even their mothers have a hard time finding their good qualities. Fortunately, there aren't too many of these types.

In between, the majority of us are sometimes lovable and sometimes not. Romance-busting people tend to make romance more difficult. They have personality traits that are less than desirable, or they simply do and say things that turn others off. People who exhibit these problems can certainly work on improving their dispositions, which might turn them into better people as well as more passionate lovers. Let's look at some of the more common types of romance-busting people.

The Sarcastic Type

Have you ever been in a grand mood, only to have someone's smart aleck comment bring you right down? It's just no fun dealing with a person who is negative and mean. Sarcasm has its place in political commentaries, but not in a romance or marriage. In the worst cases, sarcasm becomes verbal abuse. Even in milder versions, it's bad form to say something haughty or arrogant about the one you love.

Another type of sarcastic person is the one who verbally unloads on everyone and everything, even if the snide comments are never targeted at loved ones. One writer refers to such a nasty, snide temperament as "toxic."

If you tend to make derogatory comments all the time, here's what we suggest. First, place yourself in situations where optimism abounds and keep your mouth shut. See if some of it will rub off. Go to a spirited church service or listen to a speech by someone with an inspiring story to tell. Head to one of those bars where they have karaoke or sing-alongs and join in the fun. Then, when the urge strikes to cut someone down, try to think of something pleasant.

If you can't contain yourself, find outlets where your acidic comments won't hurt anyone. Make it a point to avoid voicing criticism and negativity around the one you love. Let him or her help you enjoy a more positive outlook. In more severe instances, you may want to invest some time with a counselor or mental health professional whose training and skills can help you become a more positive spouse, lover, and friend.

The Pessimist

Being pessimistic is closely related to being sarcastic. Pessimists see the dark side and the worst-case scenario, no matter what comes their way. They immediately find the downside in a stroke of good fortune. For example, on hearing that a friend won the lottery, the pessimist says, "He won't like his tax problems."

Pessimists think they'll never get promoted, never get ahead, and never catch a break. They think people who are happy are just fooling themselves, that every marriage is destined to fail, and that every relationship is moving toward a breakup. An optimist sees the glass as half full; the pessimist sees it as half empty.

Coping with a pessimist is the same as dealing with a drowning victim. The first rule of life saving is, "Don't let the victim drown you." Put some space between yourself and the pessimist, if necessary. The problem is that pessimism is contagious. The next thing you know, a happy person begins to make more caustic comments. (Unfortunately, it doesn't seem to work the other way around.) So, if you are that constantly negative person, you're going to have to make an effort to change how you see things and how you describe them to others. It's worth the effort, though. Life actually does have many pleasant moments. Figuring out how to focus on the good while sharing it with others makes you a better person in all sorts of ways.

A pessimist goes home thinking, "We probably won't have sex tonight." A romantic goes home thinking, "I can't wait until we have sex tonight!"

The Grump

One thing is certain about life: There is plenty to be grumpy about. The world gets a little more hectic every year; pollution and global warming keep getting worse; it costs a fortune to raise a family; and rude people are everywhere. It's easy to complain. But sooner or later, you'll notice that all that griping and grumbling doesn't solve anything.

Grumpy people are time thieves. They steal precious moments that you could have spent doing something more fun. For however long a bad mood lasts, you're just wasting time. The trick is to discover activities that lighten your mood. No matter what the tactic, when you're looking for love, avoid continually grumpy people and make sure you're not one yourself.

The Debater

Do you know people who always have to be right? They're probably not much fun, especially if they love to pick fights. A person who is driven by the need to win is either terribly insecure or overly opinionated. Being around someone like that is grueling. Eventually, you wear down and just give in. That's not good for self-esteem or romance.

If you have this tendency, practice holding your tongue. Figure out why it's so important to you to have the last word. A counselor may help, or even a close friend who is willing to point it out to you. Love is give and take, not debate and conquer.

The Aggressive Type

There are all kinds of aggression. None is particularly appealing unless it happens in a safe arena such as sports or business. Bullies usually have low self-esteem. Aggressiveness happens in conversation, in dealing with other people, in driving, and in handling problems and obstacles in life.

It's wise to keep your distance from overbearing, aggressive people. They can be dangerous to your self-esteem, sense of well-being, and even your health. Be very cautious around these people. If you have this trait, you may need help; it's easy to get completely out of control. Either channel this drive and energy into constructive places, or look for ways to reduce the need to dominate others. A mental-health professional can help.

The "I-Me-My" Type

One key romance-busting type is so totally self-consumed that he or she never shares or shows concern for others. You know the type. He always has to be the center of attention. Everyone knows somebody who is so self-absorbed that she never even asks, "How are you?" Someone who is that self-centered is going to be a lousy companion and probably a terrible lover.

This trait can be fixed, if you are willing to put in some effort. You just have to learn how to enjoy others' accomplishments and empathize with their problems. Life is a lot more interesting when you share it with someone else.

The Taker

Like the "I-Me-My" type, the Taker drains you. One-way relationships can never be completely fulfilling. Unrequited love is empty. It's best to keep your distance from people who are this needy. Otherwise, you'll get suckered into constantly solving their problems and spending your own emotional energy while getting nothing in return. This is not love and it's certainly not romantic. Stay away from selfish people, if at all possible.

Until they learn about their problem, they will continue to sap your strength without even knowing how badly they misuse the people who care most about them.

The Control Freak

Romance suffers when one person in the relationship always has to get his or her way. At their worst, control freaks may go behind your back and change things you've done, or insist something be done their way. They pout and argue until things go the way they want. You can cope with a control freak either by insisting on your way from time to time or by running for the hills.

Try pointing out the problem to see if the person is willing to mend his or her ways. If not, you have a less-than-equal friendship, but at least the cards are on the table. If you have control issues, start learning how to give up the reins. It's not easy, but you'll be better off in all sorts of ways. Just for starters, you'll have more free time because you won't be so busy trying to run everyone else's life.

The Glass House Issue

It's easy to judge others. We all do it from time to time. Most everyone has good qualities as well as bad. Just make sure you don't spend too much time with someone who is dominated by one of these flaws. Also, work hard to make sure you don't exhibit them. "Trying to be a better person" shouldn't just be a motto. It should be a way of life, for everyone.

Advertising classes teach students that one effective marketing technique is to turn a negative into a positive. So, for example, a restaurant with slower service can brag that they take their time to make higher quality food. One ketchup company advertises that that is why their product comes out of the bottle so slowly—it's thicker and tastes better. In life, we can improve our personalities when we take a negative trait and try to make it more positive. If you complain too much, learn how to write down your gripes and make them funny. If you find you're too critical, sit down and make a list of your ten worst habits or qualities. Then try to change them. This might make you less judgmental of those around you.

One thing we can all do is practice humility mixed with a healthy dose of the Golden Rule: Do unto others as you would have them do unto you. People who strive to be better people are superior lovers and romantic partners. It's just that simple.

Ten Steps Toward Becoming a Better Person—Today!

1. **Smile frequently.** Experts say smiling creates fewer wrinkles and actually puts you in a better mood.
2. **Compliment someone.** It costs nothing to make someone else feel good, and his or her opinion of you will also improve.
3. **Stifle yourself.** Instead of spouting off about a rude behavior, shrug and think of the last time you were rude. Maybe that person is just having a bad day. No need to make it worse.
4. **Perform random acts of kindness.** Sure, it's a cliché, but it works.
5. **Hug more often.** It lifts your spirits and cheers up someone you love.
6. **Pray regularly.** Quiet contemplative time is good for the soul as well as the demeanor.
7. **Laugh at yourself.** No one should be taken that seriously.
8. **Tell more jokes.** When you're able to make someone else laugh, everyone's day is better.
9. **Think positive thoughts.** Believe it or not, you can practice cheering yourself up. A bright outlook makes you more fun to be around. That can turn into a cycle of happiness.
10. **Take a deep breath.** Learning how to slow down and think things over keeps you from having "knee-jerk" reactions and helps you learn how to control your anger.

Romance-Busting Places

Some locations just aren't conducive to romance or love. It's important to pick your spots as you build a love portfolio and to recognize places that aren't suited to romance. Here are some examples.

The Office

Office romances happen all the time. Still, in general, it's a bad idea to try to find a romantic partner at work. For one thing, if you're spending all of your time flirting and sending signals, you're not doing your job. If the object of your attention is not interested, you can end up feeling uncomfortable on the job at best, or dealing with a sexual harassment complaint at worst.

Boss-subordinate relationships are especially troubling, because of the power aspect. It is very difficult to develop equal standing when you're dating someone higher up in the organization. When the relationship goes sour, your job can get worse in a hurry.

At the same time, people do fall in love on the job. Since they tackle the same problems and share a common language, it's not surprising that an office friendship can evolve into something more. You can't help the attraction, but you can use caution and common sense. Don't get involved with a boss unless you're willing to leave the organization. Make sure the company doesn't have a rule against employees dating (some do). Many companies also have strict rules prohibiting a husband and wife from working in the same department. Ask yourself if you would feel as strongly about the person if you worked in separate companies. Even then, recognize you're tap-dancing in a minefield. If you have strong career ambitions, you can be sidetracked by an indiscreet or ill-advised affair with a coworker.

Traffic Jams

Driving isn't what it used to be. Families used to take "Sunday drives" to relax! That tradition has long since gone by the wayside. Many people spend far too much time commuting to work, costing themselves time, energy, and quality of life. In that kind of environment, it's easy for traffic to turn into a big-time romance buster.

First, more than a few couples tense up as they drive. We confess to this problem. We hate the way each other drives. And we don't even live in a major city. Those of you who do should be aware that the stress of driving could easily incite an argument. But traffic jams and such offer you the perfect opportunity to talk with your loved one, especially if your lives are filled with kids and activities. It's not as if you can go anywhere! Take advantage of this time and keep your stress at bay.

Second, when you travel alone, the strain of coping with all those "road rage" types, bumper-to-bumper traffic, bypasses, and detours may end up affecting your mood. Unfortunately, the person you take it out on is usually the loving spouse or partner who greets you as you come through the door. To help fix this problem, two things should happen. If you're the driver, recognize that you are "taking it out" on the wrong person. If you're the person waiting at home, allow your loved one time to unwind. No sense letting the road trip ruin your night.

Whispering is always more romantic than yelling.

Third, staying out of accidents requires constant concentration, which can make you tired and irritable. On long trips, take frequent breaks, and enjoy the scenery. Try to avoid that sense that you have to push on and just get where you're going. A more relaxed pace can help make any vacation or road trip more enjoyable, so build in a few hours for downtime.

Loud Places

Doesn't it seem as though the world has gotten louder? Kids drive by with booming radios. Homes are filled with racket generated by television sets, stereos, and other gadgets. Practically everywhere you go you are greeted by noise. Even groceries and drugstores seem to think customers need to be serenaded with music played at a higher volume. Quiet has practically disappeared.

Noise is not romantic. When you go to a loud party and have to shout to be heard, mostly what you get is a sore throat. If you're in a bar or restaurant where the music is blaring so loudly that you can't hear yourself think, odds are you're heading toward a headache.

Our advice for romantic people is simple: Turn the volume down. Sure, sometimes you want to go to exciting places filled with noisy activity, but when you get home, you don't need all those decibels. Soft music and a light touch are almost always more intimate than headbanging intensity.

Scientists are looking for places in the world where only "natural" sounds are present. Even in the most remote deserts and forests of the United States, the noise produced by traffic, airplanes flying by, and other sources make this task practically impossible.

If you need background noise, consider turning off the CD player and getting yourself a nice calming water fountain. Trickling water is soothing, relaxing, and can be very romantic. At the least, it's a change of pace from the rest of your day.

Hectic Places

The classic song *Some Enchanted Evening* suggests that someday you will find the love of your life "across a crowded room." That's probably a long shot. Most of the time, crowded, hectic places only offer distractions. Although they may add excitement to some occasions, it's harder to talk and feel intimate when you're being jostled around.

Crowds have their own mindset, which is sometimes called "mob psychology." People lose a sense of individual identity and take on the personality of the group. In sports arenas or at rock concerts, this can lead to ugly incidents. In other places, the effects can be just as bad.

The time to be in a crowd is at a parade or some other event where the mood is jovial. Crowded parties and gatherings are fun; but if you're looking for romance, you'll need to leave them and find some space elsewhere. Otherwise, conversations are constantly interrupted and there is very little privacy, which is a key ingredient in intimacy.

Some of the places that are usually too hectic for anything romantic include malls and discount stores (especially during the holidays), theme parks in the summer, airplanes and airports, and busy, crowded restaurants. Compare these spots to parks, private boats, small specialty shops off-season, and picnics in the wilderness. Sound and fury inhibit romance; quiet and privacy build it.

Romance-Busting Things

Just as there are tools that help build romance, there are gadgets and issues that break it down. Some romance-busting things have positive uses, so you'll have to decide when to have them and when to leave them alone. Others are bad pretty much all the time.

Cell Phones, Pagers, and Telephones

We know that staying connected in a fast-paced world may mean you need to carry around a cell phone or pager as part of your job. Many people like having one in their cars, so that they can call for help if they're ever stranded. Beyond that, why in the world would you need to call someone the second your plane lands, just to say you're on the ground? Or, answer a ringing cell phone in the middle of a restaurant or movie theater? Is it so impossible to just take a few moments to relax? Apparently it is. What this can do to a romance is both an opportunity and a problem. The opportunity is that you can pick up one of these mobile contraptions and call your lover to say something sweet practically anywhere. You can update him or her if you're running late. Maybe you can even work a little more efficiently, so that when you get home you can set your job aside and focus on your lover.

The problem is telephone addiction. Many kids develop symptoms of the addiction as early as grade school. By the time they're teenagers, they spend countless hours talking on the phone instead of seeing each other in person. Mix in a few chat rooms and e-mail, and they practically never have to make human contact.

This is bad training for later life, because this addict will never be farther than an arm's reach away from a phone or pager. You, the helpless victim of his or her addiction, will have meals interrupted constantly by calls. Lovemaking will stop at the first little beep or ring. Instead of conversation in the living room or in your car, the addict will be busy talking to someone else. You will lose out to what is essentially a sophisticated walkie-talkie or citizens band radio.

When the phone rings and disrupts an intimate moment, it's sometimes difficult to restore the mood. While an answering machine may help, the best course of action is to turn off the phone. Weaning yourself away from instant message devices creates free time and allows you to spend time in more pleasant ways. This is nowhere more true than in your love life.

Laptop Computers

Computer addiction is rising to new heights as this century evolves, aided by online trading and real-time everything. Stroll through an airport or sit on a plane. People can't even get away from technology while traveling. You'll see husband and wives ignoring each other and their kids just to get in a few more moments online. We think that's very sad.

Many of you have probably been at a social event where someone withdrew in order to pull out a laptop to play a video game or do a little surfing. This much is for sure: A person who is deeply in love with a computer will probably ignore you. You'll forfeit handholding, kissing, lovemaking, and even conversations so that he or she can interact with a machine instead. Be cautious about a laptop lover. It's a warning signal you shouldn't ignore.

Television

We've been critical of television in several places in this book. That's because we truly believe overuse of mindless programming is a major romance buster. When you stop to think of all the time you waste seeing a show that has little value, you should ask yourself, "Why am I doing this?" Single people who are TV addicts spend less time circulating. Couples who watch television instead of talking, reading, or seducing each other are losing precious and valuable hours in their lives.

Loud television shows stifle even short conversations. Channel surfing means you don't even turn away from the set during commercials; instead, you choose to view another show. Television is a great way to keep your kids quiet so you don't have to spend any time engaging them. Think about it.

Is Technology Ruining Your Romantic Life?

Keep a diary for one month. Chart the following items:

1. How many hours did you spend watching television?
2. How many times did you stop a conversation because the phone rang and then never returned to the conversation?
3. How many hours did you spend online, answering e-mail or surfing the Web?
4. How many evening meals did you eat in front of the television?
5. How many times was your sex life interrupted by a phone or pager?

Compare your answers to questions 1 through 5 to your answers for 6 through 10. The differences will give you a pretty good indication of where your priorities lie.

6. How many times did you make love uninterrupted?
7. How many times did you give your lover a massage?
8. How many conversations did you have that lasted more than half an hour (the length of a typical TV program)?
9. How much time did you spend outdoors playing a game or sharing an activity with your children?
10. How many quiet, intimate dinners did you share with your spouse or partner?

Other Romance Busters

Besides people, places, and things that are bad for romance, several emotions and behaviors can have a negative impact. Each of these must be dealt with and resolved if you want to make your life as romantic as possible. Couples who are willing to put in the work get great payoffs. Those who aren't willing usually aren't as happy and aren't as compatible. The choice is yours.

Anger and Carryover Issues

We've all heard that you shouldn't go to bed mad. Sometimes that's impossible. Certain things make you angry for longer periods. Still, anger is a poison that rarely does anything constructive. At the extreme, people who are constantly annoyed may develop a condition called an "angry heart," where they actually secrete enzymes that damage heart tissue.

A similar thing can happen in a romantic involvement. Couples who constantly fight and are generally angry at each other waste dozens of hours that could be spent in a more pleasant manner. The issues that seem to invite this kind of conflict are most often the following:

- Money
- Sex (or the lack thereof)
- In-laws and family members
- Child-rearing practices
- Living arrangements and chores

These disagreements are rarely resolved. Instead, both parties carry them around until a festering, long-term hostility exists. This does not bode well for love, romance, or even friendship. Carryover anger becomes a self-feeding cycle of shouting and cross words.

Sadly, you can't automatically fix all of these arguments, but you can learn how to fight fairly. Avoid harsh and negative statements. Try not to make personal attacks. Wait until you are calmer and can discuss a problem rather than tossing accusations back and forth. If you truly can't get along, either get counseling as a couple or think about moving on.

Some people say fighting can lead to sensuous and passionate "makeup" sessions. We've never bought that. The idea that there is a thin line between love and hate only holds when you break up. The rest of the time, the thin line is between liking and loving someone. Respect, friendship, compatibility, and concern are simply not connected with fussing and fighting.

Anger is a poisonous emotion. It's also contagious. Being mad at one thing can easily lead to being mad at something else, where it isn't appropriate. It's tempting to "take out your frustration" on someone safe, like a spouse or partner, but it's unfair and mean.

Anger can also carry over from a past relationship into a new one. You see this happen all the time. A person who has unresolved hostility toward a previous lover or spouse takes it out on all those who follow. If you find yourself dating someone like this, you will need to quickly ask yourself, "Is this worth it?" You should only answer yes when you believe you have the patience and compassion to wait until this person has worked through all of these issues. In the meantime, you may take a verbal or emotional beating. Normally, rather than becoming some kind of emotional punching bag, you're better off letting this person solve these problems alone. If you are recovering from a disastrous relationship, wait until you can see a new romantic involvement as an exciting prospect where no hard feelings enter in. Once you enter the relationship, if these unresolved hostilities arise, it's only fair to keep them to yourself rather than subjecting an innocent person to your discontent.

Jealousy

Jealousy is a two-sided coin consisting of possessiveness and insecurity. Neither side is good. The idea of being jealous never even enters some people's minds. Usually the reasoning involved is something like this: "I know my lover is attractive, so I expect he will draw attention. I also know that he truly loves me and would never stray. If he did, it must mean someone else was better suited. And besides, it's his loss." These words are easy to say, but many people find them hard to believe.

Most of us have a bit of a protective and territorial instinct. It's easy to let these feelings get the best of you, keeping you awake at night wondering and worrying, or worse. If you are prone to this problem, you need to work on matters of self-esteem, confidence, and trust. Normally, when you feel better about yourself, it becomes much easier to ignore those little twinges. Jealousy, for the most part, is a wasted emotion. Clingy, insecure people just aren't very attractive. Take the time to rid yourself of this unnecessary anxiety that detracts from more affirming emotions.

Jealousy is a little green monster that often says more about your insecurities than it does about the one you love.

Family Rivalries and Problems

Okay, go ahead. Pick out your favorite mother-in-law joke. Some may be funny, but they reveal a sad truth: Many couples find their romantic involvements tainted by family problems. These difficulties range from a tough set of parents to brothers and sisters who create issues for loving couples. Some people can't cut the apron strings, so a husband or wife takes the place of Mom. These issues always seem to get worse around the holidays.

Many couples must work diligently to figure out how to remove themselves from family commitments that keep them from building lives together with their own traditions. It's important to make the effort. If you don't, a controlling in-law or a troublesome sibling can totally disrupt your marriage or relationship. These family members aren't playing fair and your relationship is the victim. Learn how to discuss these intrusions calmly with your partner. Make a clear plan to manage the problem.

Bad Habits

We all do things we shouldn't. Nail biting, procrastination, whining, and fidgeting are just part of being human. We're not proud of them and probably believe we can't stop them. At the same time, these habits can annoy the one you love. So work on them. Excuse yourself to a private place if you must. Have your lover point out the habits that are bothersome in a constructive manner. Then, see if you can reduce the number of times you do them the next day, week, and month. Increased self-awareness is usually beneficial, especially when it helps you get rid of some annoying little routine.

Addictions of All Kinds

Romance really suffers when a person has an addiction. The more notable, of course, are addictions to alcohol, drugs, or gambling. Obsessive behaviors take you away from the people you love and lead you to a self-involved state. Those in advanced stages of addiction will do anything to feed the habit, from lying to cheating to stealing. They become excellent manipulators. Nothing is more important than the next drink, fix, or bet.

Sometimes one of the toughest things you have to do is tell someone you love that he or she has an addiction problem. Groups like Al-Anon and Alateen can help, but at the end of the day, a person with an addiction is tougher to love.

> Sometimes the most romance-building thing you can do is to move away from your families to a "neutral" site.

The major test each of you should take is the mirror test. Can you look at yourself and truthfully say, "I don't have a problem"? No one wants to admit that he or she gambles too often or drinks too much. It feels like failure, even when it is more of an illness, and denial is a huge part of the addiction. It takes great courage to admit you need help and that you face a lifetime recovery process. At the same time, if you don't, the ones you love will begin to drift away or you'll drive them away. Even those who stay in loveless marriages dominated by an addiction have lost time and romance. Knowing this, they often mentally withdraw even while being physically present.

People who are unwilling to admit they have an addiction, or who are unwilling to try to overcome their addictions, should receive the same reaction we mentioned before: the lifesaving rule. Don't let them drown you in their problems. Life is too short and you are worth too much to be a victim. Back away.

If you know the addiction is winning, there is help. Many programs are free or low cost. It is a loving thing to tackle such a problem head-on. It's also a lifesaver and worth every ounce of effort you can give.

Whatever your addiction, there's help out there. Check the Yellow Pages or go online for information, but get help today.

Bad Timing

The final romance buster boils down to the luck of the draw. Many things that keep an event from taking place are out of our control. More than a few couples can tell you that they had a romantic weekend planned, only to come down with the flu. It's tough to feel cuddly when you're sick. A flat tire when you're out on a date has a much different meaning than "running out of gas" at a convenient time.

Timing issues come into play in lots of ways. For one, it can be the timing of when you meet. It may be that you are introduced to someone who is very attractive just as you have started getting serious with your current love interest. Or, following a bad breakup, you run into a person who in any other situation would seem perfect; but you let it go because the time is not right.

Romance is harder to get started after a tragedy, disaster, or even a bad break. An employee who has just gotten fired is probably not looking for love. An individual recovering from an accident or injury may feel inclined to wait for a better moment. There is a certain randomness to meeting the right person at the right time.

Timing also comes into play when a good evening is spoiled by something. You may be on the greatest date in the world when you see violence break out or the couple you're with gets into a major fight. Many potential downers are present on any given evening.

You married couples also know that many times your moods simply don't match. A wife may be feeling amorous while the husband wants to work on taxes. One of you may feel like socializing while the other prefers to stay home.

At the same time, timing isn't everything. You can take a bad moment and turn it into something good. Over the years, we've tuned in to the idea that if the day doesn't go well, we have to make the night better. A simple trip to buy an ice-cream cone can break the momentum of a day in which your boss chewed you out and your kids were just pills.

Beating the Busters

When you think about life, you will eventually decide what's truly important. Some people conclude money and security matter most. Others want excitement or fulfilling jobs. Still others believe religious values carry the most weight.

A truly romantic individual values other people and ideas more than self. Love of God, family, friends, and virtue finish far ahead of personal interests. This means when love reveals itself in the form of a cherished spouse or lover, that person takes the highest priority possible. Consequently, any of the personal traits, places, things, and emotions that might keep love from blooming will immediately receive attention. As we said at the start of this chapter, romance is much more than doing positives. Ironically, eliminating a negative is also one of the most positive things you can do for someone you love.

CHAPTER 13
Romantic Proposals

S ooner or later, everyone makes the bold move of asking someone out on a date, suggesting a romantic night out to a steady partner, proposing marriage, or something else along those lines. When you suggest something new or different to a romantic prospect or partner, you are, in a sense, very exposed. Feelings can easily be hurt. On the other hand, the right answer can be exhilarating. We're going to look at several different kinds of romantic proposals in this chapter. Some involve a night out while others are designed to last a lifetime. They deserve your thoughts and energy in order to increase the chances that the proposal will be accepted. After all, the whole point is to get an answer in the affirmative!

Proposing a First Date

Practically everyone can imagine, or has experienced, the trepidation of asking someone out. The range of nervousness associated with making this first dating move runs from barely noticeable on the radar screen to near-paralyzing fear. We hope, for your sake, that it's not too traumatic to pick up the phone or simply ask someone in person. Those of you who are shy or a little insecure usually have the hardest time. Either way, with some practice and a few successes, the process gets easier. Still, rejection hurts, even though it's to be expected. Here are some ideas for how to get through a dating proposal.

Do Your Homework

The first step is to make sure the person is willing to go. There are a few basic rules to follow. The entire process will go more smoothly when you can answer the following questions.

1. Is she available?
2. Has he shown any interest in me or dropped any hints?
3. Do I know what kinds of things she likes to do?
4. Am I positive about his sexual orientation?

The availability question is often an interesting one. A person rebounding from a broken relationship or divorce may have a hard time deciding to get back in the game. Someone who is swamped by work or troubled with family issues may seem available but may not be ready to date. And then there is the person who is already dating someone, but seems as if he or she might be open to dating others. The best approach is honesty. Just ask. An evasive answer will tell you all you need to know.

Expressions of interest are sometimes hard to read. Some men seem to think that when a woman smiles or is nice, she's ready to jump into the sack. Therefore, it's probably a good idea to step back and read the signals carefully. For instance, the man of your dreams says to you, "I would really like to see that movie." Was he looking at you with raised eyebrows when he said it, or was he just thinking about the movie?

Finding out what a person likes to do is also a great help. If a fellow finds out that his romantic interest loves Chinese food, for example, and she turns down an invitation to have dinner at a Chinese restaurant, he knows the rejection may be more about him and less about the activity. (Of course, the reason could also be she's just not free that night—in which case, she would probably ask about going another night.) It may smart a little, but it's still better than being told no and not knowing the reason. To get some date "data," ask her friends. Listen to conversations. Or, of course, ask her directly.

The trickiest of these questions, obviously, is sexual orientation. If the person in question is very secretive about his or her personal life, you may not know. If you ask and that's the answer, you can still keep your friendship. Remember that a good friendship is as valuable as a casual dating relationship.

If you're constantly talking about yourself, you'll never know what a potential dating partner might like to do on a night out. Show that you're interested in others and ask what they like to do.

Ladies, a piece of advice: There are lots of nice fellows out there who may be a little shy about making the first move. If you can summon the nerve to ask one of them out, you might be surprised at the pleasant reaction you get. After all, men don't always have to be the ones to do the asking.

If you want to go out with the "inviter," the response is a no-brainer. Simply say, "Yes, I'd love to!" and then work out the details. If you don't want to accept, try to be sensitive when turning someone down. There's no need to hurt feelings.

Graceful Ways to Say No to a First Date
"I'm sorry, but this just isn't a good time for me to be dating."
"I'm sorry, but I'm seeing someone."
"I can't really handle any new complications in my life."
"It is very nice of you to ask, but I'm afraid I'm going to have to decline."

Not-So-Graceful Ways to Say No to a First Date

"You have got to be kidding!"

"Yeah, right."

"Go out, with you?"

"Wait till I tell my friends. This'll kill 'em."

Just laugh.

Stand Out from the Crowd

Another great idea for starting a dating relationship is to find something unique to do on the date. Everyone is all too familiar with the dinner-and-a-movie scenario, so do something out of the ordinary, as long as it's not too crazy. Should things develop into something stronger, the first date becomes a great memory to share.

For ideas, pick up hints by watching old movies. For example, stargazing might entice some people. If you live near an observatory, that would be different. A walk through the park stopping for a burger or hot dog is another fun way to get to know someone. Or, turn a first date into a theme that matches the time of year. Watching fireworks goes with the Fourth of July. A canoe ride near sunset is a unique summertime event. A trip to the skating rink can be fun in the wintertime, if you live in a colder region.

If you don't feel you have that kind of inspiration, you can take one of two approaches. You can ask your friends about their favorite dates. Or ask your potential date, "If we were going to do something really fun and unusual on our first date, what would you want it to be?"

Try to think of something your new friend might find fun and interesting. He or she is just as tired of the routine dating game as you are, so it's a great time to call on your creativity.

Be Flexible

One dilemma some people run into when they ask someone out is to tie the date to a specific evening. For example, a woman says, "I have tickets to the Rangers game for Saturday night. Would you like to go?" When the guy says, "I'm sorry, I can't," she may find herself stuck with an extra ticket.

There is an easy way to avoid this problem. Start with a more general question, such as, "I'd like to do something with you sometime," or "Would you like to go out with me at some point?" Then, when the person says, yes, tell him about your tickets. The idea is to be flexible enough to give the other a range of choices without appearing so desperate that you'll take whatever leftover crumbs he or she is willing to let spill your way.

Enjoy Success; Get over Failure

Getting over a foiled attempt to date someone is often hard. No one likes to find out they don't measure up, even though that's not really what's going on. We believe honesty is the best policy. That is, if you're truly not interested, don't lead someone on.

After asking someone out who refuses, stay positive. If the individual has made it clear she doesn't want to date, she is saving time and emotional energy. That tactic is much more thoughtful than leading you to believe it's a personal flaw or that someday she might change her mind.

The worst-case scenario on an early date is being stood up. This form of rejection is tough to take. As a matter of common courtesy, always be perfectly honest and clear about why you have to break a date. If the problem is truly unavoidable, send a peace offering to let the wounded party know you are very sorry and want to try some other time. If you're stood up, and no apology follows, just move on. And remember this: After being stood up, don't think, "What is wrong with me?" Instead, think, "It's his (or her) loss!"

Other Date Proposals

Once you're seeing someone regularly, dating can (and should) take on some new and interesting twists. Look back to Chapter 1 at our checklist of supplies for romance. One of the items was "creativity." This time in life is unique, because it's somewhere between lonely/alone and married/settled. It's a phase to enjoy to the fullest. So, savor it as much as possible.

Guys, gallantly kissing a woman's hand on a first or early date is likely to make a grand impression.

Regular dating partners should create romantic proposals with two ideas in mind: what you want to do and how you ask. The more inspired the effort, the more romantic the night might become. Sure, those dates where you do the usual, such as going out to dinner, are the most common. The secret is to mix in spicier, more adventurous activities. We hope the ideas we've presented can serve as inspiration for what to do. That leaves you with how to ask for a date. There are, of course, the four basic options:

- In person
- By phone
- In a note or letter
- By e-mail

The goal should be to include something clever, titillating, enticing, or unusual. The main rule here is: Don't take a dating partner for granted! Be sincere, and ask nicely. Be understanding if his or her schedule isn't clear. Show respect. Cater a date request to your level of interest and involvement. For example, if you have a long-standing relationship with someone, you could ask him out by leaving a note on his windshield at night. It might seem cute. On the other hand, if you're just getting to know each other, it may look more like stalking. Use good judgment.

Unusual Ways to Ask for a Date

- Have a friend bring a note, just as you did back in grade school or high school.
- Give a gift that signifies what you'll do on the date:
    A baseball cap to go to a ball game
    A fishing lure to go fishing
    Cotton candy to go to the carnival
- Send a telegram.
- Send a date request delivered by FedEx (marked "Urgent!").
- Think up two activities, write each one down, and put one in each hand behind your back. Then ask him to pick a hand.
- Leave a series of notes that lead up to the actual request. Turn him or her into a detective trying to figure out what you're up to.

Taking the Next Step

Dating relationships vary quite a bit in this day and age. For some, sexual intimacy happens in fairly short order, even on the first date. More conservative types wait weeks, months, or even longer before doing much more than kissing. It would be impossible to spell out romantic suggestions for each individual couple, but it's clear that most relationships are marked by a series of major steps. Some of the more obvious are:

- Having sex and/or spending the night together for the first time
- Taking a trip together
- Deciding to live together
- Making joint purchases or decisions that suggest you'll be staying together for a long time or intend to marry

We don't think there should be a big rush to jump into bed. The risks of disease combined with a casual view of sex make romantic involvements more complicated. Waiting for the right moment greatly enhances the odds that intimacy will be more loving and meaningful. It's hard to find a downside to being somewhat patient. When the moment comes, here are some guidelines we'd suggest.

1. Avoid the clichés, like "I'll respect you in the morning." If you have to say that, a red flag is already up.
2. Say, "I love you" only if you mean it. Never use those words as a tactic to get what you want.
3. Don't expect spectacular sex. It takes awhile to work out preferences and details.
4. Do expect sensitivity and tenderness.
5. Remember that the moments after and the morning after are every bit as important as the act itself. Reassurance and afterglow will keep the romance going.
6. Birth control and disease prevention are not options; they are absolute necessities. If you aren't prepared, don't have sex!

It's almost always a bad idea to rush off or sneak out while your lover is asleep. The amount of vulnerability present following the first time of intimacy with someone you genuinely care about will probably never be higher. Running away is just bad form.

Taking Trips and Vacations

If you are enjoying a long-term relationship, there may come a time when you decide to take a vacation together, whether for a weekend or something more elaborate. We've already talked about the kinds of things you can do together in other chapters. The subject here is how to ask.

What is the protocol? One part would have to be honesty. It is important to see if your romantic partner views this as a big step or something that's not very dramatic. If your opinions differ, talk it out beforehand to avoid any misunderstandings about what the trip means.

The next item involved is finances. Are you splitting the costs, or is the person who makes the invitation paying the way? This is another matter you need to resolve before you pack so there are no surprises later. This one gets a little ticklish when one partner has a better-paying job. Still, if you have the nerve to go on a weekend-long date, you should also have the nerve to discuss money.

Always have a backup plan when you take your first trip together, just in case it turns into a disaster. Take enough money to book separate rooms or pay for your own bus or airfare home.

Taking trips and vacations together can create a combination of assorted feelings. You do get to go away and relax, which makes it possible to remove yourselves from daily stresses and routines. The relaxation part is counterbalanced by the tension that has to do with compatibility. You're going to find out something new about each other. You may also be spending more time together than you ever have before. Some couples travel well together. Others don't. Either way, it's a learning experience; you're probably going to view the time as a bit of a test. It doesn't hurt to acknowledge that to each other, so the lines of communication stay open.

Meeting the Parents

Another potentially traumatic trip is when you take a partner home to meet Mom and Dad. Just asking if your lover is ready to take this step is bad enough, because it's another signal. Once again, some couples won't feel as if this is a big deal, while others know it's a major indicator that the relationship is really getting serious. Consequently, as you ask, the first thing to hammer out is what the meeting means.

When the two of you agree the "meet the parents" step is a major turn of events, create a strategy. Give your partner advice on how best to approach your folks. If your parents are reserved, a handshake and a more formal greeting may be in order. If your parents are a little more gregarious, you may find your partner hugging these strangers he or she just met. Also, bring flowers or a small gift to your lover's parents the first time you meet them. Later, try to make a more personal connection with them.

When the big moment arrives, carefully avoid controversial topics like religion and politics. No sense starting an early, unnecessary disagreement. This is true even when the two of you have the same values. Never assume his or her parents will feel the same way or believe the same things.

> Just remember, the "meeting the parents" phase can be very romantic. You think enough of this person to invite him or her into your family. That's as much a cause for celebration as it is for consternation!

After the visit is over, it's wise to talk about what happened. Don't judge your lover's performance. Instead, reassure him or her that things went fine. If there were trouble spots, your lover already knows.

Places to Meet Your Partner's Parents

Parents' Home Court
- Their house
- A restaurant they choose
- At a friend of the parents' house

Neutral Site
- A restaurant you both like
- A park for a picnic
- A coffee shop
- A sports event, musical program, or some other place where there is an additional activity besides the meeting
- At a party where everyone has friends present

Your Home Court
- Your dining room as you cook them a meal
- Your living room as you serve coffee and dessert
- One of your favorite "hanging out" places

Living Together

Once again, there doesn't seem to be any kind of rules of etiquette for this step. On the one hand, it has to feel something like a marriage proposal. You are going to live much like a married couple. On the other hand, there may be this sneaking suspicion that the person doing the asking is copping out, because he or she isn't ready for more of a commitment. Either way, there are some emotions to untangle. On a practical level, here are a few of the issues and questions that would go with this step:

1. Am I sure my partner thinks living together is morally acceptable?
2. Do we see this as a greater commitment or a matter of convenience?
3. Can we work out financial arrangements we both accept?
4. Where should we live: my house, his or her house, or a new place?
5. Is one of us going to maintain a separate residence?
6. Are we sharing our old furniture or buying new?
7. What are we going to tell our parents?

By the time you've finished resolving all matters, we're a little hard-pressed to figure out how it can also be romantic. Presumably, "I want to live with you" can be said with as much romantic emotion and passion as "Let's get married." Still, once you're in and settled, the majority of romantic ideas we've presented apply equally well to folks living together as they do to married couples.

Romantic Marriage Proposals

Proposals of marriage are among those moments that are frozen in time and in your mind. Almost everyone has a completely clear recollection of the event, even fifty years later. The lion's share of these moments are romantic just because of the issue involved. Some are spur-of-the-moment inspirations while others are carefully planned and orchestrated events. To be able to make a proposal as romantic as possible, there are a few things to consider.

Who Is Present?

Probably the majority of marriage proposals are made privately, one-on-one. These are more intimate and quiet. If you're going to take this route, here are a few ground rules that might help.

- Be sure about what you want to say. Rehearse the words if you get easily tongue-tied.
- Give flowers as part of the event. Some proposals include attaching the ring to a dozen roses.
- Make certain there are no distractions. Get away from phones, pagers, and other devices that might spoil the moment.
- Make a decision about a ring.
- Have a handkerchief ready.

Of these ground rules, the ring requires some thought. For some, the idea of being able to pull out a box with an engagement ring is the crowning moment. Others may decide that the better course is to let the woman choose one she would like.

When you ask all alone, you also get to be answered in the same way. And you can choose the form of celebration that follows. Chances are, if the answer is yes, there is at least going to be some hugging and kissing going on. That's romantic, right?

You should also think about body position. Do you plan to kneel? Will you sit beside your partner or stand? Others make the proposal at dinner. For those who want a carefully choreographed proposal, these things need to be decided in advance.

Public Proposals

Public proposals can be part of a party, a dinner (at home or in a restaurant), or some other special gathering. These kinds of proposals are tricky. The clearest problem occurs when he or she doesn't want the pressure of answering in front of a bunch of people. Before making a grand public marriage proposal, carefully answer the following key questions.

- Is she as outgoing as I am, and will she enjoy sharing this with a bunch of folks?
- Am I positive she will say yes?
- How am I going to make sure the people I want to see this moment are present? Can they keep a secret?
- What will I do if she runs out of the room screaming or crying?

When you choose the public arena to make the proposal, it's like throwing a party. There is a guest list to work out. You have to decide on details, such as how long the celebration will last, who to invite, and how you'll get everyone in the right place at the right time. An additional side note is the parent issue. Do you plan to have one set present? Both? Neither? If you invite one side and not the other, you may also be inviting an early engagement fight. If you invite neither, they may not be happy that you had this most exiting moment without including them. If you invite both, and one side isn't very excited about the prospect, some real tension can result. It's a sticky wicket no matter how you proceed.

There are also those more outlandish public proposals that take place in front of total strangers, including posting the proposal on a scoreboard at a sports event or using an airplane banner to proclaim your love. Such proposals are certainly dramatic and can be romantic if you think that type of presentation would appeal to your partner. If your partner is a private person, you might want to reconsider proposing in this way.

Let's Elope!

A successful marriage that started with a couple throwing caution to the wind and eloping would make, at the minimum, a great story. There's no style guide for how to elope romantically, or any other way, for that matter. It seems to us there would be two ways to go about it: with a plan and on the spur of the moment. Romance-wise, a whirlwind decision to run off and get married has some appeal. We do wonder about second thoughts. Planning it out, on the other hand, takes away the spontaneity.

Primary spots include Las Vegas, Reno, Lake Tahoe, and anywhere else they offer quickie ceremonies. Remember, however, that you are, at some level, deliberately excluding family and friends from the process. In some ways that can seem selfish. Those who don't have a lot of family may find it to be a low-cost, adventuresome way to start a life together.

The Honeymoon

Deciding where to go on a honeymoon can be one of the great debates you have as an engaged couple. It can be delightfully fun and romantic at the same time. Surfing together on the Web for sites, going to a travel agent, or sharing brochures and magazines featuring honeymoon locations causes you to look forward together to the first few days of married life. Here are few suggestions as you and your partner exchange ideas:

- Go where you want, not where family or friends say is best.
- Don't go where your parents went unless both of you agree it's the best choice.
- Do be aware you're probably going to spend quite a bit of time indoors, so opt for a nice room.
- Include places that offer activities both of you like as part of the selection process.
- Stay within a reasonable budget. Being broke right afterward isn't all that romantic.
- If you can't go someplace exotic, start planning what you can afford as quickly as possible.
- Remember, choosing a honeymoon destination is never worth fighting about.

One of the secrets to a successful honeymoon is to avoid building expectations that are impossible to meet. This is easier said than done.

Still, remember there can be a natural letdown following the actual wedding and reception. You may feel tired and grumpy. As a result, it's a good idea to make sure a honeymoon includes time for resting and relaxing. Then it's easier to move on to other fun and games.

There may come a point in your marriage in which the most romantic thing you or your partner will ever say is, "Let's have a baby."

Anniversaries and the Second Honeymoon

It seems to be a common complaint among women that men often forget wedding anniversaries. We're not sure how this can happen. Suffice it to say, *romantic* men don't forget anniversaries; in fact, they make a big deal about them! Proposing what to do to commemorate such a major day in the year can take several forms. One spouse or the other can make the suggestion, the two of you can decide together, or there can be a surprise in the works.

In many marriages, either the husband or the wife routinely decides what to do to celebrate an anniversary. Of course, the traditional activities including dining, dancing, and getting away together. On the round-number anniversaries or those divisible by five (five, ten, twenty, twenty-five, and so on), a party may be in order. Traditional accessories for anniversaries include:

- Flowers
- Cards
- Gifts
- A sitter for the kids
- Reservations (dinner)
- Reservations (other events)

Also, you can add in a few goodies such as:

- A negligee/lingerie
- Oils and lotions
- Hot tub
- Wine/champagne
- Jewelry

In this case, the invitation or romantic proposal is more along the lines of clearing your plans to keep the night free. It's possible to spice up these plans with perfume-scented invitations, flowers sent in advance, sexy e-mails, and so forth.

To make an anniversary party more special, ask guests to bring photos or other remembrances of your time together instead of "traditional" gifts.

Deciding on anniversary plans can be fun and romantic. You and your spouse can exchange travel brochures, restaurant menus, and other ideas to turn the day into a special event.

Be a Love Messenger

People in long-term relationships make hundreds of proposals to each other over the years. Romantic proposals range from suggesting a night out to get away from it all to figuring out how to celebrate a fiftieth wedding anniversary. These love messages help you build a better romantic life together. They help create the fond memories that carry you through the tougher times.

Both people in a partnership should work hard to create romantic proposals of one sort or another. Don't leave the burden on just one person. The back-and-forth of posing questions and options to each other makes every stage of life more interesting. Even those of you who aren't good with words can plan out ways to make suggestions for evenings, special events, and new steps in your relationship. Let your partner know what you want to do, how you want to do it, and when. Then do it. As most of you already know, the best part of a romantic proposal is when it's accepted and carried out. Don't let the fear of rejection stop you. The rewards are much greater than the risks, in every stage of your love life.

CHAPTER 14
Romantic Gifts

A major part of nearly every romantic relationship is gift-giving. Presents can range from tokens of your affection to expensive expressions of love. It's important to remember that the best gifts you can ever give to your partner are your time, attention, energy, and passion. These other tokens of affection, however, are the trimmings that make romantic relationships even more special. Along the way, the gifts we give, and the ones we receive, move, amuse, charm, seduce, and intrigue us. In this chapter, we'll look at gifts from several angles, starting with the various kinds people give and what each means. Then, we'll look at giving, receiving, and exchanging gifts in the context of a romantic relationship.

Types of Gifts

Lovers give and receive all kinds of things as a relationship progresses. Some gifts are seemingly inconsequential, but they serve as expressions of interest.

Early on in a relationship, the gift should be inexpensive but thoughtful. In the previous chapter we discussed the importance of listening in terms of choosing the ideal dating venue. The same advice goes for gift-giving when you're just getting to know someone.

Lots of times the gift is as simple as providing your phone number! When you don't want to be that forward, use your imagination. Gift-giving can be a great form of flirtation at this point. The idea is to let the item serve as notice that you would be inclined to accept a dating invitation.

Gifts That Say, "I'm Interested, How About You?"

- Candy (Hershey's Kisses, lollipops, etc.)
- A card
- A cup of coffee or a soda at an opportune moment
- A flower
- An inexpensive book on a subject you know interests him or her (even if it's just a loan)
- Recordings of songs or copies of the lyrics
- A small souvenir you bring back from vacation

Traditional Gifts

Lovers of all ages tend to give traditional romantic gifts at special times and on less notable occasions. Romantic experts of all kinds recommend them. The most typical list would probably include:

- Candy
- Flowers
- Jewelry
- Perfume/cologne

There may be an upside and a downside to giving traditional gifts. The upside is that each one says you've made the effort to buy an item that signals your interest and involvement. In other words, it's hard to go wrong with flowers. This is especially true when a relationship is just beginning. The gift is in an "acceptable" category, in which the intent is to make a good impression without going overboard.

On the other hand, sometimes giving these more routine items can seem to be a cop-out. That is, they are so standard that it can appear as if the giver didn't give it any thought at all. To avoid this interpretation, it's wise to make sure you personalize each gift in some way. A box of candy should include a note that says something more original than "Sweets for the sweet." If you're not all that creative, here are a few suggestions to get you started:

"Nothing in this box is as sweet as one kiss from you."
"Life with you is like a box of chocolates: one treat after another."
"To the woman who helped me redefine 'delicious'!"
"These treats do not compare with the treat of being with you."

The same holds true for perfume and cologne. Just the bare bottle doesn't send the entire message. Fill in the blank somehow with meaningful words. Also, make sure the scent is one the recipient prefers.

Get the idea? Just remember to only say these things if you are sincere!

When it comes to jewelry, take care to find out what your romantic interest likes. Ask his or her friends what will make a big impression. Or listen carefully as you walk through a store. Sooner or later, your partner will tip his or her hand and let you know what would be best. At that point, you can pounce on the opportunity.

Somewhere-in-Between Gifts

These gifts are highly personal expressions of interests that don't suggest an engagement is pending. They are delightful to give and receive.

Gifts from Men

- Your favorite shirt to wear instead of PJs
- Simple jewelry such as a pin or a single pearl
- His pajama top or gym shorts
- A wallet photo

Gifts from Women

- A coffee cup that has some special meaning for him
- A framed picture of you
- A throw or blanket with his favorite team's insignia on it
- Tickets to a game he's dying to see

These little gifts shouldn't stop after marriage. From time to time, both partners should make the effort to give something that will have a special meaning, just to be nice. If the one you love enjoys the ocean, and the two of you have picked up lots of seashells along the way, make them into a display of some sort. It's impossible to be overly thoughtful, isn't it?

"Sweet" Gifts

During your time together, many opportunities to give what we call "sweet" gifts will present themselves. These items may not cost much, but they still pack a big romantic punch. What do "sweet" gifts mean? There are two ways to look at it. One is that you're "in the moment," and the opening was available to do something nice. That by itself makes a gift both romantic and good for the relationship. The other meaning is that these small tokens become great keepsakes. Many of us have them hidden away somewhere, especially if they were given by someone other than the person we're now with. They serve as reminders of a different time in life. And, of course, when you are settled in with that special person, these little gifts are warm reminders of the good times that took place early in the relationship. Later, you can pull out all of the movie, airplane, and theater ticket stubs; matchbooks; cards; menus from restaurants; seashells; wine bottles; and other small items and go through all of them together.

No-Cost and Low-Cost Gifts

- Anything you make by hand
- Back rub
- Compliments and kind words
- Cooking a meal (and cleaning up afterward)
- Doing any household chore unexpectedly or to free up time so you can be together
- Hair washing and drying
- A personal IOU for one really tough favor
- Photographs and videos of special events you shared together
- Picking up some little "goodie" at the store you know your partner loves
- A poem that you write about your love (it doesn't have to be serious—a lighthearted limerick works well too)
- Rub anywhere (feet, hands, neck, etc.)
- Taking his or her stuff to the dry cleaners
- Taping a show for him or her to watch later, uninterrupted

"Couple" Gifts

Bonding experiences of various kinds appear throughout a dating relationship, including those times when you find little "couple" gifts to share.

A simple, fun gift is a pass to a wine-tasting party or food fest that the two of you can enjoy together.

Couple gifts go beyond exchanging more impersonal items, which means that they take on substantially greater significance. When we knew we were getting serious, we came across a coupon for a relatively inexpensive portrait. One Saturday morning, we got all dressed up and had a portrait taken. This came at a time before our engagement. Over the years, that photo has become one of our more treasured keepsakes.

Portraits, photos, and drawings of you as a couple are bound to create the impression that you're close. In fact, anything that has both of your names on it, such as a T-shirt or sweatshirt, is a gift with special meaning. These kinds of gifts indicate you've taken another step as a couple. Each represents some unique point in time during your life together, giving it greater meaning that is easily attached to romantic memories.

Holiday/Birthday Gifts

Holiday gift-giving can be tough, especially at Christmas and on Valentine's Day. It's clear a gift is in order, but finding what's appropriate can be a challenge. During the dating years, you want to find the present that says, "You are special to me" without going overboard. Newlyweds want to give nice things without busting the budget. By the time a couple reaches their golden years, they have pretty much everything they need. Any time a gift is "expected," the challenge is in finding the right one.

It's a good idea to divide holiday gifts into two categories: regular items and grand gestures. Regular items are things you give more than once; grand gestures are more unexpected.

Regular gifts for holidays, Valentine's Day, and birthdays should be simplified as much as possible. This means communication is critical. The straightforward way is simply to ask what he or she wants. Now some of you may say this takes all the fun out of it. The alternative, of course, is to pay attention. When he says he's running out of golf balls, take notice. Write it down for the next event. When she picks up an item of clothing and says, "I love this," double back. Buy it and save it for a special day. Making a surprise out of a routine present requires a little extra effort, but that's in the nature of the romance game anyway.

For routine gifts, think in the more traditional categories. Lots of men like things such as:

- Cologne
- Sports equipment or videos of sports events
- Liquor or items for a bar
- Tools and work gloves
- Items for the office

Ladies tend to like certain routine items as well. Most fellows can feel safe when they buy:

- Bath oils, soaps, and perfumes
- Candles
- Decorations for the home
- Gift certificates from clothing stores
- Inexpensive jewelry
- Lingerie

Your lady friend may or may not want all of these things. Still, it's easy enough to figure out which ones might suit her needs during any given holiday season. It's also easy to slip into the bathroom to see what she buys for herself, or to ask her friends or her mother for some help.

If you're still stuck for ideas, try bookstores, toy stores, secondhand shops, office supply stores, dress boutiques, music stores, and hotel gift shops. Something may jump out at you for the oddest reason.

This points out another way to give regular gifts. Lots of folks have hobbies that involve collecting items. This makes shopping easier, since adding to his or her collection shows your support of the hobby with a personalized gift.

Do you want to give a nice gift, but hate going into stores and malls? Use the Internet or go through gift catalogs. Many of your partner's favorite things are sold online or by mail.

The other side of holiday gift-giving is the grand gesture variety. These gifts dramatically widen your number of choices. Everything from a dream vacation to an automobile or an expensive piece of jewelry may fit into this category. Of course, the key to a grand gesture is planning. First, how are you going to pay for it? If you're thrifty, you can set up a regular savings plan to set money aside to fund a major extravagance. Each time some cash is put in the "kitty," you can enjoy the idea of building up to a great moment. You do have to be able to convince yourself and your partner that this present is affordable and is not taking the place of something more important.

Second, make sure the gift is something your partner truly wants. There's nothing worse than going to a huge amount of effort only to find out it's not that valuable a commodity as far as your partner is concerned. Careful research is in order.

Third, question your motives. The only correct one is love. If you're working on a guilt trip (yours because of something that happened in the past or trying to create one in your partner), a grand gesture is a bad idea. Also, those who are trying to establish a big-time IOU, or who keep score in some way, shouldn't bother. It's worth remembering that no matter how grand the gesture, life will eventually return to normal. If you even vaguely suspect that some day you'll feel taken for granted when he or she stops saying thank you, a grand gesture–type of gift probably won't work the way you intend.

Ladies, find out if your partner is interested in one of those sports fantasy camps, where men play sports games against legends from their favorite teams. He may not ask to go, but he might be thrilled if you arrange one for him. Guys, look into renting time at one of those luxurious health spas where women go to focus on their health while being pampered. She'll love it.

Fourth, if it's a time-based gift, like a vacation, make sure in advance that your lover isn't booked with something else. There's nothing worse than arranging a weekend in Vegas only to find out he or she can't go. Call your partner's office and check things out with the boss and secretary. Then, ask friends and family members to make sure there are no conflicts.

Anniversary Gifts

Choosing an appropriate present for an anniversary may be even more challenging than finding the right holiday or birthday gift. Men know practical gifts like kitchen or household appliances may not be appreciated as much as more romantic gifts. Diamonds are always a safe bet, but they're expensive. What in the world can a woman get for a man as an anniversary gift? Tools and appliances make most guys happy, but they're not very romantic.

Remember two things when selecting anniversary gifts: simplicity and sincerity. To keep it simple, help your partner out with a few well-placed hints. Remember the clichés about the heart being in the right place or that it's the thought that counts. Give your partner an A for intention and effort, no matter what the gift. Also, it's possible to choose a gift together that both of you can enjoy, such as a new piece of furniture, a trip, or something else. To make it even simpler, book a night out for dinner and a hotel room. Just don't forget the "Do Not Disturb" sign.

As you can see, there are lots of different kinds of romantic gifts, intentions for giving them, and times to present them. And some people just seem to have a knack for selecting the perfect gift for every occasion. Those of you who are challenged in this regard can get better simply by putting a little extra thought and effort into the process.

Whenever a gift is given, there are at least two people involved. It's just as important to know how to receive a present as it is to give one. In this next section, we'll take a quick look at how to give and receive these tokens of affection romantically.

Romantic Gift Givers

We've talked about how being a romantic gift giver means matching the recipient with the cost, intent, and substance of the gift, and aligning all of that with the event in question. Those who are truly talented can incorporate the element of surprise into a repertoire.

When you're truly stuck for ideas, you can always make a donation in a partner's name to a favorite charity. If your friend loves animals, for example, you could make a donation in her name to the American Society for the Prevention of Cruelty to Animals (ASPCA) or the local humane society. When it's clear your partner has a passion for a charity, one of the nicest gifts to give is time or money to that organization.

The truly romantic gift giver never expects anything in return. Don't give gifts expecting to get something back. The key word in being an effective gift giver is "gracious." A great gift giver is one who sincerely tries to please the recipient. Most of us have been taught that it is better to give than to receive. Whether you believe that idea, you can derive great joy out of making someone else happy.

Romantic Gift Receivers

Why is it that sometimes the hardest words to say are, "thank you"? Some people are just lousy receivers. They downplay the significance of a gift, question the giver's motives, act embarrassed, or in some other way manage to spoil the moment. Part of being a real romantic is knowing how to savor any offering rendered by your partner, from a small peck on the cheek to a night out or an expensive engagement ring.

Rent a limo or a convertible for a day and be your partner's chauffeur for a special occasion.

The best way to receive a gift is to be genuine and honest in your acknowledgment. When you receive something that touches you deeply, say so. There's a kind of backward Golden Rule in place. Think about the last time you gave a present. Didn't you feel a great deal of joy when the receiver was genuinely excited? Any act of generosity deserves to be appreciated. Simply fit the response to the situation, even when you're caught off guard.

Is Honesty Always the Best Policy?

There are times when someone you love offers you a present that simply doesn't work. You may not like the item, it may not fit, or you know it's something you'll never use. In those situations, it's better to be honest. Thank the person for the intention and then gently point out the problem, at some later time. On the other hand, there are times when a little white lie is better than the truth. If you know you won't see the giver often, thank him or her graciously for the gift, then quietly exchange it at the store for something else, or give it to someone you know can use it.

Romantic Gift Exchanges

In most relationships, there are treasured times when the two of you quietly exchange special gifts without anyone else around. These intimate moments are unique opportunities to connect with each other. To make the most of them, there are several details to consider.

First, save your most personal gifts for these times. Garments and other more personal effects are the best candidates. At holiday and birthday and anniversary celebrations, hold back the one gift you would most prefer to give privately. Set aside a time for the two of you to be alone. A surprise gift can be shared in this way as well. If you've stumbled on an object that you just can't wait for him or her to have, bide the time until you can be alone. Chances to do something special like this don't come along that often, so enjoy them for all they're worth.

Second, create the right atmosphere. These gift exchanges can be great romance builders when the setting is right. Besides privacy, there are several ways to make gift exchanges more romantic, including:

- Beverages (anything from hot cocoa to champagne)
- Mood music (soft and romantic)
- Proper lighting (think candlelight)
- Scents and flowers

Remember, there are dozens of places besides home where you can give gifts. Many anniversary presents have been delivered across the table at a nice restaurant. You can be outdoors, on vacation in a hotel room, or hidden away in an unused room at the office when presenting a gift. A change of venue helps when you're trying to include the element of surprise. Consequently, whenever possible, make picking the site part of the fun of giving the gift.

Third, don't let any kind of distraction interfere. Turn off the television and unplug the phone so there won't be any interruptions.

Finally, make sure you exchange gifts when you're both relaxed and can appreciate them fully. The words offered as the gift is opened are just as meaningful as the item itself. To make the gift exchange more romantic, try to convey a sentiment along these lines:

"I know you've always wanted one of these."
"I am so happy I finally found this."
"I love you so much. I hope you like it."
"This is just a small example of how much you mean to me."
"Is this cool, or what?"
"I can't wait to see you wearing this."

When you say the right words, you are going to need time for smooching and saying thank you. A romantic gift-giving session may quickly evolve into other more intimate activities. Be sure to clear the calendar well ahead of the big night!

Love Is the Greatest Gift

We're going to finish where we began this chapter. The greatest gifts loving couples give to one another are their time, energy, and passion. The rest is really window dressing. Still, these little extras can be a great part of a life together that continually evolves in some wonderful ways.

Always bear in mind that money is not the key to successful gift-giving. Remember O. Henry's story, "The Gift of the Magi," in which a woman cuts and sells her long beautiful hair so she can buy a gold chain to go with her husband's pocket watch? At the same time, he sells the watch to buy beautiful combs for her hair. The moral? Don't go broke trying to impress each other. Do communicate so you both don't end up taking out major loans to finance holiday gifts. Focus on the idea that being together is what matters more than anything. Love will always be the most valuable gift you give to each other.

CHAPTER 15
Romance and Sex

This book is not supposed to be a "how to" manual about sex. Instead, in this chapter, we will look at the relationship between sex and romance. As Dr. David Reuben wrote years ago, in *Everything You've Always Wanted to Know about Sex But Were Afraid to Ask*, there are at least three basic motives for sex: procreation, recreation, and as a profound expression of love. When you play your cards right, romance is part of all three. All time spent together in one version or another of physical intimacy has the potential for romance. Unfortunately, sometimes there are obstacles to overcome. Let's get them out of the way first.

Romance Interruptions

How many articles have you read about things that can disrupt your love life? It seems that there are far too many distractions in the modern world. They can cause you to spend less time in the bedroom and more time bickering or tackling the day's problems, and stop you from being intimate for other reasons. Just as there are times when seduction and lovemaking seem easy and natural, there are also times when getting together seems almost impossible. To make the most out of your sex life, in a romantic sense, you need to become aware of things that shut it down. Here are some of the major problems.

Mood Busters

Practically everyone who has been in a long-term sexual romance knows there are plenty of things that can shatter the mood. You start out with the best intentions, but the next thing you know everything has gone sour. It seems as though romance and sex are delicately balanced and easily disturbed.

Money problems can turn just about any evening away from lovemaking and toward bickering about spending and saving. Any top-ten list of problems that couples encounter includes money, whether you're just starting out or have been together for a long time.

Since good sex begins in your head, bad moods are big-time romance busters. If you're feeling irritable because of work or other issues, don't inflict it on your partner. Go for a walk, soak in the tub, take a bike ride, or do whatever will make you feel better.

Tough times on the job can easily spill over into your home life. There are days when it's difficult to leave the job at the office. Instead of thinking about tickling his or her fancy, you find yourself brooding over some incident at work. Before you know it, the night has passed and the opportunity is lost.

A foul mood can easily reduce interest in sex. Besides work and money, dozens of other daily battles take away your sex drive. They can be as minor as a burned dinner or an argument over who controls the remote, to much more serious issues such as worries about the stability of your marriage and bouts of depression.

Life Circumstances

Certain stages of life tend to interfere with sex and romance. For example, having a baby or toddler in the house can constantly interrupt you and drain romantic energy. Later, grade-school kids can run you ragged getting to and from all of their activities. Then, teenagers come and go so abruptly it's hard to schedule times for intimacy.

Besides your kids, there are other life circumstances that don't bode well for romance. Some people simply overbook themselves with activities and commitments; they fail to leave enough time for the really important stuff. There can be so much company and other kinds of traffic in your house that you simply don't slow down. An auto accident or other kind of disaster can take away a great deal of time as you work toward fixing the problem. Then there are more serious life circumstances, such as when you lose a loved one or close friend. Feelings of grief, loneliness, or anger associated with the loss can prevent you from reaching for intimacy.

Physical Conditions

Sometimes the problem is health related. Pregnancy is a time when many couples lose sexual interest. It's also possible that your doctor will recommend abstinence for medical reasons. Pregnancy creates an interesting contradiction for most couples. On the one hand, you are sharing the joy and excitement of this period; but on the other, she's worn out and probably feeling a bit insecure about how she looks. That's going to lead her to ask all of those tough questions: "Am I still pretty?" or "Do I look fat?" Early on, morning sickness gets in the way. Later on, there are other obstacles.

Illnesses and injuries can also be culprits. Various medications can lessen desire, as will chronic drug and alcohol abuse. Some people are simply in poor health, due to things beyond their control, or as a result of bad lifestyle choices such as smoking, lack of exercise, and an unhealthy diet. Further, many males may experience impotence at some point in a relationship. Arising as it does from various physical and mental causes, impotence may make you wary of any new sexual contact. Later in life, we all start to worry about the physical deterioration that is part of aging, wondering if we are as attractive and desirable as when we were younger.

All of these factors may slow down sexual frequency. It's a frustrating list. What can a couple do? As with practically every aspect of creating a more romantic life together, the answer includes honest communication, careful thinking, and greater effort.

Building and Rebuilding Sexual Interest

The majority of folks who are in committed relationships or in the early stages of marriage have relatively few problems getting in the mood. When life's complications begin to intervene, however, it takes a little more planning to find your way into the bedroom. It may feel as though the great spontaneity of your early years without kids is lost, but that's not really the point. The point is to arrange it so you are able to continue to experience the joys of a rich and fulfilling sex life. Here are some suggestions.

First of all, admit to your circumstances in life; then work around them. For example, we think the most important thing to remember about pregnancy, on both the sexual and romantic fronts, is that she doesn't stop wishing to be a desirable woman anymore than he stops wishing to be a manly man. With all that common ground, it's simply a matter of working out the details. For one, the environment can play a major role. By continuing to engage in familiar romantic rituals, like candlelit dinners and evenings filled with music and good food, the rest may readily fall into place. Naturally, the man is going to have to be more careful and considerate, but the goal can be reached. Loving each other in these circumstances comes so easily that romantic nights are easily constructed.

If you have young children, set firm bedtimes that allow you the chance to be alone together at the end of the day. It's better for the kids as well as the parents. Baby sitters, overnights with neighborhood friends or relatives, and dozens of other methods are available to guarantee you some time alone to drink a glass of wine, talk, and eventually crawl into bed.

Next, assign a high priority to sex. Although you may not like the analogy, sex is like exercise. It's easy to fall out of the habit and get lazy. At the extreme, you may even want to keep a calendar and count the number of times per month for a while, just to help you emphasize to each other how important it is to be together. It helps to figure out regular times and then to build on that foundation.

This leads to the third issue, flexibility. An evening that does not go as planned shouldn't lead to finger pointing or frustration. Instead, simply be determined to find time for a "make good" as soon as possible. It may also be necessary to allocate twenty minutes instead of a full night, when you're in a "catch as catch can" mode. Still, it's better than the alternative.

Couples who make sure they take time for love are going to be more relaxed and patient with their kids.

Finally, if there are physical issues standing in the way, deal with them. See a doctor to find out what can be done. It is possible to build sexual energy by making lifestyle improvements. Mild exercise, proper diet, and more rest may just do the trick. When medications decrease libido or interfere with sexual function in other ways, there are still numerous methods to stimulate a partner to achieve feelings of sexual intimacy. Rather than abandoning everything, explore these alternatives. Alcohol and drug abuse issues may require counseling and assistance. No matter what the hindrance, the attempt to overcome the problem is a major romantic and loving step.

We know that in this world of dual careers and multiple family commitments, sex can easily take a backseat. This is bad for every aspect of your life, from mental well-being to feelings of love and romance toward each other. And we're sorry to start off this chapter with the bad news. At the same time, that leaves us with all of the good things. Building a great sexual and romantic relationship is one of the most fulfilling things you'll do as a couple. Therefore, you should work hard to make sure you take time, make time, and enjoy time together physically. Here are some suggestions on how to add spice to your romantic sex lives.

Many seductions begin hours before you're anywhere near the bedroom. A kind word or deed coupled with a gentle touch may be all that's needed to put everything else into motion.

Romance and Seduction

There's an old joke that says foreplay, to some extent, consists of the words, "Brace yourself, Betty Lou." It's crass, but it does point to one problem, and that is not giving full attention to the seduction ritual, which is an important part of romantic sex. These rites can pass quickly or take hours, and they are important to getting things going in the right way. Let's break down foreplay into two categories, long-term methods and fast-track approaches, and take a quick look at each.

Long-Term Methods

Here's where you talk about sexy lingerie, hot tubs, massages, oils, creams, whipped cream, scents, lotions, and all of those other tactics designed to lead to ecstasy later. Many couples know the joy of bathing or showering together as a prelude to having sex—or following it. We all love being caressed in just the right places. Even the right words can get the mood going.

Those of you in longer-term romantic relationships know that building expectations can be half the fun. The whole idea is to prolong the "waiting period" with the goal of amplifying the outcome. How you choose to do this depends on how familiar you are with each other, the boundaries you've drawn, and your individual tastes and preferences.

As you may have guessed by now, we think sex in a long-term relationship, especially marriage, is, to put it directly, better. You have time to work out all of the nuances. You know exactly where to go to get the right response. You learn to "read" each other as things progress. Both the act of seduction and the act of consummation are more familiar.

Some people say all this familiarity leads to a dull routine. We couldn't disagree more. It is so easy to avoid the "same-old, same-old" problem by expanding what you try over time and simply mixing up the routine. That, of course, leads us to the other side of seduction.

A Laundry List of Seduction Techniques

- In a crowded restaurant, discreetly tell your lover that you're not wearing underwear.
- Touch him under the tablecloth.
- Call the office near the end of the day to let her know what's coming when she gets home.
- Greet him at the door naked.
- Talk dirty while you're driving.
- Buy whipped cream and tell her she's dessert.
- Buy scented oils and give him a lengthy massage.
- Take a bath or shower and have your lover dry you off.
- Blindfold your lover and feed her various foods with your fingers. Have her guess what they are.
- Do a striptease.
- Play "doctor."
- Share a shower, bath, or hot tub.
- Walk into the living area as you're drying off after a shower; then let the towel drop.
- Breathe on her neck, ear, and later, on other places.
- Unplug the phone and say, "The next hour is all yours."
- Go to a place where there's a risk of getting caught. See how he reacts.
- Touch yourself inappropriately while he's watching the game. Tell him he can score later.
- Role-play; be Scarlett and Rhett or nurse and patient. You can even rent costumes.

- Book a hotel room for a night out.
- Go to a favorite old make-out spot.
- Smooch at the movies.
- Sit at a table and write down every seductive thing you've ever done. See where it leads you.
- Sit at a table and write down every seductive thing you want to do. See where that leads you.
- Read aloud to each other the corny sex scenes from a romance novel.
- Pretend you and your lover are stars in a porno film. Video is optional.
- Play one of those sex board games sold in novelty shops.
- Take turns writing down descriptions of various acts of foreplay on small pieces of paper and put the pieces in a hat. Draw them out and follow the instructions.
- Be blunt—tell your lover you want him or her, right now.

Fast-Track Approaches

Never underestimate the power of a quickie to make a day better. There are those instances when you just want to "get down to business" right away. It may be before you head off to work in the morning, just before the kids get home from school, or in some other unique situation where you just grab for the gusto.

Short little bursts of sex can lighten your mood while reminding each other how great it is to be together. Often, you'll discover the most romantic part of a quickie is the time you spend later appreciating each other's willingness to go with the flow.

The most important part of a fast-track seduction is making sure your partner is in the same mood; otherwise, it can be a recipe for disaster. Among other things, this means you'll need to develop a set of signals that can easily be discerned. The signals should include signs that say both yes and no. It can be something as simple as a passionate kiss that you both know might get out of hand quickly. She can jump in the shower with you, or he can say, "Are you in the same mood I'm in?"

Both fast-track and long-term seduction rituals can lead to various kinds of sex. Sometimes it's raunchy; sometimes it's quiet and intimate. Every version is good when the two of you are on the same page. What comes next? The act itself.

Romantic Sex

There are certain things that seem to make sex more romantic. Settings, words, and actions are the most prominent. If you are trying to make your relationship more romantic, you may need to reconsider how exactly sex plays out. Then, it is possible to intensify the romantic elements in this key part of a relationship.

Settings

The lion's share of sexual events takes place, as they probably should, in the bedroom. There are many things you can do to make the bedroom more romantic. For example, install a dimmer switch so you can turn the lights down low without making the room completely dark. Being able to see each other in soft light is romantic. Candles serve the same purpose, so have them available. To get the same result, keep a dark scarf handy to throw over a lamp. Other ideas include:

- Placing your contraception in a bedside drawer so you don't have to get out of bed
- Having access to soft music
- Adding soft scents to the room, such as scented candles, a touch of fragrance on the sheets, or a vase of fresh flowers
- Shutting out all other noises and distractions

Remember, the bedroom is only one of several romantic sexual settings. Others include a quiet corner of the park, a deserted beach, and even a car or van, if it's the only place you can be alone. A private balcony at a hotel can be a highly romantic and seductive setting.

In general, the features that make a setting romantic include quiet, intimate lighting, privacy, and a soft place to lie down. These are easy enough to find on a daily basis. We think it's a grand goal to enhance places that are already good settings while you look for others. It's also a good idea to identify the places you can go as a couple to gain the kind of inspiration that later leads to sexual intimacy. Knowing where they are adds a great tool to your romantic arsenal.

The Romantic Settings Quiz

Rate the romantic potential of each of these places, in terms of how strongly it puts you in the mood, on a scale of 1 (not at all) to 10 (highly seductive). Compare your score with your lover's. Then, frequent the places you both like!

1. A candlelit restaurant _____
2. The beach _____
3. The mountains _____
4. A drive-in movie or theaters of any kind _____
5. A picnic in a park or in the country _____
6. Your living room or den _____
7. The bathroom shower, tub, or hot tub _____
8. The bedroom _____
9. A train _____
10. A hotel room _____
11. Backseat of a car or cab _____
12. Semipublic places _____

Romantic Words

Lovemaking involves all of the senses; seeing, smelling, tasting, and touching seem to come naturally. The one to work on is hearing. Romantic couples say loving things while they're intimate. Here is a sampling of romantic things to say while you and your lover are between the sheets:

"You feel good."
"I am so secure when I'm with you."
"This feels so right."

"Touching you is special."
"I feel so close to you right now."
"I want to spend my whole life with you."
"You are the best lover ever."
"We are so good together."
"Can't we just stay like this forever?"
"You are so (big, small, soft, hard, good, bad, etc.)"

And, of course, the ever popular . . .

"I love you."

Quiet whispers of passion, affection, and love help make sex even more romantic. Combined with the natural moans and rhythmic breathing that just happen, these sounds add a new dimension to the experience. There is nothing quite like that.

Romantic lovers want to please each other more than anything else.

The other key use of words while being intimate is to make sure your lover is getting the kind of attention he or she wants and needs. It never hurts to ask what a romantic partner desires. You may find he or she wants prolonged foreplay, some specific form of gratification, or even just to move on to intercourse quickly. Communication during sex is a great asset. When both partners are willing to express their desires and preferences, each becomes more likely to be satisfied with the time together. This is not a matter of being selfish, because it works in both directions.

Romantic Actions

Is romantic sex slower paced? In general, we believe the answer is yes. Romantic sex should include more eye contact, lots of touching, soft words, and lingering kisses. These things take time. Besides, the idea is to savor the moment, not rush through it.

The actual act of lovemaking, of course, takes many forms and positions. Romantic lovemaking, however, should include three ingredients.

First, both of you should share the same mindset. This happens naturally most of the time. Still, it never hurts to say something along the lines of, "I'm feeling especially close to you," as you begin. This will set the stage properly, increasing the tenderness of the moment. Second, romantic lovemaking often is focused less on orgasms and more on passion, feeling, and experiencing each other. The whole point is to be joined as one. This union goes beyond sex into a different realm. There is no feeling quite like romantic sex. Third, while it may begin slowly, sometimes it doesn't stay that way. A truly romantically entangled couple reacts to each other as the event progresses. There is a certain power in this kind of intercourse that is not the same as a session designed to be more athletic in form. All versions are satisfying in different ways, including sex for fun. Still, from time to time, lovemaking stands out because of the connection made. That's when romantic sex is truly taking place.

Some folks believe that lighthearted episodes are equally bonding experiences. For example, greeting your husband at the door naked while holding a martini would be an attempt at romance. So would grabbing a quickie in a coat closet or wrapping yourself in cellophane or wrapping paper, complete with ribbon and bow. We're not going to dispute this view. The point is to find that form that fits your demeanor and approach to love and sex.

The following are suggestions for sexy stuff to wear: ankle bracelet, bikini briefs, flowers in your hair, muscle shirt/gym shorts, silk shirt (with several buttons undone), silk stockings and high heels, tight sweater, or a toe ring.

Afterglow Issues

Romantic sex leaves people feeling especially close in longer-term relationships and probably more vulnerable in newly emerging relationships. Both circumstances seem to cry out for reassurance and additional romantic activity. We know that men tend to get pretty sleepy after sex, because it's simply a natural physiological reaction. At the same time, afterplay can last a long time, especially if you include the part of the day when you're dressed again and going about your business. A gentle hug combined with a comment about how great it was or how much you love your partner extends lovemaking into the night.

Hugging several times a day is often a great sexual mood builder for later that night.

Stage of Life Issues

Romantic sex undoubtedly changes as a couple goes through various stages of life. Each era offers different challenges and opportunities. Long-term love means enjoying each one to its fullest and adjusting as the stages change. Here are some general categories.

Young, Single Sex

We're not going to debate the morality of having sex before marriage, but we feel it's wise to point out that sleeping together without any long-term commitment can leave you emotionally vulnerable. When a relationship ends, the odds increase that one person or the other will feel used sexually. Those who are willing to take this risk know that sex at this stage of life can be wildly exciting. That's because several advantages are present.

First of all, more often than not, this is the time when a couple has more time and energy to devote to sex. Without kids, it's easy to slip away to enjoy some time together. Nights, weekends, vacations, and holidays can be spent indulging in sexual revelry. Your libido is likely to be at or near its peak (especially men, according to physiological experts). Given the time available, this may lead to having intercourse several times in the same evening or day. The same freedom means you can hop into the tub or shower without worrying about being interrupted. It's not surprising that many married couples lament that their sex lives don't resemble these carefree days, but it's like trying to compare apples and oranges because of the circumstances.

Those who aren't married but are sexually active must be aware of all the diseases lurking out there. Careful protection is in order to keep you and your partner safe and to prevent unwanted pregnancy. This may dampen some of the enthusiasm, but it is essential. Also, the lack of familiarity may impede "gratification," in some sense of the word. It takes awhile to become accustomed to a partner, which can lead to a few early disappointments.

In general, people who choose to have sex in dating relationships without greater commitment run risks, but they may also find that intimacy changes how they feel about each other. The net result can easily become greater romantic involvement and an increasing commitment to each other.

Young Married Couples

Newlyweds enjoy all of the advantages of single sexual partners, with a few additional benefits. There may be an even greater sense of freedom associated with lovemaking, which leads to fewer inhibitions and more experimentation. And, since most young married couples have less disposable income, sex is a great way to entertain yourselves for free! For many partners, these years will create rousing memories that they'll cherish through the rest of life. At that point, dramatically romantic sexual encounters are mixed in with more recreational moments. After all, this is the closest you may ever come to constant sexual availability.

Remember to build the relationship while you and your partner indulge in all of these sexual opportunities. In other words, don't forget to talk and share.

Normally, the single biggest concern at this stage of life is contraception. There are many options, from birth control pills to condoms. Of course, there is always the enormous temptation to test fate when the weather is bad and you don't want to go out to the drugstore— but unless you and your partner want a baby, don't do it.

Couples with Kids

We've already talked about the challenges that occur when there are kids in the house. It can be a time when desire diminishes and couples grow apart. If you have children at home, consider the variety of ways you can spice up your romantic life and then think up some new ones. Always remember to lock the door before you start. This is the time to use intelligence, energy, and talent to keep things going with the one you love.

Empty Nesters

There is a new sense of freedom awaiting those of you who are about to become empty nesters. This freedom can be used to build and strengthen a marriage and a flagging sex life. In some ways, for those who carefully manage it, this period may be the greatest sexual era of your lives. Most couples at this stage have more money. They can book trips and give gifts without the financial pressures that lead to fights about money. That alone may increase bedroom time.

Several other factors also come into play. You don't have to worry about being interrupted. It may be possible to abandon contraception. Physiology may also play a role. By now, the two of you have probably marked out all of the sexual territory you're willing to explore and know exactly how to make each other feel great.

A man who stays sexually active in middle age may discover he has quite a bit more "staying power" than in his earlier years. He is able to substitute this advantage for frequency (one long, fulfilling session versus several short "bursts"), and she may be the greatest beneficiary. Couples who work at remaining intimate at this stage in life are likely to report the highest levels of life satisfaction and satisfaction with a romantic partner of any group.

Second honeymoons, anniversaries, and other sojourns can become great sexual adventures for empty-nest couples. The hilarious part is that your kids think you're over the hill, just at the point when you may be setting all kinds of new sexual records. Irony is a wonderful thing.

The Golden Years

Those of you who follow celebrities' lives have read about men who father children very late in life. Sex is available even as you pass retirement and head into your final years together. The secrets are medical care and understanding how the process works. Taking time to read a few materials and visiting a doctor can mean that sex will be part of your entire lives.

The biggest worry for men over sixty-five is, of course, prostate cancer. It's advisable to get regular PSA tests and checkups. There are options available to help you overcome the disease. Even those who lose the ability to perform can remain sexual and romantic partners. The parameters may change, but the intentions and emotions do not.

Some Warnings

Of all the things that can quickly damage a relationship, sex is near the top of the list. The combination of emotional and physical responses, plus the vulnerability involved, mean that you must exercise due caution when entering into a sexual relationship. There are many pitfalls to avoid with regular sexual partners as well. Here is a standard list of no-no's.

Sex As a Commodity

Far too many couples think of sex as something to trade in a relationship. It may go back to that old adage, "Women give sex in order to get love; men give love in order to get sex." If this applies to your relationship, you're off to a bad start. Viewing sex in that way leads to many misdeeds, including:

- Using sex as a method to get your way
- Withholding sex for revenge or to express anger
- Feeling that you are "owed" sex after you do a favor, give a gift, or spend a lot of money on your date

Sex is never something you owe or trade. Thinking of it in that way demeans the act and makes real intimacy far less likely.

Sex As Power

Playing power games in a relationship is generally a bad idea. When they move into the bedroom, a disaster soon follows. Sadly, in many long-term romances, men complain about lack of frequency, while women complain about lack of intimacy. As both partners become more frustrated, the "power card" of withholding sex can emerge. Such a move is a sure sign the romance is in trouble, because it easily becomes a game of negative "tit for tat" in which other power moves associated with money or household chores emerge. Sex should never be about who is in control.

 One of the worst things that can happen to couples is an unexpected and unwanted pregnancy. Therefore, it is never worth the risk to go without protection. In addition, dating couples must be aware of other sexually transmitted diseases. Failing to do so makes sex risky and less fulfilling.

Sexual Martyrdom

Closely related to thinking of lovemaking as a commodity or as power is being cast in the role of a sexual martyr. When one partner says to the other, "You got laid, didn't you?" the message is, "I went through the sex act in a self-sacrificing way." (It's also just a crude thing to say to someone you love.) Doing things that are uncomfortable or that you simply don't want to do will raise feelings of frustration, anger, and other negative emotions or thoughts. Sex is not, and should not become, a one-way street. When a person engages in sex because he or she feels as if it's necessary ("I have to do this, even though I don't want to"), or has sex that feels phony or forced, the relationship is likely to break down. The bottom line: If you're not in the mood, gently say so. When your partner turns you down, show respect and wait for a better time.

When you fall into one of these traps, sex loses its meaning and potential as an expression of love. It is easy to start "keeping score" in a game that no one wins. Sex, especially romantic sex, should always be a matter of mutual consent with no strings attached.

Some couples are able to substitute sexual activities when one is not particularly agreeable. Also, sometimes when a partner makes a move and you're not in the mood, you'll feel differently if you give it a chance. Sensitive romantic partners know when to press on and when to give up. The net result is more frequency and a long-term situation in which each of you becomes more open to the possibility, even when things don't seem right at first. The trick is to use a great deal of caution and never simply impose your will.

A Great Love Life

As you can see, we view romantic sex in a special way. The world has become quite promiscuous in the past century, which has been good in some ways and bad in others. At the end of the day, we know sexual compatibility is a great treasure in a romantic involvement, and basically there's only one way to find out if you are compatible. On the other hand, when sex becomes so casual that it is part of the everyday banter of television, something very precious is being lost.

As you grow old together, sexual memories and moments may be one of the strongest forms of glue that keeps you connected. Love of family, shared adventures, and other bonding experiences are equally important, but there is nothing as unique as your sex life. We believe a strong connection exists between feelings of deep romantic love and those spiritual stirrings that rise up among us. Pure love—whether it is love of God, love of a family member, or love of a spouse—is a poignant emotion that has no equal. Sex is one way to express these strongly held feelings and thoughts.

The wonderful part is that a romantic couple learns how to blend these raw and powerful loving emotions with fun, frivolity, fantasy, and other indulgences. A great love life is part well-kept secret and part bragging rights. We'll leave it up to you to figure out which is which in your relationship.

CHAPTER 16
Romance Revisited

Romances begin and end for various reasons. This chapter is about picking yourself up off the floor and getting back in the game following the end of a relationship. Revisiting romance can be tough, depending on the circumstances that caused you to be suddenly single. Getting over anger, depression, guilt, frustration, a sense of loss, and feelings of failure may not be easy. Even then, deciding to once again risk possible pain by becoming involved with someone makes you feel vulnerable when your morale is already weak. So, why bother? It's worth trying again because the rewards far outweigh the problems. The idea is to find times and places where you can reconnect in comfortable ways. It may not be easy, but it can be done.

The Loss of a First Love

Do you ever completely get over breaking up with your first true love? For many people, thoughts and memories linger for years. At the time it happens, parting ways with this person who has tugged at your youthful heartstrings is often very painful.

One natural tendency is to compare anyone new to the previous love of your life. This can work for or against you. A bitter or angry breakup may lead you to relief that a new romantic interest is nothing like a former boyfriend or girlfriend. Or, through that "successive approximation" idea we talked about in Chapter 11, a new dating partner may have many of the same characteristics of the former romantic interest, but without some of the rough edges. Those who don't break this habit are doomed to repeat it in future dating relationships and breakups.

The alternative occurs when a person remains so smitten with the previous partner that no one new can measure up. This is unfair to everyone concerned. Those who still think a past love cannot be matched should concentrate on doing other things until the feelings pass (and they will, with time).

As the world continues to change, fewer and fewer high school sweethearts end up getting married. Most teens endure breakups. For the most part, this is good. Empathy, sympathy, and consideration may grow through the loss of a first love, making the individual a better romantic partner the next time around.

Several things can be carried away from the loss of a first love. First, you can still recall the innocence and joy of that era. In fact, you may remember some kind of idealized version of this former lover. This isn't a problem as long as you recognize that it's not the real lover or relationship that you're recalling but rather a bit of fantasy mixed with reality. After all, you're never going back, so it's okay to make this person more than what he or she really was. Just get on with life at the same time.

A learning curve is also present. Paying attention to what went wrong makes it easier to avoid repeating it. Many teenagers learn that they need to grow up and be more considerate. Others discover that being clingy, jealous, and possessive is neither attractive nor conducive to romance.

The other lesson has to do with pain. Breaking up is upsetting. We hope that this means that as young people encounter this kind of pain, they learn not to toy with someone else's feelings. Some may even pick up this information vicariously, by watching a close friend go through a breakup.

Coping with Your First Breakup

- Take some time off from dating to fully understand your feelings.
- Use the time you spend mending to enjoy evenings with friends. Don't sit home and sulk for too long.
- Make a list of the things you loved about the lost partner. Make a list of the things you didn't like. Learn from both lists.
- Date casually when you first decide to start circulating again.
- If you're still angry with your previous partner, don't take it out on a new date. Find a better way to express it.
- Be aware of the "rebound" effect. You are vulnerable.
- Don't fret if love takes awhile to find you again. When the time is right, it will arrive.

The Breakup of a Serious Relationship

One concept we've heard more about recently is the idea that romantic involvements often play out through what is called "serial monogamy." In other words, a person joins with one partner, but the relationship eventually goes sour. Then, he or she moves to another solo partner. Instead of juggling a dance card with a series of dates and boyfriends, the individual always remains loyal to one at a time.

No matter whether you are serially monogamous or juggle several lovers simultaneously, there will be breakups that affect your life to some degree. For example, the college couple who separates around the time of graduation has some major adjustments in store. Recall what we said back in Chapter 2 about making yourself more interesting to help attract a new lover or friend.

Single people who break up run into various complications as part of the process that may serve as a precursor of things to come if they marry and get divorced. For example, when you have mutual friends, there is tension associated with how and when you will spend time with them. Minor relationships may end up as friendships, meaning the larger circle of friends remains intact. Catastrophic romantic collapses may leave you feeling as if you have to create a whole new social life, because you just can't hang with the same old gang. Even then, those who live in small to midsize towns run the risk of bumping into each other, creating an awkward moment. This gets just a bit worse if the encounter happens in a nightspot or restaurant the two of you used to frequent and your ex shows up with someone new.

One nasty situation occurs when a couple has been living together or sharing so many overnights that they may as well be living together. Personal possessions must be separated, keepsakes divided or discarded, and items jointly purchased require some resolution—all at a time when you really don't want to see each other.

Besides these details, some emotional baggage remains. Disenfranchised lovers may start to wonder if they'll ever find Mr. or Ms. Right. Others question how attractive they are, or begin to wonder if they deliberately sabotage relationships. Negative thinking takes over, and people end up lonely, alone, and often bitter.

Rebounding from a longer-term, more serious romantic relationship takes time. It's a good idea to be alone for a while so you can step back and think more clearly about what went wrong. Being alone allows you to put the former relationship to rest, start to heal, and perhaps reach the conclusion that it was for the best. Being alone doesn't mean you should lock yourself in your home with just the TV for company, however. Take walks, work out at the gym, see a movie, or take yourself out for lunch. During this time of healing, it's especially important to be good to yourself and treat yourself gently.

Once you start feeling a little better about things, you need to go out to stay in circulation. Having friends around builds confidence and is entertaining. Socializing is like a form of exercise. If you get lax and lazy, you'll find it tougher to start up again. Going to church, having dinner out with friends, and staying involved in other activities will help make the transition from being "paired" to being single again an easier adjustment.

> After breaking up with a serious partner, expect tears and remorse. Things that remind you of your time together (songs, restaurants, activities) will hurt. If they don't, the relationship wasn't that serious in the first place.

Divorce

It's a sad fact of modern American life that one out of every two marriages ends in divorce. There are dozens of factors that contribute to this statistic, but this book is not the place to discuss them. We will say this: In the United States, there is a prevailing idea that you should be happy. When you're in an unsatisfactory marriage, you're not happy. What is confounding, however, is that getting divorced and becoming single doesn't mean you will immediately turn into a happy person. In fact, many divorced people sink into a greater state of unhappiness or depression following the end of a marriage. Against this backdrop, friends start trying to set you up, you feel sexual yearnings that are unfulfilled, and eventually you start wishing for a new romantic partner. It is not going to be easy, but most divorced people who live in the United States eventually do remarry. This means they first rejoined the ranks of the dating. Let's take a look at what's in store.

Childless Divorce

Some marriages terminate fairly quickly. The good side is that usually these couples don't have kids or a great deal of personal property with which to contend. The bad side is that the hurt, frustration, and "what if" stuff is present. It's never a clean break.

The decision to date again following a childless divorce is easier in some ways than if children are present. You don't have to worry about how the children will feel about you dating again or that they won't like your dating partners. Still, it's wise to be cautious. A former spouse may quickly remarry and even have kids, leaving you filled with questions and resentment, especially if you wanted children and your spouse didn't. It's easy, under those circumstances, to question yourself: "Wasn't I good enough for him?" or "Why would she have kids now, and not with me?" Self-doubt can rear its ugly head as jealousy and unresolved anger, and you have no good place to vent it. It makes for a tough dating situation, because you may find yourself dumping far too much on someone who just wants to enjoy drinks and dinner.

Focus on the positive side of this new era in your life and look at rejoining the dating scene as an adventure.

To make it work, the best approach is to think about the exciting aspects of going out once again. There is the intrigue of meeting someone new. Getting to know a person better can be enjoyable. The challenge of presenting yourself well may lead you back to the gym or to the library to catch up on reading, so you'll have something interesting to say.

Ten Signs That a Romance Is Over

1. You'd rather polish the silver than have sex.
2. He says he's going to walk the dog and is gone for three days.
3. The complaint-compliment ratio drops to 10:1.
4. All of the time you spend with friends revolves around talking about how miserable you are.
5. Fighting with your partner just isn't worth the bother.
6. You fantasize daily about being free.
7. You're thrilled when he asks to take a weeklong trip with friends.
8. Seeing a happy couple makes you want to hurl.
9. You constantly invent reasons to work so you don't have to go home.
10. You begin discovering signs that your partner is seeing someone else.

Divorce with Kids

Trying to date while raising a family is one of the more difficult complexities of modern living. A vast range of issues comes into play. Each one has the potential to slow down a blooming romance and even lead to the end of a promising relationship. Of course, the alternative is to wait until the kids are grown, an option some people choose. For those who intend to try to find a new lover, here's a quick look at some of the complications.

Item #1—Finding time. Every child from one day old to eighteen years demands a significant amount of time and emotional energy. Early on, there are diapers and feedings. Later, practices, lessons, school meetings, sick days, and lots of unexpected events take up hours and days. Preteens require a unique kind of chauffeur service, while those who drive worry you sick with their comings and goings, not to mention all of the temptations lingering out there.

    If you're trying to date with these distractions, the first rule of business is to learn how to compartmentalize. You have to be able to set aside time and energy for a romantic prospect as well as time for yourself. If you don't, it's not going to be right for your partner or for you. Sitters, grandparents, and friends can make a huge difference. It's critical to balance your social life with some personal time to spend alone, and with your kids. Otherwise, guilt may play a major role, even when someone is watching them for you.

Item #2—Budgets. As a divorced parent trying to raise children, you usually have to think about money, especially if you've gone from two incomes to one. Besides funding all of your children's current activities and the monthly bills, there are worries about a college fund, plus money for emergencies. Paying for a night out can be a budget-buster in those circumstances. And, as we mentioned in Chapter 6, you have to figure out the issue of who pays for both the date and a sitter. It's bad enough that married couples fight about money. Here you are trying to work out financial arrangements with someone you're seeing casually.

The keys to these potential budget battles are honesty and candor. You simply have to tell your date that you're financially strapped. Another great remedy the two of you can work out is cheap dates. You may not want to include the kids at first, but you can split the cost of a sitter, and then just go for a cup of coffee, a drive, a picnic, or some other inexpensive date. Reducing the cash flow problem means you're more likely to relax and enjoy the time together.

Item #3—How the kids react. This is a tough one. You don't want to run your kids through a whole series of dating partners, each of whom reacts differently to them. This can create a confusing home. On the other hand, it's impossible to pretend you're not dating or seeing anyone. Somewhere in between are the times when your date is exposed to your kids, and vice versa. They are probably going to resent this individual for a while. It gets complicated quickly.

We suggest keeping lovers away from your home life for as long as possible. To some extent, how long depends on the ages of your children. When you reach the point when you know the involvement is more than just a passing fancy, the time is right to slowly and carefully introduce this new person to your children. Expect blowups and rude behavior from your kids. It is vital to show compassion and concern. Let your children know they are still the most important part of your life.

Those who don't have children but are seeing romantic partners who have kids have the toughest job of all, especially if the children are old enough to realize what's happening. The best you can do is to be kind, friendly, and patient. Many mixed families and dating couples manage to deal with this issue, but it isn't always smooth sailing.

The greatest complication of all is the "Brady Bunch" effect, in which two adults, each with children, date and then marry. There are a number of potentially difficult problems in blending two families. Everyone has to adjust to everyone else. You'll need all of the compassion, caring, empathy, and love that you can muster to make this situation work.

Item #4—New sexual partner. Another major entanglement is sex. For one, the first time you make love with a new partner, there are going to be some odd feelings. After all, you had a child with your previous lover, and no matter what you think of him or her now, that echo is present. Also, every single partner is a little different. The sex may be fabulous and fulfilling, or it may be stilted. That alone is cause for discomfort.

Then there are additional issues such as whose bed are you going to use. Making love to a new partner in an old marriage bed is likely to feel very strange. Having sex in a hotel room may feel "cheap" at some level. Going to his or her place is probably the solution, but even then the new environment feels strange. Do you stay the night? If you rush home, what kind of signal does that send? And all of this takes place as you struggle with other issues such as sexual history and safe sex and contraception protocols. Putting it mildly, we don't envy people going through this stage in a relationship. There are no easy answers and there are lots of questions. As with everything else, good communication is key. It also helps to have a friend and confidant you can talk to freely. It's not so much advice you'll be looking for, as emotional support and understanding.

Give your children time to adjust to your new romantic partner, but remember that you are entitled to happiness, too.

Item #5—The ex-factor. Divorced couples with children usually work out some type of arrangement for the kids to spend time with both parents. Among other things, this means an ex will soon find out that you're seeing someone, and may even get reports from the kids on how serious the new relationship has become. Some former spouses are hurt, angry, and depressed by the news because they have unresolved issues. For example, they may secretly wish to get back together. As a result, you may find yourself dealing with some chiding or anger from a former partner. There are also those inevitable comparisons between past and present loves, which don't do anyone any good.

The flip side may also turn up. You may find out that your ex now has a new boyfriend or girlfriend. There may be a natural tendency on your part to want to "compete" or "get even" by seeing someone yourself. That's not going to bode well for a new relationship. Work hard to avoid falling into this trap.

Later-Life Divorce

Another unpleasant scenario is that of midlife to late-life divorce. The kids may be grown and the financial arrangements worked out, but the bitterness and baggage that results can be awful. Of course, the relationship that tends to get most of the press is the man in a midlife crisis who leaves his wife of many years for a younger woman. Other couples just grow apart over the years. When the kids have left the nest, the parents discover they have nothing left to share.

Date because you want to date, not because of anything your ex is doing.

Later-life divorces create a variety of individual dilemmas. The hurt of the breakup may affect how a person views him- or herself and others. It's easy to become suspicious of others and to resent people of the opposite sex. The sense of abandonment may be overwhelming. Others may be so relieved to be out of the relationship that they feel guilty about feeling so good. Even then, showing up to a party or dinner without a companion may make everyone feel a little awkward. After all, your friends are used to seeing you as part of a couple. And they aren't quite sure about your mental state. You may not want sympathy, or you may be begging for comfort.

To make matters worse, even after time has passed and you decide to take the big step, you may not have dated for a quarter of a century or more. Certainly the rules of the dating game have changed. You may not know how to ask for or accept an invitation. Clearly, the things you did on dates as a young person are not the same things you would want to do now. And, just to make matters a little more complicated, there are fewer potential dating partners.

If you divorce in later life, our advice is to find a way to rediscover a sense of adventure and a willingness to take emotional risks. It won't be easy, and it can't be forced. We've noticed that people who've had to deal with late-life divorce seem to have a tendency to panic, leading them to "settle" for someone they know is less than an ideal match in order to avoid loneliness. Unfortunately, such a move often leads to yet another divorce or breakup. Use caution and listen to your friends' candid advice.

The Death of a Spouse

Of those most stressful things that happen in life, losing a spouse is about the worst, probably only eclipsed by losing a child. The stages of mourning, from denial to acceptance, don't account for the difficult time that follows. Loneliness remains. Heartbreak never completely goes away. Many times anger is present. Grieving is vital, but it's also difficult.

At what point is a widowed individual ready to re-enter the world of romance? The answer varies from person to person. At some level, there must be a willingness to move on. The right potential partner must come along. Both people must be ready.

Those who make the leap into dating may run into resistance. Family members may say it's too soon or dislike the new choice. Many times a new romantic partner becomes the focus for the family's unresolved grief and other negative emotions, even when the widowed person has been able to let go and get on with life.

If you've lost a parent, you may at some point wish to signal you're okay with your remaining parent dating again. If so, throw him or her a "coming out" party, or invite that new dating partner to your home for an evening.

Intimacy is particularly tricky. Revived feelings of guilt and grief may emerge. Then there may be a concern about the morality of sleeping with a new partner without marrying that person. All in all, the waters are rough but negotiable for those ready to make the journey—and the destination can be fabulous. A new friend and source of support suddenly enters your life. Remember that companionship at any age is crucial. Finding a person who truly understands what you're experiencing—perhaps someone who has also lost a spouse—is worth his or her weight in gold.

Over time, romantic feelings beyond friendship may re-emerge. Passion is possible at any stage of life. Although this may not be the road the majority of widows or widowers choose, this new relationship can be a godsend for some. Be happy for those who find love and companionship, at any stage of life.

Recovery from Other Broken Relationships

Other broken relationships can affect your romantic life. The death of a parent profoundly affects many people, and, during that mourning period, it may be very difficult for them to feel amorous toward their partner. The loss of a close friend can have the same effect. Such a period is a time for a partner to really stretch his or her romantic muscles by being supportive, understanding, kind, and patient. When a child dies, the power of grief is so great that it can break up the most stable couple. Counseling, prayer, and the support of family and friends may help, and the pain will ease, but it will never go away completely. Sharing this kind of grief can either bring a couple closer together or tear them apart.

Most of us will experience these kinds of losses in our lives. Part of being a romantic spouse is to prepare for them as best you can. Knowing how to offer support is one key. Reminding yourself that the grief will subside and life will return to a more normal state also helps. Those who are truly in love will do their very best to work through these difficult periods And may end up achieving a profound new sense of attachment and love.

Keep Your Sunny Side Up

Our circle of friends includes those who have been divorced, widows, widowers, and single friends of all ages who have overcome separation and loneliness only to discover love once again. Most of these people are optimistic, open-minded folks who know that when you open yourself to the possibility of finding a new love, there is always a risk of rejection and pain. Having seen the excitement of a person finding a new romantic partner convinces us that it can and does happen every day.

At the same time, we know getting back into the game isn't for everyone. Those who believe they've lost a lifelong soul mate may feel a connection that extends beyond the grave. These people can derive comfort and support from family and friends while basking in the memories of a great romantic life. That's not all bad either, which leads us to another point. It's vital to remember that the simplest way to revisit romance is to recharge the relationship you have, rather than look for greener pastures. If you are fortunate enough to have a romantic partner, you should always consider that there was a point at which you saw something special enough in that person to expand your relationship. Many times, that makes the relationship worth salvaging.

No matter which course you choose, try to remain as open as possible to the idea that love often finds folks in the most unusual places and times. Revisiting romance can be a surprise guest at an odd time. Those who open the door and let love in stand to gain what can be one of life's greatest pleasures: the company of a new romantic partner.

The easiest way to revisit romance is to recall the fond memories of the relationship you're in. Keep loving the one you're with!

CHAPTER 17

Romance Forever!

One of Don's wise mentors is Dr. Robert Trewatha, who took Don under his wing nearly two decades ago. At his recent retirement party, Bob said he believed the future of a successful company is not going to be determined on the Internet but, rather, by using a VCR. The twist was that VCR stands for *Values, Commitment,* and *Relationships,* which he thinks are the keys to a thriving business. In this chapter, we will show you how to use the VCR approach to romantic living.

The VCR Approach

It makes a great deal of sense to us that you can employ a VCR-approach to loving, romantic relationships. Values come into play in a couple of ways. First, lifelong love is much more likely when you share the same values. Agreeing on what you enjoy doing together (and what you should do separately) helps make shared time more pleasant and romantic. Second, loving relationships are much more likely to succeed when they include spiritual values, family as a high priority, and faithfulness to each other.

Commitment means many things to romantic partners. The obvious, of course, is commitment to each other. The common lament that a man is "afraid of commitment" gets at this issue. However, once a commitment has been made to a monogamous relationship, it should be expressed in words, deeds, and the intense desire to have the relationship succeed. Compromise, effort, and constant attention are needed to nurture a new love affair into a long-term partnership.

Don't let outside interests such as work or hobbies get so out of balance that they interfere with a romantic partnership.

When your "VCR" is working properly, romance is forever. Life will unfold in uncertain ways and there will always be bumps in the road. Still, when you maintain your zest for living and your love for each other and you make a concerted effort to maintain romance, the journey is more exciting and enjoyable.

In this final chapter, we want to wrap things up. By now, you have probably decided you know just as much about romance as we do. That's great. Fill in the blanks we left with the innovations you create. If we have prodded you to think more about the topic and given you a couple of ideas, we've succeeded.

Keep Falling in Love

Dating and romance, as we've tried to describe them, are adventures in which discovery is a key element. Meeting and falling in love with a person who will become a long-term partner involves an exchange of information. Each side finds out more about the other. Some of what you learn is attractive; some is not. On balance, a romance takes off when each new discovery makes the couple feel closer and more excited about sharing time together.

In a very real sense, falling in love is rarely a one-time event. When two people start dating, the normal routine is to become more and more connected over time. Odds are that romance grows and love builds in a series of steps, so you keep falling deeper and deeper in love with each other over time.

One of the keys to keeping a marriage or partnership romantic is to make sure the falling-in-love process does not stop at the altar. Each stage of life reveals something new about a partner. As we learn more about each other, romance and love can and should continue to grow. Truly romantic partners find new things to love about a spouse as time goes by. Here are some of the highlights.

Keep a separate scrapbook or journal of romantic and passionate moments and events. Share it on occasion to remind yourselves of the great romantic times in your past.

Deciding to Make a Baby

In today's world, the great majority of pregnancies can be planned. Sure, accidents happen, but most married or cohabiting couples can make a proactive decision either to have kids or not. Deciding to go ahead and try is romantic and connecting on a series of levels. The commitment a couple makes to each other builds with the decision to start a family. The sense of security that it takes to reach this decision means you're in a strong ongoing relationship, which is very reassuring. Also, bonding takes place in the physical act of making love, and, for those who are fortunate enough to succeed, throughout the pregnancy.

Growing Older Together

A couple married for five years has probably gone through a great deal of sexual and interpersonal exploration. Even after that phase is over, romance can blossom in other ways. One of you may decide to return to school or tackle a new hobby. It is easy to find joy in watching a partner grow and to become even more attracted to him or her.

Renewing Experiences

Another great way to keep falling in love, believe it or not, is to occasionally spend some time apart. The first time one or the other leaves for a business trip, or even a solo vacation, represents the opportunity to find out what life alone is like. When you get back together, a unique discovery event is possible.

Maintain Your Sense of Humor

Many years ago, an anonymous writer said, "We're all going to die, so why be pompous about it?" The writer went on to suggest that romantic relationships are built, in part, by keeping a sense of humor about things. The ability to laugh at yourself and make others feel better through humor is one of God's greatest gifts. Humor is good for physical as well as emotional well-being. A well-timed joke can tame many stressful, tense, frustrating moments by putting them in perspective. If you really want a forever-romance, it really helps to learn how to laugh.

Enjoy Life's Funny Moments

Couples that laugh together often love more. For those of you who are humor-challenged, start with easy things. Choose more comedies when you watch television. Go to funny movies together or rent them from a video store. Try a comedy-based theme bar or attend a comical play.

Next, build on the experience. Actively recall the funnier moments of what you've seen. Buy a book of jokes or something from the humor section of a bookstore. Remember, while different things are funny to each person, there are still many concepts most of us share. Couples often develop a common sense of humor. Sharing laughs is part of bonding as partners. Later in life, mutual ideas about what's funny will probably be passed on to your kids. Enjoying whimsical moments keeps daily life less mundane.

Grab the Gusto

Love flows freely when you embrace situations and enjoy them to the hilt. Finding the humor in any circumstance keeps life going along much more pleasantly. So, when you see something funny as you drive down the highway or walk through the mall, share it with your partner. You can even build in little games. For example, go into a store and make up funny stories about people you see shopping. Turn them into spies, famous people, and forlorn lovers looking for "dates" in each scenario. Make up an entire scene. Try to think up a punch line for each one. Any form of play that goes with a situation you share can be both romantic and entertaining.

Research suggests that men and women who idealize each other, just a bit, tend to stay together. By seeing the good side of a spouse or lover and accentuating those characteristics in your own mind, it's easier to handle the tough times and bad moments. In general, brag about your partner publicly ("My husband/wife is the best") and praise him or her privately.

Tease Your Lover

Teasing your lover effectively is the emotional equivalent of a senior seminar in a major course of study. Far too often, teasing is mean-spirited or delivered by someone who is oblivious to the fact that he or she is hurting a lover's feelings. Therefore, unless you are certain, you shouldn't tease a friend, your lover, or your kids.

On the other hand, couples in genuinely romantic relationships often playfully tease each other, handholding, hugging, and kissing all the while. The secret, here, is that you have to know that the person you are teasing has no underlying insecurity about the subject.

When teasing is a form of play, it is intellectually challenging trying to come up with some clever turn of phrase. It also means you know your lover so well that you have worked out the boundaries and the ground rules. Many couples use teasing and humor as part of a seduction ritual, laughing all the way to the bedroom. That's a great approach. Who hasn't giggled about getting too loud while having sex at their parent's house? Sex isn't always solemn seduction and romantic passion. Sometimes it's just funny and fun.

Drink It All In

The final piece of advice we'd like to offer is to remember to pay attention. Notice things as they happen. File romantic moments away in your memories, scrapbooks, photo files, and videotape drawers. Revisit them often even as you generate new moments.

We looked over many books in the love, relationships, and romance sections of various bookstores and libraries before we started writing this one. We found that many of them seemed to suggest you have to spend money, go places, and buy things to be romantic. Either that, or you had to be doing something sexual. We respectfully disagree.

Much of what we have enjoyed as significant romantic moments, both as single people and as a married couple, didn't cost a dime. Memories fit into that category. Revisit them often. When you do, you will find yourself lovingly looking at this wonderful person you chose to share life with. He or she, not knowing your thoughts, is likely to receive a tender touch or kiss out of the blue. That makes romance a kind of self-fulfilling prophecy and a positive cycle of tenderness.

Romance is an emotion, an activity, a feeling, and sometimes a fantasy. The emotion is love, care, concern, passion, and friendship all rolled into one. The activities include both the smallest favor and the grandest gesture that say, in no uncertain terms, "I love you!" The feeling is indescribable. You feel safe, reassured, content, happy at times, and comforted when you are in sorrow.

As you go through your life's journey, take in all of the sights and sounds life offers. You have been granted the greatest gift of all: the chance to live and love. Never forget how special it is that you found someone to share a romance with. Never take it for granted. Soon enough, the time is gone. If the Beatles are right, "the love you take is equal to the love you make." Even if they're not, a life in love is a great deal more interesting than one at the office. Be the best romantic partner that you can. The rewards of giving love to another are far richer than any other kind of wealth in the world. What you receive back is greater still. Have a great romantic life!

The greatest legacy you can leave is a life filled with love.

APPENDIX A

Great Romantic Getaways

Agetaway as a couple, even for a night or two, is like a first-aid kit designed to patch up an ailing romantic life. When you have the money, it's always a good idea to get away together. Quality time alone is often tough to find in our fast-paced world, so you may have to work at it. When you do, you may be asking, "Where shall we go? What shall we do?" In this appendix, we give you a list of romantic places throughout the United States. The prices for rooms vary from quite reasonable to a little bit extravagant (prices are subject to change; call to check). For each listing, we have also displayed one or more featured activities. Check this list to jump-start a romantic weekend or vacation!

ALABAMA

The Beach House Bed & Breakfast

9218 Dacus Lane
Gulf Shores 36542
(334) 540-7039

Rooms: 5
Rates: vary by plan

Special feature: on the dunes of the Gulf Shore next to a National Wildlife Refuge

Radisson Admiral Semmes Hotel

251 Government Street
Mobile 36602
(334) 432-8000

Rooms: 170
Rates: $150 +

Special features: whirlpool in courtyard, health club

The Secret Bed & Breakfast Lodge

2356 Highway 68
West Leesburg 35983
(256) 523-3825

Rooms: 6
Rates: $95–$150

Special feature: on top of a mountain

ALASKA

Lynne's Pine Point Bed & Breakfast

3333 Creekside Drive
Anchorage 99504
(907) 333-2244

Rooms: 3
Rates: $85–$90

Special features: tennis courts, cross-country ski trails

Pearson's Pond Luxury Inn & Garden Spa

4541 Sawa Circle
Juneau 99801
(907) 789-3772

Rooms: 3
Rates: $169–$229

Special features: private hot tubs with spectacular views, surrounded by rain forest, on a pond created by a glacier

Yukon Don's Bed and Breakfast Inn

2221 Yukon Circle
Wasilla 99654
(907) 376-7472

Rooms: 8
Rates: $85–$135

Special features: the majesty of the Matsu Valley, a 360-degree viewing room

ARKANSAS

Inn at the Mill—A Clarion Carriage House

3906 Greathouse Springs Road
Johnson 72741
(501) 443-1800

Rooms: 48
Rates: $99–$109

Special feature: décor of rooms inspired by famous artists

Heartstone Inn & Cottages

35 Kingshighway
Eureka Springs 72632
(800) 494-4921 or (501) 253-8916

Rooms: 10 rooms,
2 suites, 2 cottages
Rates: $68–$125

Special feature: theme is "Lose your heart in the Ozarks"

Oak Tree Inn

1802 W. Main Street
Heber Springs 72543
(501) 362-7731 or (877) 362-7731

Rooms: 4 rooms,
3 cottages
Rates: $85

Special feature: in the foothills of the Ozark Mountains

ARIZONA

Arizona Inn

2200 E. Elm Street
Tucson 85719
(520) 325-1541

Rooms: 86
Rates: $195–$245

Special feature: Audubon Bar looks like the bar in the movie *Casablanca*

Bisbee Grand Hotel

61 Main Street
Bisbee 85603
(520) 432-5900

Rooms: 11
Rates: $52–$115

Special feature: murder mystery weekends

The Mine Manager's House Inn

601 Greenway Drive
Ajo 85321
(520) 387-6505

Rooms: 5
Rates: $82–$150

Special features: 30-mile desert view, Organ Pipe National Cactus Park

CALIFORNIA

Babbling Brook Bed & Breakfast Inn

1025 Laurel Street   Rooms: 13
Santa Cruz 95060   Rates: $145–$195
(831) 427-2437

Special features: waterfall; near redwoods, ocean, and boardwalk

Blue Whale Inn Bed & Breakfast

6736 Moonstone Beach Drive   Rooms: 6
Cambria 93428   Rates: $170–$210
(805) 927-4647

Special features: on the bluffs overlooking the Pacific Ocean, near Hearst Castle

Cypress Inn

P.O. Box Y   Rooms: 34
Carmel-by-the-Sea 93921   Rates: $165–$295

Special feature: afternoon tea in a garden courtyard

COLORADO

China Clipper Inn

525 2nd Street   Rooms: 11
Ouray 81427   Rates: $85–$160
(970) 325-0565

Special feature: view of snow-capped peaks from hot tub

Riverbend Bed & Breakfast

42505 Highway 160   Rooms: 5
Mancos 81328   Rates: $75–$125
(970) 533-7353

Special features: canyons, ski hills, Mesa Verde National Park

Queen Ann Bed & Breakfast Inn

2147-51 Tremont Place   Rooms: 14
Denver 80205   Rates: $75–$175
(800) 432-INNS or (303) 296-6666

Special feature: "Romance Package" arrangement including horse-and-carriage rides, catered candlelit dinners, and musicians for private serenades

CONNECTICUT

Blueberry Inn

40 Bashon Hill Road   Rooms: 3
Bozrah 06334   Rates: $85–$135
(860) 889-3618

Special features: forests and blueberry bushes

Griswold Inn

36 Main Street   Rooms: 30
Essex 06426   Rates: $90–$115
(860) 767-1776

Special feature: in operation since 1776

The Inn at Chester

318 W. Main Street   Rooms: 42 rooms, 2 suites
Chester 06412   Rates: $105–$185 (rooms)
(860) 526-9541 or $215–$245 (suites)
(800) 949-7829

Special feature: art gallery

DELAWARE

Hotel DuPont

11th & Market Streets   Rooms: 217
Wilmington 19801   Rates: $149–$279
(302) 594-3100

Special features: 1,200-seat theater; over 800 original works of art

The Inn at Montchanin Village

Rt. 100 and Kirk Road, P.O. Box 130   Rooms: 33 (25 suites)
Montchanin 19710   Rates: $170–$450
(800) COWBIRD or (302) 888-2133

Special feature: on the National Register of Historic Places

Sea Witch Manor Bed & Breakfast

71 Lake Avenue   Rooms: 5
Rehoboth Beach 19971   Rates: $135–$170
(302) 226-9482

Special feature: wraparound pool near beach

FLORIDA

Lightbourn Inn

907 Truman Avenue
Key West 33040
(305) 296-5152

Rooms: 10
Rates: $158–$178

Special features: teddy bear collection and signed memorabilia

Little Palm Islands

28500 Overseas Highway
Little Torch Key 33042
(800) 343-8567 or (305) 872-2524

Rooms: 30 suites
Rates: $350–$850

Special feature: private island (your own "Bali Hai")

Seminole Country Inn

15885 SW Warfield
Indiantown 34956
(561) 597-3777

Rooms: 23
Rates: $75–$95

Special features: Charles Dickens Christmas and tree lighting

GEORGIA

Ballastone Inn

14 East Oglethorpe Avenue
Savannah 31401
(800) 842-4553 or (912) 236-1484

Rooms: 13 rooms, 3 suites
Rates: $195–$225

Special features: riverfront 1853 Italianate mansion, listed in *Bride's Magazine*

1906 Pathway Inn Bed & Breakfast

501 S. Lee
Americas 31709
(912) 928-2078

Rooms: 5
Rates: $75–$125

Special feature: recreates 19th-century living

Whitworth Inn

6593 McEver Road
Flowery Beach 30542
(770) 967-2368

Rooms: 9
Rates: $65–$85

Special features: winery, golf, sailing

HAWAII

Chalet Kilauea—The Inn at Volcano

Wright Road
Volcano Village 96785
(808) 967-7786

Rooms: 12
Rates: $125–$395

Special features: lava tube walks, lava trees, freshwater tidal ponds

Hale Kai Bjornen Bed & Breakfast

111 Honolii Pali
Hilo 96720
(808) 261-0316

Rooms: 2
Rates: $75–$80

Special feature: set in a peaceful tropical garden

Merryman's Bed & Breakfast

P.O. Box 474
Kealakekua 96750
(808) 323-2276

Rooms: 4
Rates: $75–$125

Special feature: underwater sea life park

IDAHO

The Blackwell House Bed & Breakfast

820 Sherman Avenue
Coeur d'Alene 83814
(800) 899-0656 or (208) 664-0665

Rooms: 8 (3 suites)
Rates: $75–$140

Special features: built as a wedding gift, near Lake Coeur d'Alene and "world's longest floating boardwalk"

Idaho Heritage Inn Bed & Breakfast

109 W. Idaho Street
Boise 83702
(208) 342-8066

Rooms: 6
Rates: $90–$105

Special features: skiing, trout fishing, old mining towns

J. J. Shaw House Bed & Breakfast

1411 W. Franklin Street
Boise 83702
(208) 344-8899

Rooms: 6
Rates: $79–$129

Special feature: piano player in sitting room

ILLINOIS

The Checkerberry Inn

62444 County Road 37	Rooms: 13 (3 suites)
Goshen 46526	Rates: $112–$325
(219) 642-4445	

Special feature: horse-drawn buggy tours through Amish country

Market Street Inn Bed & Breakfast

220 E Market Street	Rooms: 8
Taylorville 62568	Rates: $75–$125
(217) 824-7220	

Special features: skydiving and golf

Queen Anne Guest House

200 Park Avenue	Rooms: 4
Galena 61036	Rates: $85–$105
(815) 777-3849	

Special features: riverboat excursions, greyhound races, artist and photographer shops

INDIANA

Creekwood Inn

Rt. 20/35 at Interstate 94	Rooms: 13
Michigan City 46360	Rates: $123–$168
(219) 872-8357	

Special features: charter fishing, winery tours, set in 33 acres of woods

The Sherman House

35 S. Main Street	Rooms: 23
Batesville 47006	Rates: $51–$66
(812) 934-2407	

Special features: Raspberry Fest and Apple Harvest Festival

Varnes-Kimes Guest House Bed & Breakfast

205 S. Main Street	Rooms: 5
Middlebury 46540	Rates: $75–$85
(219) 825-9666	

Special feature: gardens lit by candlelight nightly

IOWA

Die Heimat Country Inn

4430 V Street	Rooms: 19
Amana 55236	Rates: $59–$69
(319) 622-3937	

Special features: original stagecoach stop for the Colonies, canopy beds

President Casino's Blackhawk Hotel

200 E. 3rd Street	Rooms: 191
Davenport 52801	Rates: $79–$129
(319) 328-6000	

Special features: fitness center, sauna, gambling

Squiers Manor

418 W. Pleasant Street	Rooms: 8
Maquoketa 52060	(includes 3 suites)
(319) 652-6961	Rates: $75–$195

Special feature: a whirlpool tub nestled in a garden—your own Garden of Eden

KANSAS

The Grand Central Hotel

215 Broadway	Rooms: 10
Cottonwood Falls 66845	Rates: $129–$179
(316) 273-6763	

Special features: biking, hiking, horseback riding, fishing

The Inn and Willowbend

3939 Comotara	Rooms: 41
Wichita 67226	Rates: $102–$185
(316) 636-4032	

Special feature: Willowbend golf course

The Senate Luxury Suites

900 SW Tyler	Rooms: 52
Topeka 66612	Rates: $80–$90
(785) 233-5050	

Special features: landscaped courtyards, balconies

KENTUCKY

Beautiful Dreamer Bed & Breakfast

440 E. Stephen Foster Avenue
Bardstown 40004
(502) 348-4004

Rooms: 4
Rates: $89–$119

Special feature: sing-alongs with piano

Bed & Breakfast at Sills Inn

270 Montgomery Avenue
Versailles 40383
(800) 526-9801 or (606) 873-4478

Rooms: 12
(including suites)
Rates: $69–$159

Special features: 1911 Queen Anne Victorian mansion, heart-shaped whirlpool tubs

Four Seasons Country Inn

4107 Scottsville Road
Glasgow 42141
(502) 678-1000

Rooms: 21
Rates: $70–$130

Special features: hiking trails, Mammoth Cave National Park

LOUISIANA

Bed and Breakfast As You Like It

3500 Upperline Street
New Orleans 70125
(504) 821-7716

Rooms: 2
Rates: $80–$150

Special features: casino nearby, zoo, river cruise

Delta Queen

Robin Street Wharf
1380 Port of New Orleans Place
New Orleans 70130
(800) 543-1949 or (504) 586-0631

Rooms: 873
(Victorian staterooms)
Rates: approx. $200

Special features: three-day to two-week cruises, learn to play the steam-powered calliope on board

La Maison de Campagne, Lafayette

825 Kidder Road
Carenco 70520
(318) 896-6529

Rooms: 4
Rates: $110–$135

Special features: biking by Wilderness Trail and Vermillion River

MAINE

The Elms Bed & Breakfast

84 Elm Street
Camden 04843
(207) 236-6250

Rooms: 6
Rates: $85–$95

Special feature: lighthouses

High Meadows Bed & Breakfast

2 Brixham Road
Eliot 03903
(207) 439-0590

Rooms: 4
Rates: $80–$90

Special features: whale watching and sandy beaches

Inn at Canoe Point

Eden Street, Route 3 Box 216
Bar Harbor 04609
(207) 288-9511

Rooms: 5
Rates: $80–$245

Special feature: ocean cove

MARYLAND

Antrim 1844 Country Inn

30 Traveanion Road
Taneytown 2178
(800) 858-1844 or (410) 756-6812

Rooms: 23 (8 suites, 3 cottages)
Rates: $200–$350

Special features: formal gardens, croquet, lawn bowling

Beaver Creek House Bed & Breakfast

20432 Beaver Creek Road
Hagerstown 21740
(301) 797-4764

Rooms: 5
Rates: $75–$95

Special features: nearly 400 antique stores, horseback riding

Chesapeake Wood Duck Inn

Gibsontown Road
Tilshman Island 21671
(410) 866-2070

Rooms: 7
Rates: $135–$215

Special features: waterman's village ambiance, sailing

MASSACHUSETTS

Candleberry Inn
1882 Main Street
Brewster 02631
(508) 896-3300
Rooms: 9
Rates: $124–$145

Special feature: summer festivals

Jenkins Inn
7 West Street
Barre 01005
(978) 355-6444
Rooms: 5
Rates: $95–$135

Special features: antiques, sightseeing, listed on Historical Register

Wheatleigh
West Hawthorne
Lenox 01240
(413) 637-0610
Rooms: 17
Rates: $165–$625

Special feature: in the Berkshires with lake view and private palace

MICHIGAN

Deer Lake Bed & Breakfast
00631 E. Deer Lake Road
Boyne City 49712
(616) 582-9039
Rooms: 5
Rates: $85–$105

Special features: private balcony over the lake, fishing, tennis

Grand Hotel
Mackinaw Island 49757
(906) 847-3331 or (800) 334-7263
Rooms: 324
Rates: $160–$485

Special features: golf, horseback riding, tennis, dancing, carriage tours

The Kirby House
29 W. Center Street
Douglas 49453
(616) 857-2904
Rooms: 8
Rates: $100–$135

Special feature: candlelit buffet breakfast

MINNESOTA

Finnish Heritage Homestead
4776 Waisanea Road
Embarrass 55732
(218) 984-3318
Rooms: 4
Rates: $69

Special features: pick domestic and wild berries, Finnish wood-fired sauna

Fitger's Inn
600 E. Superior Street
Duluth 55802
(218) 722-8826
Rooms: 60
Rates: $90–$250

Special features: microbrewery and dinner theaters

Thorwood Inn
4th & Pine
Hastings 55033
(612) 437-3297
Rooms: 7
Rates: $97–$167

Special feature: 23-foot-tall steeple room with fireplace and whirlpool

MISSISSIPPI

Cedar Grove Mansion Inn
2200 Oak Street
Vicksburg 39180
(800) 862-1300 or (601) 636-1000
Rooms: 16 rooms, 8 suites, 5 cottages
Rates: $85–$165

Special feature: antebellum home with rooftop garden overlooking Mississippi River

The Linden
1 Linden Place
Natchez 39120
(601) 442-2366
Rooms: 7
Rates: $90–$120

Special feature: fashioned after Tara in *Gone with the Wind*

Rosswood Plantation
Route 1, Box 6
Lorman 39096
(601) 437-4215
Rooms: 4
Rates: $115–$135

Special features: heated pool and spa

MISSOURI

Branson Hotel Bed & Breakfast Inn

214 W. Main   Rooms: 9
Branson 65616   Rates: $95–$105
(417) 335-6104

Special features: Branson music shows, author Harold Bell Wright stayed here while writing novels

Red Bud Cove Bed & Breakfast Suites

162 Lakewood Drive   Rooms: 8
Hollister 65672   Rates: $79–$115
(417) 334-7144

Special features: pontoon boat rentals, scenic roads

St. Charles House

338 South Main Street   Rooms: 1 suite and
St. Charles 63301   1 cottage
(800) 366-2427 or (314) 946-6221   Rates: $120–$150

Special features: near the Arch and the St. Louis Art Museum

MONTANA

Izaak Walton Inn

Off Highway 2   Rooms: 31 rooms,
Essex 59916   2 suites,
(406) 888-5700   4 cabooses
     Rates: $98–$150

Special features: moonlit dinners on a caboose's private deck, near Glacier National Park

Lindley House

202 Cindley Place   Rooms: 5
Bozeman 59715   Rates: $95–$250
(406) 587-8403

Special features: hot tub, sauna, mountain bikes, massage

Sacajawea Hotel

5 North Main Street   Rooms: 32
Three Forks 59752   Rates: $65–$100
(406) 285-6515

Special feature: near Yellowstone National Park

NEBRASKA

Barn Again Bed & Breakfast

170549 Country Rd Lane   Rooms: 4
Scottsbluff 69357   Rates: $75–$80
(308) 632-8647

Special features: golf course, museum, antique shop

Golden Hotel

406 E. Douglas   Rooms: 34
O'Neill 68763   Rates: $37–$42
(402) 336-4436

Special feature: historic hotel

Plantation House

401 Plantation Street   Rooms: 6
Elgin 68636   Rates: $55–$80
(402) 843-2287

Special feature: old farmhouse turned into a mansion

NEVADA

Bliss Mansion

710 W. Robinson   Rooms: 4
Carson City 89703   Rates: $165–$175
(775) 887-8988

Special feature: the name says it all!

Gold Hill Hotel

Highway 342   Rooms: 12 rooms,
Virginia City 89440   2 houses
(702) 847-0111   Rates: $45–$150

Special feature: lectures by local historians

Steptoe Valley Inn

220 E. 11th Street
Ely 89315-1110
(775) 289-8687

Rooms: 5
Rates: $84–$90

Special feature: reconstructed from a 1907 grocery store

NEW HAMPSHIRE

The Inn at Thorn Hill

Thorn Hill Road
Jackson 03846
(800) 289-8990 or (603) 383-4242

Rooms: 19 rooms,
3 cottage suites
Rates: $150–$250

Special features: Victorian elegance, candlelit dining

The Notchland Inn

Route 302
Bartlett 03182
(800) 289-8990 or (603) 383-4242

Rooms: 17 rooms,
3 suites
Rates: $185–$275

Special features: hiking, waterfalls, sleigh rides

Three Chimneys Inn

17 Newmarket Road
Durham 03824
(603) 868-7800

Rooms: 23
Rates: $169–$189

Special features: Jacuzzis, authentic tavern

NEW JERSEY

The Bernards Inn

27 Mine Brook Road
Bernardsville 07924
(908) 766-0002

Rooms: 20
Rates: $145–$215

Special features: one-hour train ride from New York City, piano bar

Gingerbread House

28 Gurney Street
Cape May 08204
(609) 844-0211

Rooms: 6
Rates: $125–$240

Special feature: historic district with nearby beach

The Woolverton Inn

6 Woolverton Road
Stockton 08559
(609) 397-0802

Rooms: 10
Rates: $90–$210

Special features: antique shops, boutiques, canoeing nearby

NEW MEXICO

Casa del Granjero

414 C de Baca Lane NW
Albuquerque 87114
(505) 897-4144 or (800) 701-4144

Rooms: 6
Rates: $79–$159

Special features: rose garden, lily pond, waterfall, gazebo, pygmy goats

Hacienda Vargas Bed & Breakfast Inn

1431 S.R. 313 (El Camino Real)
Algodones 87001
(505) 867-9115

Rooms: 8
Rates: $69–$139

Special features: horseback riding, casino gambling, trading post

Yours Truly Bed & Breakfast

160 Paseo de Cerrales
Corrales 87048
(505) 898-7027

Rooms: 4
Rates: $89–$100

Special features: river rafting, hot-air balloon rides

NEW YORK

Another Tyme Bed & Breakfast

7 Church Street
Hammondsport 14840
(607) 569-2747

Rooms: 3
Rates: $60–$70

Special features: scenic drive, vineyards, wine tasting

Genesee Country Inn

948 George Street
Mumford 14511
(716) 538-2500

Rooms: 9
Rates: $85–$145

Special features: trout fishing, golf

Old Drovers

Old Route 22, P.O. Box 100
Dover Plains 12522
(914) 832-9311

Rooms: 4
Rates: $350-450
(weekends)

Special feature: Elizabeth Taylor and Richard Burton stayed here after filming *Cleopatra*

NORTH CAROLINA

The Banner Elk Inn Bed & Breakfast

407 Main Street E.
Banner Elk 28604
(828) 898-6223

Rooms: 4
Rates: $90–$120

Special features: hiking, swimming, boating, picnic tables

Greystone Inn

Greystone Lane
Lake Toxaway 28747
(828) 966-4700

Rooms: 33
Rates: $265–$525

Special features: Lake Toxaway, all water activities, golf, tennis, croquet

Theodosias' Bed & Breakfast

2 Keelson Row
Bald Head Island 28461
(910) 457-6563

Rooms: 10
Rates: $165–$255

Special feature: no cars on the island (golf carts instead)

NORTH DAKOTA

Badlands Motel

P.O. Box 198
Medora 58645
(701) 623-4422

Rooms: 116
Rates: $75–$125

Special feature: the scenic Badlands

Best Western 7 Seas Inn

2611 Old Red Trail
Bismark 58854
(800) 597-7327 or (701) 663-7401

Rooms: 103
Rates: $75

Special feature: nautical décor

Hartfield Inn

509 3rd Avenue W.
Dickinson 58601
(701) 225-6710

Rooms: 4
Rates: $59–$89

Special feature: historical architecture

OHIO

The Inn at Brandywine Falls

8230 Brandywine Road
Sagamore Hills 44067
(330) 467-1812 or (330) 650-4965

Rooms: 6 (3 suites)
Rates: $94–$185

Special features: Cuyohoga Valley National Park (33,000 acres), romantic waterfall

Misty Meadow Farm Bed & Breakfast

64878 Slaughter Hill Road
Cambridge 43725
(740) 439-5135

Rooms: 3
Rates: $120

Special features: nightly bonfires, bass fishing

The White Oak Inn

29683 Walhonding Road (S.R. 175)
Danville 43014
(740) 599-6107

Rooms: 10
Rates: $100–$150

Special features: hiking, fishing, canoeing

OKLAHOMA

Island Guest Ranch

Ames 73718
(800) 928-4574 or (580) 753-4574

Rooms: 10
Rates: $75–$125

Special features: working ranch (herd cattle, ride horses), fishing, pow-wows

McBirney Mansion Bed & Breakfast

1414 Galveston
Tulsa 74127
(918) 585-3234

Rooms: 8
Rates: $119–$225

Special features: overlooks Arkansas River, jogging trails

Monford Inn Bed & Breakfast

322 West Tonhawa   Rooms: 15
Norman 73069   Rates: $90–$195
(405) 321-2200

Special feature: casts from many films, including *Twister*, stayed here

OREGON

Morical House Garden Inn

688 N. Main   Rooms: 7
Ashland 97520   Rates: $110–$160
(541) 482-2254

Special features: local drama and music festivals

Stephanie Inn

2740 S. Pacific   Rooms: 50
Cannon Beach 97110   Rates: $249–$409
(503) 436-2221

Special features: beach, Pacific Ocean views, mountains, rose petals placed on beds

Tu Tu Tun Lodge

96550 North Bank Rogue   Rooms: 16 rooms,
Gold Beach 97444   2 suites, 2 houses
(800) 864-6357 or (503) 247-6664   Rates: $135–$325

Special features: jet-boat and whitewater Rogue River trips

PENNSYLVANIA

Intercourse Village Bed & Breakfast

Rt. 340 Main   Rooms: 12
Intercourse 17534   Rates: $89–$199
(717) 768-2626

Special feature: heart-shaped Jacuzzi

Quill Haven Country Inn

1519 North Center Avenue   Rooms: 4
Somerset 15501   Rates: $75–$95
(814) 443-4514

Special features: Frank Lloyd Wright architecture, fishing, summer theater

Scarlett House

503 West State Street   Rooms: 4
Kennett Square 19348   Rates: $95–$135
(610) 444-9592

Special feature: hot-air ballooning

SOUTH CAROLINA

Beaufort Inn

809 Port Republic Street   Rooms: 13
Beaufort 29902   Rates: $125–$224
(843) 521-9000

Special features: carriage tours, museums, horseback riding, sidewalk cafés

Charleston's Vendue Inn

19 Vendue Range   Rooms: 45
Charleston 29401   Rates: $150–$315
(843) 577-7970

Special features: wine and cheese serving, rooftop terrace overlooking the harbor

Woodlands Resort & Inn

125 Parsons Road   Rooms: 19
Summerville 29483   (includes 3 suites)
(800) 774-9999 or (843) 875-2600   Rates: $290–$350

Special features: fresh flowers and champagne in rooms, all-natural day spa

SOUTH DAKOTA

Deadwood Gulch Resort

Highway 85 S. (Box 643)   Rooms: 98
Deadwood 57732   Rates: $75–$125
(800) 695-1876 or (605) 578-1294

Special features: casinos, creek-side restaurant, amusement park

Historic Town Hall Inn

215 W. Main   Rooms: 12
Lead 57754   Rates: $69–$99
(605) 584-2147

Special feature: near Homestake Gold Mine Tours

State Game Lodge

U.S. 16 A
Custer 57730
(605) 255-4541

Rooms: 47
Rates: $87–$130

Special feature: buffalo safari Jeep ride

TENNESSEE

Bluff View Inn

411 East 2nd Street
Chattanooga 37403
(423) 265-5033

Rooms: 16
Rates: $100–$250

Special features: bluff view, art district, cafés; gardens

Richmont Inn

220 Winterberry Lane
Townsend 37882
(423) 448-6757

Rooms: 10
Rates: $105–$150

Special feature: café provides dinner baskets for private picnics in nearby Great Smoky Mountains

Whitestone Country Inn

1200 Paint Rock Road
Kingston 37762
(423) 376-0113

Rooms: 12
Rates: $85–$160

Special features: sauna and steam room, in waterfowl/wildlife refuge

TEXAS

The Columns on Alamo

1037 S. Alamo Street
San Antonio 78210
(210) 271-3245

Rooms: 11
Rates: $89-$165

Special features: the Alamo, Riverwalk

Hotel St. Germain

2516 Maple Avenue
Dallas 75201
(214) 871-2516

Rooms: 7
Rates: $245–$600

Special feature: the "dangerous liaison" suite

The Texas White House Bed & Breakfast

1417 Eighth Avenue
Ft. Worth 76104
(817) 923-3597

Rooms: 3
Rates: $105

Special features: Ft. Worth Zoo, botanical gardens

UTAH

Angel House Inn

713 Norfolk Avenue
Park City 84060
(800) 264-3501 or (435) 647-0338

Rooms: 9
Rates: $85–$285

Special feature: an abundance of angels, cherubs, cupids, roses, pearls, ribbons, and lace

The Mayor's House Bed & Breakfast Inn

505 Rose Tree Lane
Moab 84532
(435) 259-6015

Rooms: 6
Rates: $89–$150

Special features: whitewater rafting, bike trails

Sky Ridge, A Bed & Breakfast Inn

950 E. Hwy 24
Torrey 84775
(435) 425-3222

Rooms: 6
Rates: $93–$138

Special features: mountain views, red rock–canyon country

VERMONT

The Inn at Weathersfield

Jct. Routes 100 & 100A
Plymouth 05056
(802) 672-3748

Rooms: 12
Rates: $120–$150

Special features: grand piano, Finnish sauna

The Peak Chalet

South View Path
Sherburne 05751
(802) 422-4278

Rooms: 4
Rates: $80–$145

Special feature: panoramic view of Killington and Green Mountains

The Village Country Inn
Route 7A, P.O. Box 408   Rooms: 33
Manchester Village 05254   Rates: $160–$300
(802) 362-1792

Special features: French country inn, offers Enchanted Evenings dinners and Blooming Affairs lunches in the garden

VIRGINIA

Cedar Gables Seaside Inn
6095 Hopkins Lane   Rooms: 4
Chincoteague 23336   Rates: $150–$175
(757) 336-6860

Special features: canoeing, sea kayaking

Clifton: The Country Inn
1296 Clifton Drive   Rooms: 14
Charlottesville 22911   (10 suites)
(888) 971-1800 or (804) 971-1800   Rates: $150–$315

Special features: 48 acres with waterfall, Monticello (Thomas Jefferson's home) and Montpelier (home of James and Dolley Madison) nearby

Piney Grove at Southhall's Plantation
16920 Southhall Plantation Lane   Rooms: 4
Charles City 23030   Rates: $160–$170
(804) 829-2480

Special features: mint juleps on porch swing, hot toddies by the fire

WASHINGTON

Edenwild Inn
Lopez Road   Rooms: 8
Lopez Island 98261   Rates: $100–$155
(360) 468-3238

Special features: arrive by ferry landing or seaplane, ride in 1973 limo to the inn

A Harbor View Bed & Breakfast
113 W. 11th Street   Rooms: 4
Aberdeen 98520   Rates: $65–$120
(360) 533-7996

Special feature: walking tours of historic homes

Schnauzer Crossing
4421 Lake Drive   Rooms: 3
Bellingham 98226   Rates: $120–$200
(360) 733-0055

Special features: lake view, Jacuzzi, fireplace

WEST VIRGINIA

Bavarian Inn
Route 480 & Shepherd Grade Road   Rooms: 73
Shepherdstown 25443   Rates: $95–$160
(304) 876-2551

Special features: German food specialties, European-style pub

Cottonwood Inn
Mill Lane & Kabletown Road   Rooms: 7
Charles Town 25414   Rates: $75–$120
(304) 725-3371

Special features: near Civil War battlefields, large reading library

The Glens Country Estate
New Hope Road, P.O. Box 160   Rooms: 8
Berkeley Springs 25411   Rates: vary
(304) 258-4536

Special features: hot tubs, massages, limousine pickup

WISCONSIN

Canoe Bay
West 16065 Hogback Road   Rooms: 17
Chetek 54728   (includes cottages)
(800) 568-1995 or (715) 924-4594   Rates: $225–$375

Special features: Frank Lloyd Wright architecture, lots of privacy

Fanny Hill Victorian Inn

3919 Crescent Avenue
Eau Claire 54703
(715) 836-8184

Rooms: 11
Rates: $119–$199

Special feature: dinner theater

Harbor House Inn

12666 S.R. 42
Gills Rock 54210
(920) 854-5196

Rooms: 15
Rates: $54–$149

Special feature: Washington Island ferry nearby

WYOMING

Davey Jackson Inn

85 Perry Avenue
Jackson 83001
(307) 739-2294

Rooms: 12
Rates: $169–$229

Special features: ride through Snake River rapids, outdoor hot tub

Rainsford Inn

219 East 18th Street
Cheyenne 82001
(307) 638-2337

Rooms: 7
Rates: $95

Special features: the Moonlight and Roses suite, hidden staircase

Spahn's Big Horn Mountain Bed & Breakfast

70 Upper Hideaway Lane
Big Horn 82833
(307) 674-8150

Rooms: 5
Rates: $90–$140

Special feature: mountainside over Sheridan Valley

APPENDIX B

Reading Resources

I f you'd like more information on the topics covered in this book, check out these resources.

DATING AGAIN

Barash, Susan Shapiro. *Second Wives: The Pitfalls and Rewards of Marrying Widowers and Divorced Men.*

Belli, Melvin, and Mel Krantzler. *A Complete Guide for Men and Women Divorcing.*

Caine, Lynn. *A Compassionate, Practical Guide to Being a Widow.*

Clapp, Genevieve. *Divorce & New Beginnings.*

Goldfarb, Daniel A., and Gary S. Aumiller. *Red Flags: How to Know When You're Dating a Loser.*

Kelly, Susan, and Dale Burg. *The Second Time Around: Everything You Need to Know to Make Your Remarriage Happy.*

Kingma, Daphne Rose. *Coming Apart: Why Relationships End and How to Live Through the Ending of Yours.*

Pistotnik, Bradley A. *Divorce War! 50 Strategies Every Woman Needs to Know to Win.*

Tessian, Tina. *The Unofficial Guide to Dating Again.*

Wallerstein, Judith S., Julian M. Lewis, and Sandra Blakeslee. *The Unexpected Legacy of Divorce: A 25 Year Landmark Study.*

FOODS AND RECIPES

Better Homes and Gardens New Cook Book.

Boynton, Sandra. *Chocolate: The Consuming Passion.*

Brownley, Margaret. *Chocolate Kisses.*

Child, Julia, and Jacques Pepin. *Julia & Jacques Cook at Home.*

Desaulniers, Marcel. *Death by Chocolate: The Last Word on a Consuming Passion.*

Hopkins, Martha, and Randall Lockridge. *Intercourses: An Aphrodisiac Cookbook.*

Pillsbury's Complete Cookbook.

Rombauer, Irma, Marion Rombauer Becker, and Ellen Becker. *The New All-Purpose Joy of Cooking.*

Rubalcaba, Stacey Rae. *In the Kitchen with the Chippendales.*

Stewart, Martha. *The Martha Stewart Cookbook.*

RELATIONSHIPS IN GENERAL

Beattie, Melody. *Beyond Codependency: And Getting Better All the Time.*

Chapman, Gary. *Your Gift of Love: Selections from the Five Love Languages.*

Cook, Marshall. *Time Management.*

Cousens, Gabriel. *Depression-Free for Life.*

Covey, Stephen R. *The 7 Habits of Highly Effective People.*

Ellis, Albert, and Marcia Grud Powers. *The Secret of Overcoming Verbal Abuse.*

Forward, Susan, with Donna Frazier. *Emotional Blackmail: When People in Your Life Use Fear, Obligation, and Guilt to Manipulate You.*

Freeman, Arthur, and Rose DeWolf. *Woulda, Coulda, Shoulda: Overcoming Regrets, Mistakes, and Missed Opportunities.*

Furman, Leah, and Elina Furman. *The Everything® Dating Book.*

Glass, Lillian. *Toxic People.*

Harrell, Keith. *Attitude Is Everything: 10 Life-Changing Steps to Turn Attitude into Action.*

Haynes, Cyndi. *2002 Ways to Cheer Yourself Up.*

Haynes, Cyndi, and Dale Edwards. *2002 Things to Do on a Date.*

Hogan, Eve Escher, and Steve Hogan. *Intellectual Foreplay: Questions for Lovers and Lovers to Be.*

Hollander, Dory. *101 Lies Men Tell Women and Why Women Believe Them.*

Katherine, Anne. *Where to Draw the Line: How to Set Healthy Boundaries Every Day.*

Kearney, Katherine G., and Thomas I. White. *Men and Women at Work: Warriors and Villagers on the Job.*

Kinder, Melvyn. *Mastering Your Moods.*

Klauser, Harriette Anne. *Write It Down, Make It Happen: Know What You Want—And Getting It.*

Kubler-Ross, Elisabeth, and David Kessler. *Life Lessons.*

Luhrs, Janet. *Simple Loving.*

McKay, Matthew. *Self-Esteem.* 3rd ed.

Niven, David. *The 100 Simple Secrets of Happy People.*

Richardson, Cheryl. *Take Time for Your Life.*

Wieder, Marcia. *Making Your Dreams Come True.*

Rowe, John W., and Robert L. Kahn. *Successful Aging.*

SEXUAL INTIMACY

Bechtel, Stephan, Lawrence Roy Stains, and the editors of Men's Health Books. *Sex: A Man's Guide.*

Bright, Susie. *Full Exposure: Opening Up to Sexual Creativity and Erotic Expression.*

Cane, William. *The Art of Kissing.*

Chia, Mantak, Maneewan Chia, Douglas Abrams, and Rachel Carlton Abrams. *The Multi-Orgasmic Couple.*

Comfort, Alex. *The Joy of Sex.*

——. *More Joy of Sex.*

Corn, Laura. *101 Nights of Grrreat Sex* and *101 Grrreat Quickies.*

Hooper, Anne. *Anne Hooper's Ultimate Sex Pack: A Lover's Guide to the Secrets of Sexual Pleasure.*

——. *Anne Hooper's Sexual Intimacy: How to Build a Lasting & Loving Relationship.*

The Kama Sutra.

King, Bruce. *Human Sexuality Today.*

Lacroix, Nitya. *The Art of Erotic Massage.*

Masterton, Graham. *The 7 Secrets of Really Great Sex.*

——. *How to Drive Your Woman Wild in Bed.*

——. *How to Drive Your Man Wild in Bed*

Schoenewolf, Gerald. *The Couples' Guide to Erotic Games.*

Schwartz, Daylle Deanna. *How to Please a Woman in & out of Bed.*

Stubbs, Kenneth Ray. *Erotic Massage: The Tantric Touch of Love.*

Wright, Janet. *Erotic Massage: Body Magic.*

VACATION GUIDES

AAA 1999–2000 Guide to North American Bed and Breakfasts, Country Inns and Historical Lodgings.

Dyson, Katherine D. *100 Best Romantic Resorts of the World.*

Fodor's Great American Vacations.

Heiderstadt, Donna. *Consumer Reports Best Travel Deals—2001.*

Savageau, David, with Ralph D'Agostino. *Places Rated Almanac.*

Stern, Steven B. *Stern's Guide to the Greatest Resorts of the World.*

Index

picnics, 122–123
Pinot Noir, 115
plays, 153
Poe, Edgar Allan, 133
poetry, 131–134
power, sex as, 237
pregnancy
    planning of, 255–256
    sexual intimacy and, 223, 224
    see also contraception
premonitions, 168
professor, crush on, 37
prom night, 109
proposals, romantic, 193–208
    for anniversaries, 207–208
    for first date, 194–197
    of marriage, 203–206
    for regular dating, 198–203
prostate cancer, 236
puppy love, 34–35, 240–241

Q

quizzes
    about interpersonal chemistry, 169–170
    about kissing, 82–83
    about musical compatibility, 96–97
    about romantic settings, 230
    about seasonal romantic compatibility, 69–70

for divorced romantic, 43
Love-O-Meter, 2–4

R

reading, 128
    of books, 128–131
    of newspapers/magazines, 134
    of poetry, 131–134
recovery, from broken
    relationship, 239–251
    death of spouse, 249–250
    divorce, 243–249
    first love, 240–241
    serious relationship, 241–243
restaurants, 119–120
retirement, 45–46
Reuben, Dr. David, 221
romance
    different from being romantic, ix
    gestures of, 9–10
    legacy of, 48
romance busters
    gadgets, 183–185
    miscellaneous, 186–191
    people, 174–179
    places, 180–183
romance-busting people, 174–179
    aggressive type, 177
    control freak, 178
    debater, 176

grump, 176
"I-me-my" type, 177
pessimist, 175–176
sarcastic type, 174–175
taker, 177–178
romance-busting places, 180–183
    hectic places, 182–183
    loud places, 181–182
    offices, 180
    traffic jams, 180–181
romance-busting things, 183–185
    cell phones, pagers, telephones, 183–184
    laptop computers, 184
    technology, 185
    television, 184–185
romance novels, 129–131
routine, avoiding, 12
Ruby Cabernet, 115
Rufenol, 31

S

sarcastic type, 174–175
Sauvignon Blanc, 115
scents
    aromatherapy, 161
    combining of, 161–162
    fragrances and, 158–160
    other romantic, 160–161
    unpleasant, 161